ALWAYS LOOK ON
BRIGHT SIDE OF

ALWAYS LOOK ON THE BRIGHT SIDE OF LIFE

ROBERT SELLERS

FOREWORD BY MICHAEL PALIN

JOHN BLAKE

Published by Metro Publishing Ltd,
3 Bramber Court, 2 Bramber Road,
London W14 9PB, England

First published in hardback in 2003

ISBN 1 84358 064 0

British Library Cataloguing-in-Publication Data:

A catalogue record for this book is available from the British Library.

Design by ENVY Design

Printed in Great Britain by CPD (Wales), Ebbw Vale, Gwent.

1 3 5 7 9 10 8 6 4 2

Papers used by Metro Publishing are natural, recyclable products made from wood grown
in sustainable forests. The manufacturing processes conform to the environmental
regulations of the country of origin.

Pictures reproduced by kind permission of Alpha, Camerapress, HandMade Films,
Monty Python Begging Bowl Partnership, Michael Palin and Python (Monty) Pictures Ltd.

Every attempt has been made to contact the relevant copyright-holders, but some were
unobtainable. We would be grateful if the appropriate people could contact us.

*To my family and friends ...
and George.*

CONTENTS

FOREWORD

HandMade Films was born in mischief. George Harrison wanted to call it British HandMade Films but wasn't allowed to. So one of the most successful British independent production slates was, thanks to bureaucracy, never allowed to proclaim the country it sprang from.

Mischief was afoot in London, too, in the spring of 1978. Lord Delfont, the head of EMI finally got round to reading one of the films his minions had commissioned. It was called *Monty Python's Life of Brian*, and what he read appalled him so much that he became determined to extricate his company from anything to do with it.

Unfortunately, it wasn't as easy as that. A thousand miles away, on the Mediterranean shores of Tunisia, designers, art directors and carpenters were already building Brian's Jerusalem.

Monty Python desperately needed a saviour. Eric Idle approached his friend George Harrison, knowing him to be a Python fan and having a few bob. So began one of the fastest bail-outs in film history. By the end of the summer, Brian was being chased through the marketplaces of a new Jerusalem and the pay cheques were coming in from a company which was being hailed as the messiah – HandMade Films.

Stories don't usually end like that. The good guys rarely win so easily. But George persuaded his manager Denis O'Brien, who had once looked after Peter Sellers, that he was happy for considerable amounts of his money to be made available to a comedy group with, at that time, only two modestly performing movies to their credit. His reason was, as he said simply later, 'I wanted to see the film.' Generally, and inaccurately, portrayed as the quiet, retiring Beatle, George was always busy. He had a restless mind and a very sharp one, too. He felt a duty to instruct and encourage new talent and he had an uncomplicated fondness for comedy, especially of the Pythonic variety. So, in a sense, everything that drove George fused into HandMade Films, and though it was born in mischief, it thrived as a pretty complete reflection of George's personality – a generous, engaged, committed and occasionally quite silly man.

While Denis took care of business, George remained true to his belief in the integrity of the artist, backing Mai Zetterling's powerfully controversial prison film *Scrubbers*, and saving John Mackenzie's classic *The Long Good Friday* (which introduced Bob Hoskins to the silver screen) when no distributor dared take it on.

To start with, George and Denis kept their cool and their principles intact, investing in projects that were by no means guaranteed earners – Terry Gilliam's *Time Bandits*, Bruce Robinson's *Withnail and I*, and Alan Bennett's *A Private Function* – as well as keeping faith with Bob Hoskins in *Mona Lisa* and my own comedy *The Missionary*.

There were bound to be mistakes. It just happened that one of them, *Shanghai Surprise* – despite bringing together the apparent dream-team of Sean Penn and Madonna – was not only a mistake, but also their most expensive film to date.

I have the feeling that George never quite recovered from that. He remained generous, but felt compromised and he began to draw back. Once that happened, the end was in sight. HandMade had many able people at the helm, but the spirit that drove the ship had to come from George.

Even allowing for a few flops, the HandMade record is formidably impressive. Twenty-three films made in ten years – films of extraordinary range and diversity – giving a huge number of actors, writers and technicians the chance to show what they could do, with the minimum of interference.

George believed in creativity. He was curious about where it came from and how it could best be encouraged, and this respect for the artist underpinned much of the success of HandMade Films.

I remain deeply grateful to HandMade for the faith they had in me, and I know there are many more like me who believe that, if there were a HandMade around today, the British film industry would be the better for it.

All the more puzzling then that, until now, HandMade's achievements have been so overlooked. The gonged and medal-led film establishment never saw fit to welcome George into their ranks, nor, to be honest, would George have wanted that. Speeches and self-congratulation were not his thing at all. This is why Robert Sellers's book is so timely. It is, after all, the story of one of the most successful and original independent film producers since the war.

Read, celebrate … and learn.

MICHAEL PALIN

ACKNOWLEDGEMENTS

It would have been quite impossible, and a plain waste of ink, for me to have even attempted to write this book without the enthusiastic willingness I received from so many people who wished to share their memories of HandMade Films. I should like to thank those who gave me interviews: Steve Abbott, Alan Bennett, Tony Bill, Michael Blakemore, Don Boyd, Ralph Brown, John Cleese, Dick Clement, Carol Cleveland, Robbie Coltrane, Sean Connery, Ray Cooper, Hilary Davis, Paul Freeman, Terry Gilliam, John Goldstone, Richard E. Grant, Richard Griffiths, Barry Hanson, Bernard Hill, Terry Hughes, Eric Idle, Terry Jones, Neil Jordan, Barrie Keefe, John Kelleher, John Kohn, David Leland, Richard Loncraine, Jonathan Lynn, John Mackenzie, Paul McGann, Patrick Meehan, Alan Metter, Malcolm Mowbray, Peter Nichols, Michael Palin (extra thanks for a great foreword) Wendy Palmer, Denis Quilley, John Reiss, Simon Relph, Alan Shearman, Brian Shingles, Mark Shivas, Jonathan Wacks, David Wimbury and Steven Woolley. Special thanks must also go to John Blake for his decision to publish the book, and Doug Cooper whose idea it first was.

'I have a sort of kamikaze side to me that is optimistic.
I have to trust Denis O'Brien's business sense
and hope he's not going to bankrupt me.'

GEORGE HARRISON, 1988

CHAPTER 1
SAVING PYTHON'S BRIAN

Out in Tunisia, a couple of sand dunes along from where George Lucas shot *Star Wars*, the Monty Python team were preparing their own little contribution to late twentieth-century culture – *Life of Brian*. EMI, Britain's leading film production company, had kindly stumped up the cash, a little over £2 million. On the cusp of flying out to the North African location, the rug was unexpectedly yanked from under them on the direct order of EMI's 69-year-old Chief Executive Lord Delfont. The moment is still remembered with incredulity. 'They pulled out on the Thursday,' Terry Gilliam recalls. 'The crew was supposed to be leaving on the Saturday. Disastrous! It was because they read the script ... finally. Bernie Delfont hadn't read the script. I just thought it was very good; at least the Jews were protecting the Christians, in Bernie's case.'

Royally shafted by EMI, the Python's found themselves marooned in pre-production limbo. Already in way too deep to back out now, there began a desperate scramble to raise new funds. Convinced there was no other way of financing it from within the UK, producer John Goldstone left for California with one of the Pythons, Eric Idle, who says of the trip, 'We went to see several people, all millionaires and billionaires, companies and corporations, and we'd sit there and do our pitch. We got

1

in to see these people because Python was kind of popular, but nobody was very keen to finance it'.

By coincidence, a recent arrival in town was George Harrison, a Python fanatic with a private library of records and film of just about everything the comedians had ever done. He also happened to be an extremely close friend of Idle's. They'd first met in 1975 at a screening in Los Angeles of *Monty Python and the Holy Grail.*

Terry Gilliam remembers that he and Eric 'went to some do afterwards and there was George Harrison and we were sort of plonked on either side of him and became friends.' It was Idle, though, who maintained a much closer friendship than Gilliam. Eric says of his new-found friend, 'We used to hang out quite a lot together ... we had a lot of fun, a lot of drinks and a lot of laughs. He also helped me through a tough stage in my life *[in 1975, Idle was in the process of divorcing his wife, Australian actress Lyn Ashley]* ... he was very, very good to me. We'd natter to each other, he'd go on about his recording and I'd go on about my writing. He did a guest spot on my *Rutland Weekend Television* show and we both got shit-faced afterwards.'

Upon hearing that George was in Hollywood, Idle instinctively got in touch. 'I kept calling George, telling him that we were looking for money. I was just filling him in on what was happening and where we were at, and every time he'd say, "Don't worry, I'll get it." And I sort of put that out of my head. I just didn't believe anybody could actually pay for it. Then eventually he said, "Look, I'll pay for this. I'm going to set this up." '

Goldstone was dumbstruck at the possibility that one individual, be he a Beatle or not, could single-handedly finance a project on this scale, but time was pressing and he was willing to listen to any offers, however crazy they sounded. 'We went up to see George at his house in the Hollywood hills,' Goldstone says. 'I can't remember whether he'd read the script already or not ... it didn't really seem to matter ... he said, "I'll do it, I'll do the whole thing." I just couldn't believe it, I felt ... rock 'n' rollers, no sense of reality at all. He said to get in touch with his business manager Denis O'Brien, who was in Switzerland at that point, in his chalet, but he was going to be back in London, and he'd work things out.'

Everyone was taken aback by Harrison's generosity, not least Eric Idle. 'This was totally unheard of. It was a spectacular move for somebody to say, "I will pay $4 million for this movie," it was really unheard of, that's like $40 million now, a huge sum of money, and without which *Life of Brian* would never have been made.'

The sound of jaws dropping on to the floor resounded throughout the entire film industry. Harrison later described his benevolence and desire to see the movie made as 'the most expensive cinema ticket ever issued'.

When news reached the other Pythons that *Brian* was back in business, the mood was one of undiluted celebration. John Cleese particularly had begun to believe that the comedy might never be made and was actually on the verge of leaving for Vienna to make a picture with Peter Sellers. To some, the identity of their benefactor came as no real surprise. Terry Jones remarks, 'When Eric rang George and asked, "What can we do?" George said, "Well, you know, when The Beatles were breaking up, Python kept me sane, really, so I owe you one." All The Beatles had been Python fans. It was just happening at the time they were breaking up and George said they used to watch the shows, and they kept him sane, kept him going.'

Life of Brian went on to become one of the most successful and critically acclaimed comedies ever made. And perhaps the most controversial, too, guaranteed to offend anyone and everyone with delicate sensibilities from every minority. 'Some of whom one would have wished to have offended ...' adds John Cleese. More crucially, it heralded the birth of HandMade Films, the creative amalgamation between the quiet Beatle and Monty Python, six of the finest British comics since the Goons. HandMade succeeded in establishing itself as the most popular and significant independent British movie company since Ealing. Eric Idle once said of their 1980s track record, 'If you looked at the British film industry and took HandMade's films out, there would be almost nothing left.'

Much of the company's output still stands today as some of the best home-grown films of the last 30 years. And yet the company allowed itself to spiral out of control and broke itself apart amidst accusations of betrayal and financial wrongdoing.

* * *

Life of Brian's origins go back to 1975 and a press conference in New York. 'It all started as an ad lib,' Eric Idle remarks. 'The press asked us what our next movie was and I said, "*Jesus Christ — Lust for Glory!*" God knows where that came from. It was just a joke for ages and then we went off to Amsterdam for a publicity tour where Gilliam and I went out and got a little bit drunk in a bar and we did a lot of carpenter jokes. We loved the idea that Jesus was a carpenter and this cross had been very badly fixed and kept falling over and he was giving them advice on how to keep it erect. We did a lot of blasphemous jokes. Then when we came back, people said, well, actually this is quite an interesting area to do comedy because nobody ever dares tackle religion, because you get killed!'

Seized by the comic possibilities of a biblical parody, the Pythons approached the subject with methodical earnestness. Michael Palin remembers 'quite a lot of group discussions, just what our feelings were about the shape and tone of the film, mainly tone. We all thought it was a great idea, but then we had to think, well, what do we really want to say? We all suggested various books that each other might read … it was a very academic approach. We read books about the Bible story and that period, the Dead Sea Scrolls and various new interpretations of the Gospels, that sort of thing, just because we all felt, well, we can't just do silly jokes about people being knocked off donkeys, there's got to be a kind of philosophical approach as well.'

Days were also spent sitting in a private screening room watching one or two reels each from as many biblical epics as they could endure — stuff like *Samson and Delilah* and *The Greatest Story Ever Told* — sanctimonious twaddle peddled by the Cecil B DeMille school of Hollywood religious movies that was ripe for send-up.

The first concerted writing session was held in December 1976 and the whole *Life of Brian* movie evolved just like any other Python project. John Cleese remembers writing 'on our own or in pairs as we usually did. Me and Graham Chapman; Terry Jones and Michael Palin; and Eric Idle on his own. Then we would get together for read-throughs where Terry Gilliam would join us. Overall, it was a very easy project, it came together remarkably well because we all seemed to know almost instinctively what we were writing about and we got a story together that was a lot better than the stories we usually came up with.'

Very early in the writing process it was unanimously agreed not to single out Jesus Christ for personal ridicule. 'We didn't have any quarrel with Christ himself,' Terry Jones said at the time. 'My feelings towards Christ are that he was a bloody good bloke, even though he wasn't as funny as Margaret Thatcher.' So what started life as a Christ parody quickly turned into a far more warranted satirical rant against religion and religious authority. Eric Idle says, 'By reading up on the Bible, we gained respect for certain things that are good in religion and realised where the target lay, which is in the churches and their ability to kill people in the name of peace. So it isn't just "Let's do a college revue sending up religion", it is actually much more specifically focused on the problems of religion. Laughter is a way of finding the truth about things ... you can make blasphemous jokes over dinner but that doesn't hold up in a movie or any serious look at what the subject is, and religion is a very serious subject. It's a good question and needed addressing and I think we did it in a pretty good way.' Graham Chapman also saw the film as very much pro-Christ, but anti-church.

And so the character of Brian was born, a mythical counterpart of Christ born in a less lavish manger down the road. In early drafts he was the luckless thirteenth disciple who never quite got a mention in the New Testament because he was always late for miracles and managed to miss the last supper altogether because his wife had friends round that evening. Another rejected idea was someone pretending to be the Holy Ghost and getting the Virgin Mary up the duff, palming the unfortunate Mother of God off with lines like, 'Don't worry, darling. I'm a messenger from God.' Early working titles included *The Gospel According to St Brian* and *Brian of Nazareth*. The story proper has the adult Brian, working at the local amphitheatre selling snacks like otter noses, badger spleens and wrens' livers – 'Get them while they're hot!' – suddenly hailed as the Messiah by an ignorant populace in the grip of religious fanaticism.

Having scored big with the immaculately conceived *Fawlty Towers*, John Cleese was the Python with the highest box-office value so might have been expected to take the lead role. Cleese says, 'I was hoping to play Brian. I thought it would be much more interesting to try and sustain a role the whole way through a movie which, at the age of nearly 40, I'd never done. But, in the end, the others – and they were absolutely right – decided that it was much better to have Graham doing Brian and me doing the funny stuff. It was the correct decision on their part. I remember being disappointed for three or four hours, but it didn't last, and I must say Graham did it tremendously well.'

The 'funny stuff' to which Cleese refers included roles such as a Roman centurion, a priest officiating at a public stoning as if he were a schoolmaster on an ill-disciplined rugby field, sending one of the crowd to the back for chucking a rock before the whistle ('There's always one, isn't there?') and, best of all, Reg, leader of the extremist People's Front of Judea, a stinging dig at petty-minded, political, militant-style armchair revolutionaries who are all talk and no action.

The other Python members also play multiple characters; indeed, *Monty Python's Life of Brian* boasts the best ensemble acting the team ever gave. Terry Jones is Brian's putrefying hag of a mother Mandy (a Cleese / Chapman creation) and a hermit forced to break his 20-year vow of silence after Brian's followers scoff all his juniper berries. Eric Idle pops up memorably as the endearing Mr Cheeky, described as 'nice to the point of being brainless', and a would-be transsexual revolutionary called Stan (though he prefers Loretta) who believes it's every man's right to have babies.

Terry Gilliam's blood-and-thunder prophet and Neanderthal jailer are pure grotesques, which had been his stock in trade on the television show. He says of his acting, 'I like not being recognised. I like hiding behind lots of make-up. I feel very ill at ease being me in a film or something that looks like me.'

Graham Chapman is the title character, Brian, a half-Jewish, half-Roman bastard, the result of his mother's dalliance with a passing centurion. A keen drinker since university – an addiction that at its height saw him consume three pints of gin a day – Chapman was famed for his eccentric behaviour. Once, when presented with a showbusiness award at some swish function by Lord Mountbatten, Chapman crawled to the stage on all fours, clasped the prize between his teeth, squawked, then returned to his table. This was not normal behaviour, even for a comedian. On another occasion, he arrived for a university lecture dressed as a giant carrot, stood at the podium in utter silence for ten minutes, then left. Warned that if he continued drinking he'd be dead within a year, Chapman gave up the booze shortly before filming *Life of Brian* and turns in a truly memorable performance that's all the more tragic since his fate was to be the most underachieving and underrated of all the Python team.

Finally, there's Michael Palin, who steals the film from his colleagues with a veritable galaxy of memorable characters, notably an ex-leper finding it hard begging once Christ has cured him, but who still hops out of habit, and the effete Pontius Pilate who mispronounces his 'R's and defends his friend, Biggus Dickus, by proclaiming, 'This man wanks as high as any man in Wome.' How the actor kept a straight face handling such gems is a minor miracle. Well, actually he didn't … Palin does admit to corpsing on film. 'It's when I'm talking to Chris Langham's Roman sentry, you can see my mouth turn up as I'm biting the inside of my cheek trying to stop me laughing. One has to be professional about these things and realise that Pilate had to take himself absolutely seriously … there's no glimmer of humour, except at his own jokes which were not really very funny.'

The first satisfactory draft of *Brian* arrived around July 1977 and proved so bulky that a great deal of material had to be jettisoned or else the film, joked the Pythons, would have lasted three-and-a-half days. In January 1978, the Pythons flew out for a two-week break in Barbados for some fine-tuning. Terry Jones recalls, 'It had got by that stage very difficult to get everyone to concentrate. In the old days, people would come and spend the whole day and work, but it was getting increasingly difficult, people were always on the phone to accountants and other business partners. So the idea of shutting ourselves away for a fortnight … well, I thought it was a funny idea … but it actually worked out very well. We stayed in a very nice house all together so we could really concentrate, get rid of the rest of the world and just concentrate on writing the film.'

The odd interruption was provided by a steady stream of celebrity visitors like Mick Jagger and Keith Moon, a close friend of Chapman's. The Who drummer and notorious hellraiser was to have appeared in *Brian* as a mad prophet, but sadly died a week before cameras rolled.

As luck would have it, Barry Spikings, Managing Director of EMI, who'd done rather well out of distributing *Holy Grail*, was holidaying on the island and got wind of the project. Back in London, he lost no time in telephoning John Goldstone. 'I hear there's a new Python film,' he prompted eagerly. 'We'd really like to see it and we'd be really interested in financing it.'

Goldstone told Spikings they were after £2 million, by far the highest budget any of the Pythons had worked with and considerably more than the paltry sum spent on *Holy Grail*, which was gloriously marketed as making '*Ben Hur* look like an epic'. Goldstone remembers, 'Spikings called me back 24 hours later. He'd fallen out of bed reading the script he'd laughed so much and he wanted to make a deal.' During the three-hour meeting, Goldstone insisted they were to have sole artistic control over the film and final cut approval, something EMI had never conceded before. Spikings agreed. The two men shook hands and celebrated the deal over a glass of champagne.

With backing secured, pre-production began in earnest and that meant finding a suitable location. Israel was out for a start, as Chapman was quick to inform reporters. 'If we'd gone there with loads of crosses and nailed people to them, I think there would have been some objections.' So the two Terrys, Gilliam and Jones, went on a recce of Tunisia and Morocco. Their biggest obstacle turned out to be a carpet Gilliam bought in Tunisia which he was busily tying up in the airport. Jones says, 'We let somebody else go in our place in the queue as Terry tied up this carpet, and when it came to our turn they said, "Sorry, the flight's closed." I said, "What do you mean? We've been standing here, you can't just close the flight." So we couldn't get on the plane to Morocco. I mean, I went berserk, eventually managing to demand to see the head of Royal Air Maroc and then started calling him names. I'd absolutely lost my rag at this stage and it ended up with the head of Royal Air Maroc taking his jacket off and we were about to have fisticuffs in the middle of the airport. Terribly funny now, but I was really livid.'

Driving around Morocco, it became clear that Tunisia was going to be the safer bet, not least because the President's nephew had set up a film company next door to a series of grandiose sets left over from the television mini-series *Jesus of Nazareth*, which the Pythons brilliantly exploited, lending their film a look and scope that was truly epic but at little extra cost. Ironically, some of the locations scouted in Morocco Gilliam subsequently used for *Time Bandits*. Jones remarks, 'Maybe Terry was quite keen to keep those places for himself, I don't know. Anyway, we decided it was going to be simpler to do it in Tunisia.'

With the April start date looming, the pace of pre-production quickened. But there was to be a nasty surprise waiting in the wings. 'We'd had a draft agreement from EMI,' Goldstone recalls, 'but there were still things to iron out, to clarify, but everything seemed to be going in the right direction. I'd set up a meeting with Barry Spikings really just to go through the final points of the contract. It turned out to be a very strange meeting. Barry seemed very negative about a lot of the points and I sensed there was something wrong. So I asked, "Well, what's going on?" And he said that Bernie Delfont had given the script to Sir James Carreras, who was on the board and formerly the head of Hammer Horror Films and a Catholic, and Jimmy had said to Bernie, "Bernie, this is blasphemous, we can't possibly make this!" And Bernie had instructed Barry to give us the boot. So it was a bit of a shock.'

EMI tried to claim their dramatic U-turn was due to Python's dogged insistence on artistic control and the company's own financial constraints. The recent hiring and firing of The Sex Pistols had cost the company dear, as well as making them look like idiots. Whatever the reason, Lord Delfont never regretted his decision, even when the film scored a box-office bull's-eye, believing as he did 'that there are some subjects not to make – however talented the film-makers'. The ultimate irony of Delfont's snub and George Harrison's rescue job was that *Life of Brian* played in EMI cinemas in Britain and reaped a fortune for the beleaguered company. Adding salt to the wound, Harrison once travelled back from New York on the same flight as Delfont. After reading the film's encouraging box-office figures in that week's *Variety*, Harrison waved the trade paper at Delfont triumphantly, remarking, 'Thanks for backing out.'

The question of who should direct *Life of Brian* came with barbed thorns and considerable baggage. The choice was between Terry 1 and Terry 2. Making the TV series, Gilliam and Jones seemed always to be of the same mind when it came to how things should be done, particularly on the technical side, harbouring as they did ambitions to carve out post-Python careers as directors. When *Holy Grail* came along, the pair jumped at the chance to co-direct it. Gilliam says, 'But in the course of directing *Grail*, two things happened: I discovered Terry and I weren't always as much in agreement as we both thought; and I also found directing the group a pain in the arse because I knew what we were trying to make it look like and to do that required certain things sometimes, and the guys didn't like getting into uncomfortable positions for a good shot. I had been so much on my own doing animation for so long that I had no skills in convincing people to do things that they don't want to do. So I often just said, "Fuck this! All right, you wrote it, fuck it, if you don't want to do it. I'm trying to salvage your fucking script here, you don't like it, fuck it." There was one day I just walked away and went off in a huff, lay in the grass and Terry took over, so the advantage of two directors was considerable sometimes. But, in the end, we kind of decided that he would talk to them and I would stay back with the camera and deal with how we were shooting it. And the design was all my influence. And it kind of worked out reasonably well, that relationship.'

But too often the opposing directorial styles of Gilliam and Jones caused rifts on the *Holy Grail* set. Carol Cleveland, who acted in the film, comments, 'Having two directors was not a good idea … you're working with two maniacs, really. One maniac director's enough, but to have two of them … so there were lots of rows.' Cleveland was Python's resident actress, the seventh member in all but name.

Travelling up to Scotland to film her sequence as Mother Superior in *Grail*'s Castle Anthrax sequence, she noticed an assortment of long faces among the crew and a squalid on-set atmosphere. Something was wrong. 'The crew were just about ready to down tools literally that very day. And I could see why, because the way Jones and Gilliam worked was to designate different scenes between them, and on this particular one Terry Jones was doing the first half and Terry Gilliam the second. So Terry Jones had been around all morning with the crew putting my set together and then later on in the day Terry Gilliam comes along, takes one look and says, "No, no, no, don't want that," and tells this crew who had been working on it all day to change it all. And they were literally pulling their hair out.'

By the time of *Life of Brian*, Gilliam had already branched out as a solo director with the uneven but pictorially majestic *Jabberwocky*. 'I did that on my own. I said, fuck, this is great. I don't really like working with Python, we know each other too well. So after doing *Jabberwocky* on my own, that's what I wanted to do. I just really felt directing Python, so much of the work is dogsbody work, just dealing with rather recalcitrant people.' So the deal on *Brian* was for Gilliam to act as production designer and the other Terry to point the camera and say 'Action' a lot. Jones felt 'it seemed like a better division of labour really for Terry Gilliam to concentrate on the look of the film. Production design was something he wanted to learn about anyway, so it was useful for him to learn that side of it. And that's his great gift.'

However, even here the relationship was strained as sometimes Gilliam would design a set to be shot a certain way then despair when Jones lined up his camera from a different angle. Gilliam admits, 'I changed my title from designer to resigner. No, I mean I love *Life of Brian*, I just didn't have the patience or skills to deal with the others enough. Terry loved all that. Terry is a great ball of energy, he just leaps in there and has so much enthusiasm. He doesn't seem to fall into the dark moody bits that I fall into. I get really crazed.

'Directing a film for me is just hard work because it never seems to be as good as the idea in my head, so I'm constantly getting depressed and having terrible states. And Terry's just so bubbly all the time. He works perfectly with the group.'

Six months after the withdrawal of EMI, filming on *Monty Python's Life of Brian* got under way on 16 September 1978. The 41-day shoot progressed remarkably smoothly. Cleese comments, 'It was extraordinarily efficient. I'll always remember on the first day I played the priest in the stoning sequence. We got out there at 8 o'clock and by lunchtime we had the scene shot and I was in the hotel swimming pool. It was most extraordinary to have that finished by lunchtime. Usually, it takes about three days 'til you get to know everyone on set, it's like moving to a new football team, you don't know how people play, but *Brian* was different. Terry Jones was very well prepared and the camera and sound people were working like a well-oiled machine. I enjoyed making that film; everything was pointing in the right direction and there was a sense that we knew what we were doing. God smiles on some projects and he smiled on that one.'

Looking back on it today, all the Pythons remember the filming with fondness. Palin recalls, 'It was all reasonably pleasant. I remember Graham Chapman was also the unit doctor; he used to administer medicines to people, he was really enjoying it. It was the most organised of the Python films, the one in which everybody pulled together. It was quite different in that way from *Holy Grail* which had the problem of two directors and *Meaning of Life* which wasn't a totally co-operative effort.'

An early visitor to the set was George Harrison, keen to watch his comic heroes in action and perhaps curious to see how his money was being spent. Cleese remembers George coming out to Tunisia at one point 'and he stayed for a day or two and had dinner with us. Denis O'Brien came along, too, although we didn't know Denis very well. George was very easy to be around; of course, he knew Eric well, so I think he felt comfortable with the rest of us. It always felt very comfortable around him.'

Harrison even appears in the film, a hastily written blink-and-you'll-miss-it part as Mr Papadopoulis. As Michael Palin commented in a brilliant speech he made at HandMade's tenth anniversary party, 'It marked the beginning and end of George Harrison's film career. George had been persuaded to appear in a short cameo and was given the little-sought-after role of 314th Jewish Man in Kitchen during the scene in which Brian returns home and finds a huge Messiah-expectant crowd lying in wait for him. For George, the shock of finding himself in a crowd mobbing someone else was too much and he took early retirement and went back to his previous career as a musician.'

Another familiar face among the crowd is Spike Milligan. The former Goon happened to be staying in the same hotel as Cleese and, before he could raise any resistance, found himself playing one of Brian's obsessional followers in the scene where they find his discarded sandal and treat it as a holy relic. After taking the master shot, Jones was in the process of organising close-ups when a miscreant cloud manoeuvred itself across the sun, halting work. After an hour, it still hadn't budged. 'At this point,' says Terry Jones, 'Milligan said he'd had enough, he was really on holiday, so he pissed off. And I don't blame him at all, but it meant that we had to shoot the rest of the scene without Spike being there, so I couldn't get any close-ups of him.'

As was achieved with the medieval era on *Holy Grail*, the torture, filth and hardship of biblical times is convincingly realised. No nicely manicured Hollywood extras here. Much of the film's humour derives from the juxtaposition of historical settings and modern-day characters. Palin explains, 'We just looked at the sort of people who would be around nowadays, so you had the agonising liberal centurion, who I play, who's actually completely hopeless, riddled with awful guilt about what he's doing, and yet he's the one who's actually sending people off to be nailed up. And there's Eric's cheeky Cockney. So we just put in a lot of fairly modern sort of London characters and that seemed to carry it through.'

Photographically, *Life of Brian* stands as the most accomplished Python film. Amazing then to learn that something like 60 per cent of it was shot using a hand-held camera. Jones says, 'For some reason, I had a thing against putting cameras on tripods in those days.' One of the more grandiose images, of a crowd swarming up the mount to hear a sermon from Christ as the sun slowly sets, wasn't planned and came about purely by accident. The crew had been shooting all day on a deserted hillside when at 4.00pm the extras suddenly disappeared. With most being local women, the excuse was that they had to go home and cook their husbands' dinners. 'But we haven't finished shooting!' yelled Jones, sending his assistant director off to herd the largely unwilling crowd back up the hillside. Eric Idle was beside Jones and tapped him on the shoulder. 'It looks terrific,' he said. 'Turn the camera on them quick.' Jones frantically spun round and reeled off as much footage as he could of this mass migration of people scrambling back up the mount. And that's the shot they used.

Indeed, all the extras in *Life of Brian* were derived from the local population. Jones remembers, 'They were all very knowing because they'd all worked for Franco Zeffirelli on *Jesus of Nazareth*, so I had these rather elderly Tunisian extras telling me, "Well, Mr Zeffirelli wouldn't have done it like that, you know." '

Another testing moment involving the locals was Graham Chapman's nude scene. Famously, Chapman opens the shutters of his room stark-bollock-naked only to discover hordes of disciples waiting outside. The problem was that half of the 300 extras were women, and Muslim women to boot, whose law forbade them to see such wanton aberrations. 'It's absolutely forbidden for them to even think of viewing naughty bits,' Chapman later recalled. 'So when I flung open the shutters, half the crowd ran away screaming.'

In January 1979, a two-and-a-quarter-hour rough cut of *Brian* was screened in London to an invited audience and over the next few months scenes were jigged about, cut, reinstated, then cut again. Originally, the film was to have opened on three shepherds in a field nonchalantly discussing the merits of sheep, '… while in the background you get a star going across, you get wise men going past, you get the angel coming down,' Terry Gilliam explains. 'This great event is taking place while they're facing towards camera talking about sheep.' Very funny, but apparently not a rousing enough comedy set piece to start off the film with the requisite bang. So out it went.

Other cut scenes included Cleese dragged up as Pontius Pilate's wife and, most significantly of all, Eric Idle's Jewish terrorist Otto, recalled fondly by Gilliam. 'Otto is this character fighting for a state of Israel that will last a thousand years; no riff-raff, no gypsies. He had this terrible armour and I was pleased I turned the star of David into a swastika. It was a big mistake leaving it out. I think Eric, who wrote the sketch and played the lead, was spending a lot of time in Hollywood and he suddenly thought too many Jewish friends were going to take offence at this, but I thought it was such a funny scene, it was outrageous.'

Idle, of course, recalls events a little differently. 'I think Otto is what got the Jewish population very upset, mainly because old Gilliam had put a swastika on the star of David, which is like a red rag to a fucking bull. It was also out of place. I was responsible for pulling it out at the end and the reason was I felt the movie moved better without it because you suddenly had Otto come in at about the seventieth minute, a totally new character with totally new ideas and it was when the film is starting to wrap up and head towards the exit; it unbalanced it. If he'd been introduced in the twentieth minute, that's fine.'

Four hundred years ago, the Pythons might well have been burnt at the stake for making *Life of Brian*. But this was, after all, the late twentieth century and the rather antiquated British blasphemy laws were something of an irrelevance. That was until July 1977, when Mary Whitehouse, self-appointed guardian of national morals and all-round spoil-sport, won a blasphemy libel case against *Gay News* for publishing a poem about a Roman centurion's homo-erotic leanings towards the crucified Christ. It was the first successful prosecution for blasphemous libel since the 1920s and had a personal resonance within the Python camp, for Chapman had helped launch *Gay News* and was an ardent supporter of gay rights. The possibility of being found guilty of blasphemy over *Brian* was now a very real, if distant, threat, something that so enraged Cleese particularly that he publicly declared his wish to go to prison rather than yield to the Mary Whitehouse lobby. In such a climate, it was decided to open *Life of Brian* first in America where freedom of speech and religious choice is enshrined in the constitution. Or so it was thought.

Monty Python's Life of Brian received its world première in New York on 17 August 1979, the same week as *Apocalypse Now* and *The Muppet Movie*. Critics cited the film's extreme tastelessness, but neither were they blind to its obvious comic majesty. The *New York Times*'s description of it being 'a non-stop orgy of assaults, not on anyone's virtue, but on the funny bone' was fairly typical. *Newsweek* loved it, too. 'Though the pious will blanch, Pythonmaniacs should find this film a treasure trove of unborn-again humour.'

One of the few detractors was the noted New York critic David Denby who called *Brian* 'a truly lousy movie. The boys try very hard to be outrageous but most of their work is dumb, repetitive and unfunny.'

The opening salvo in what became a heated and often surreal religious war of words arrived on 19 August from Rabbi Abraham Hecht, President of the Rabbinical Alliance of America who claimed to speak for half a million Jews. Hecht denounced *Brian* as 'blasphemous and sacrilegious'. Speaking in *Variety*, the film industry's bible (no pun intended), he declared, 'Never have we come across such a foul, disgusting, blasphemous film before.' Hecht went on to make public his view that *Brian* 'was produced in Hell'.

Hecht's genuine if misguided fear was that *Brian* would weave a corrupting spell over the impressionable minds of young cinema-goers, leaving them with a contaminated view of religion. 'This film is so grievously insulting that we are genuinely concerned that its continued showing could result in serious violence.' This was no idle threat on Hecht's part; already, patrons outside some New York cinemas were being barracked by placard-waving demonstrators. 'Repent all ye who enter this place,' the opponents would wail, 'you are all vile sinners. Turn away from this film.'

After Rabbi Hecht's denunciation, outraged religious leaders queued up to vent their spleen to any hack with a microphone, in stark contrast to other more liberal churchmen who defended the film's right to be shown.

The voice of Protestant protest belonged to Robert E A Lee of the Lutheran Council, whose tirade against *Brian* – 'crude and rude mockery, colossal bad taste, profane parody. A disgraceful assault on religious sensitivity' – was broadcast over 1,000 radio stations. Not to be outdone, the Catholic film-monitoring office rated *Brian* 'C' for 'Condemned' and implored its flock not to visit theatres where it was playing, it being a sin to do so.

Embarrassed by the gathering storm of controversy, Warner Brothers, the US distributor of *Brian*, issued a statement regretting any offence that may have been caused. 'The film is a satire,' it read, 'and should be viewed in this context.' Indeed, the Australian film journal *Cinema Papers* suggested that *Brian* was saved from blasphemy by its sheer vulgarity, dismissing it as merely an expensive piece of slapstick, 'as if the writers of the *Carry On* films have teamed with the design staff of Dino de Laurentiis'.

And, if anything, the protests increased. Failing in their bid to bring a prosecution against the Python movie, assorted religious groups combined to march as one upon the Warner Communications building at the Rockerfeller Center. Gilliam says of that time, 'I thought at least getting the Catholics, Protestants and Jews all protesting against our movie was fairly ecumenical on our part. We only missed out on the Muslims. And I thought that was pretty fantastic to see, marching in the streets with placards against *Brian*. We had achieved something useful.'

Naturally, the protests and marches only served to heighten *Brian*'s media profile and so increase its box-office take. Nothing sells better than when it comes attached to the whiff of notoriety. When the shit started hitting the fan Stateside, the original plan to open *Brian* on 200 screens nationwide snowballed to nearer 600. 'They have actually made me rich,' Cleese ribbed on an American chat show. 'I feel we should send them a crate of champagne or something.'

Generally classed as Britain's comedy bad boys, Python were no strangers to controversy, it's true, so perhaps their reputation preceded them. But one should remember that, in America circa 1979, they were scarcely mainstream, more of a cult. 'When *Life of Brian* opened,' Terry Jones remembers, 'we organised a party in our New York hotel and the only people who came were us.' Perversely, the *cause célèbre Brian* provoked was probably what shot Python into the US popular culture spotlight. John Cleese adds, 'You see, the first movie, *And Now For Something Completely Different*, had done no business at all in America, and *Grail* was only a very mild hit. We were beginning to get known and we were on television, but *Brian* moved us up a couple of divisions so far as notoriety was concerned.'

In September 1979, *Life of Brian* opened across America and trouble was quick to boil over in the southern states of the Bible Belt, where fundamentalism and reactionary politics is a way of life. Cinemas were picketed and theatre managers faced the prospect of prosecution for criminal blasphemy. Often, *Brian* would open only to close again due to local pressure. In at least two states, it was banned outright. In Columbia, South Carolina, *Brian* lasted just 24 hours before being pulled from screens, leading to counter-protests where pickets held up signs urging 'Resurrect *Brian*. – Crucify Censors'. Neither was the madness restricted to the Bible Belt. In Waco, Texas, one theatre showing *Brian* received a bomb threat.

In Britain, the war against *Life of Brian* was fought a little differently. The most vociferous critics were the Nationwide Festival of Light, a watchdog association working in league with Mary Whitehouse, who opened the batting by lobbying the British Board of Film Censors to refuse *Brian* a certificate. They failed and it was passed uncut as an AA (the equivalent of a 15 today) after much legal advice. The then British censor James Ferman publicly defended the decision. 'We took the view that 14-year-olds are quite capable of telling the difference between a lampoon and a serious attack upon people's religious beliefs.' Unperturbed, the Festival of Light, supported by the Church of England Board for Social Responsibility, began circulating anti-*Brian* literature and even encouraged their Christian members to pray for the film's downfall.

With protest against the picture almost inevitable, distributors CIC moved cautiously, deciding to launch *Brian* in just one London cinema, waiting until after the religiously sensitive Christmas period before putting it out on general release. So *Life of Brian* opened exclusively at the Plaza, Lower Regent Street, on 8 November 1979 and, in spite of hymn-singing demonstrators outside, went on to break box-office records, raking in £40,000 in its first week, smashing the previous house record set by *Jaws*.

The film was backed by an ingenious advertising campaign in which each Python recruited either a relative or friend (Gilliam's mum, Palin's dentist) to present their own radio spot. By far the best was Cleese's 80-year-old mother Muriel, who reads an appeal to listeners claiming she is 102 years old and kept in a retirement home by her son, and that unless enough people see his new film and make him richer, he will throw her into the streets where she will assuredly perish. The ad won a delighted Muriel an award for best radio entertainment commercial of 1979.

The press certainly were on *Brian*'s side, calling it the group's most disciplined and consistently funny movie yet, running the whole gamut of Python humour from fourth-form gags to inspired lunacy and high satire. 'At the risk of hellfire, I recommend it,' wrote the *Sunday People*. 'An incorrigible delight,' raved the *New Statesman*. 'You have to respect a film that can make as many enemies as *Life of Brian*,' purred *The Times*. Perhaps the *Daily Mirror* summed it up the most astutely: 'If anyone's faith is to be shattered by an outrageously funny parody, then that faith is not worth a fig.'

The day after the London opening, John Cleese and Michael Palin famously appeared on a late-night BBC2 discussion programme hosted by Tim Rice, himself no stranger to religious controversy as the lyricist of *Jesus Christ Superstar*. Their inquisitors were Mervyn Stockwood, the Bishop of Southwark, and Malcolm Muggeridge. Both harangued *Brian* from the outset calling it 'a squalid little film ... tenth rate', and no amount of measured argument on Python's part would dissuade the pious double act of their firmly held belief that *Life of Brian* mocked Christ. Michael Palin recalls, 'We went on that programme and we'd done our homework, thinking we were going to get into quite a tough theological argument, but it turned out to be virtually a slinging match. We were very surprised by that. I don't get angry very often but I got incandescent with rage at their attitude and the smugness of it. And it was really the way they played to the audience that got me. We weren't defeated in argument at all. John was brilliant. What they were trying to do was to sort of smirk at the audience and belittle what we'd done and that seemed so out of touch and so stupid and so mistaken. I mean, how do they think the film was made? That we go in there one night, write the script and the film's made the next morning? They don't realise we'd been working on it for two years, we'd studied, that we had an opinion and we had an attitude, but they wouldn't let us have that. So it was their condescension that really got me irritated.' Gilliam remembers having never seen Palin quite so pissed off before.

As the debate reached its conclusion, Stockwood, dressed grandly in purple cassock and pompously fondling his crucifix in a way that was devastatingly lampooned by Rowan Atkinson a week later on a *Not the Nine O'clock News* sketch, delivered his parting shot of, 'You'll get your 30 pieces of silver.' Cleese sums up the affair best, observing dryly, 'I always felt we won that one by behaving better than the Christians.'

It was only after the show that the Pythons learnt that both Muggeride and Stockwood had turned up at a preview of the film late so had missed the first 15 minutes. Jones fumed, 'So how they had the fucking cheek to sit there pontificating about "Of course, Brian is really Christ" when they'd missed the beginning. That's actually typical, really, of people who were up in arms against it … usually they'd never seen the film.' Chapman also felt aggrieved that most churchmen condemned *Brian* out of hand without watching it first. 'But then,' he argued at the time, 'that's the prerogative of a bigot, isn't it?'

When *Life of Brian* opened across Britain in the new year, the battle lines altered dramatically and Python became a victim of regional censorship. 'There was a loophole in the law,' Palin says, 'local authorities had power over certain cinemas through health regulations and they used this extraordinary clause to ban Monty Python because it was unhealthy. I don't know if they thought it would spread diseases in cinemas. This was the obscure clause that they used, so it meant that local authorities could ban our film from their cinemas wherever it had been licensed. It was a very odd state of affairs, but it didn't half help the film, as things like that do. I mean, a ban only really works if something disappears completely. It was banned in Swansea so people went to a little cinema in Porthcawl which was just about to go bankrupt and suddenly people were coming in coach-loads, students coming out from Swansea.'

Life of Brian ended up being banned in Harrogate, parts of Surrey, East Devon (where councillors refused even to watch it, arguing, 'You don't have to see a pigsty to know that it stinks') and Cornwall (where, after one screening, a local councillor rather overstated the case by arguing for all the participants in the film to be locked up in Broadmoor). Gilliam noted, 'In Britain it was banned in different towns; what that meant was that people in those towns organised charabancs and went to the neighbouring town where it was showing. But in the States they banned it in the Bible Belt area and nobody went. You see, the British can't be controlled and the Americans can ... that's what we learnt over that.'

Incredibly, *Life of Brian* remained banned in Swansea until 1997 when it was finally permitted to be shown in cinemas in aid of Comic Relief. Informed of the ban's lifting, Eric Idle told the press, 'What a shame. Is nothing sacred?'

With *Brian* raking in £20,000 a week in London's West End alone, those renegade councils presented no problem financially speaking; indeed, their actions continued to keep the film in the media spotlight and helped it become the fourth most successful picture of the year in the UK, the only British-made film in an otherwise American-dominated top ten. Surely a case for some patriotic pride.

Censorship problems weren't the sole domain of America and Britain, though. When *Life of Brian* went global, it was banned outright in Ireland whose distributors didn't even try getting the film past the Republic's strict censorship laws. It was the same in Norway, where the country's Film Control Board decided unanimously that *Brian* was both blasphemous and against Norwegian law. Not to be outdone, Python flogged it to Sweden with the slogan: 'The film that was so funny it was banned in Norway'.

Even in 1985, *Life of Brian* was still courting controversy when the Independent Broadcasting Authority ordered Channel 4, who owned the television rights, not to go ahead with any broadcast as, 'it would undoubtedly cause offence to a large number of practising Christians'. They said nothing about those who'd already got the hang of it. The decision infuriated Channel 4's then Chief Executive Jeremy Isaacs, who later admitted that *Brian* was 'the film I fought hardest for and lost every round over'. Finally shown in April 1991, Channel 4 was predictably showered with complaints, the main bulk of which it received prior to transmission.

It would be naïve in the extreme to suggest that Python never anticipated some flak over *Brian*, but the sheer volume of the controversy did genuinely surprise all of them, Cleese included. 'We thought a few people might be offended, but it's the sort of offence that seems to last about 12 months and then they forget about it. Very frequently, the people who protest are the heads of organisations and they feel that they should protest in case any of their members criticise them for not doing so. It's one of those slightly ritual dances that you go through.'

Eric Idle adds, 'I didn't expect that level of response because I thought we'd been quite good, we'd avoided being specifically rude to specific groups. But some people, they don't want free speech, they don't want people examining it because a lot of it is just rubbish. A lot of religion is good and a lot of it's true, and a lot of it isn't. Everybody can't be right in religion; every one of the seven major religions can't all be right, somebody's got to be wrong. If you intimidate people by fear, use the word God, then you're restricting their views, you're saying, "We are the people who tell you what God says." That's obvious nonsense.'

Terry Gilliam agrees. 'What always intrigued me was my mother who was a diligent churchgoer from year dot and she saw the film and didn't understand what the problem was. She said, "Well, it's not Jesus, it's very clear, there's the one born in the other stable, here's the guy in the sermon on the mount. It's not Jesus." We were so careful about that.'

Terry Jones remembers when they started doing the script actually saying, 'Gosh, you know we might get religious nuts taking pot shots at us, it could be quite tricky,' adding, 'But I have to say, after Salman Rushdie's experience, I think we might have thought twice about it.'

Michael Palin observes, 'What I'm proud of about *Brian* is it did actually force people to take up sides. Some people took up the wrong side and some people obviously thought a little more about it and took up the reasonable side. The wrong side was just saying, "This is a completely worthless film." But I know vicars and religious people who've said since that they think it's a really good film and they show it to their congregation because it tells you something about what real belief is – don't be fooled by false messiahs, they can see it for what it is. So people who just dismissed it completely were made to look fairly foolish. The Bishop of Southwark was one of them … extraordinary! Malcolm Muggeride, very intelligent man, another. Bernard Delfont, who refused to have anything to do with it. And the great thing is that HandMade was created by people's inability to see that this was a reasonably well-thought-out, intelligent film. It was sort of born out of other people's bigotry. So good for George. And George loved it, loved the idea that he'd taken on the forces of reaction and won. It was a very Beatle-ish thing to do.'

What drew the most criticism, of course, was the gloriously tasteless finale which even Mel Brooks might have balked at perpetrating, that of Brian and what seems like the entire cast being crucified. 'We thought, How on earth are we going to do something so serious and important to so many people?' Palin says. 'It was difficult to do it in a way that wouldn't have so many people throw up their hands in horror because the crucifixion is the most intensely felt part of the Christian religion.' In the end, Palin, writing with Jones, finally cracked it. The approach was to accept the historical fact that crucifixion was a common form of Roman capital punishment long before it was invested with religious significance. Gilliam admits, 'I love the fact that the Christians wanted to claim the crucifixion as their own, nobody else got crucified. It's kinda like the Jews claiming the Holocaust as their own, there weren't any gypsies or homosexuals in there. Wait a minute, there were a whole lot of people in there, folks, let's not forget those people. It just becomes kind of an industry, the church, that cross is theirs and nobody else's.'

It might have been an omen, but on the day the crucifixion sequence was shot fears were voiced whether it could be attempted at all after heavy storms overnight. Jones recalls, 'What happens is that the wadis [dry river beds] flood and you get cut off. And as we were driving through this torrential rain about six o'clock in the morning to this location, lorry drivers were coming back the other way waving their hands saying, "Don't go on because you'll get cut off." But we went on anyway, and when we got there the rain cleared up and we were able to get everybody up on the crosses to shoot it. But it was bitterly cold. You'll notice John is wrapped in a blanket … everybody else is braving the cold.'

In fact, Cleese was suffering from a bad chest infection and had been bed-ridden for three days. 'When I had to get up to go on the cross, I remember thinking, Having bad 'flu and then having to be crucified on top of it – not ideal.' Nor was it particularly comfortable for the others. Idle says, 'We were up on these crosses and we had three ladders and if you wanted to piss you had to scream, "Hey, I need to get down quick!" '

Blasphemous or not, this scene has entered film folklore, not least because of the foot-tapping ditty 'Always Look on the Bright Side of Life' that the cast merrily sing as they dangle on a row of crosses. Idle explains, 'We'd got to the point at the end of the movie where everybody is going to be crucified and we decided wouldn't it be funny if we sing something. We realised it would have to be a very cheery song, ridiculously cheerful, and we started to giggle at the idea of people kicking their legs up and doing a dance routine. So I went straight home and banged it out; it didn't take me very long. I used a lot of jazz guitar chords. I came back and sang it and people really liked it. And then I recorded it and I did it very straight, with a big jazz swing arrangement, but not a very convincing vocal from me. When I got to Tunisia, I thought, this is not really selling, so I got the sound guy to come with me and we took a room in the hotel and we put mattresses all up around the walls. I had a little bottle of wine and we had a drink or two and then I sang it live whilst the sound guy's lying on the floor with the backing track. And I just made the vocal Mr Cheeky, and it suddenly changed the perspective of the song, sold it a lot better. So on the film that's a live track recorded in the hotel.'

Astonishingly, years after *Brian*'s release, the song found a life of its own, much to Eric Idle's delight. 'It was re-discovered by the soccer fans in England who'd sing it on the terraces whenever they were being hammered five-nil, and my friend Gary Lineker said, "You know they're singing your song." And Lineker had a pal who was a DJ, Simon Mayo, who played it every morning on Radio 1 and then Virgin re-released it and it suddenly shot up the charts. It was amazing. There's also a story that at the height of the Falklands conflict when HMS Sheffield was hit by an Exocet missile, and because they had nuclear weapons on board, the entire British fleet steamed in the opposite direction as a precaution. The sailors had about four hours to wait and they sat on the deck singing 'Always Look on the Bright Side of Life', which is fabulous because, of course, that's what the song is about, people facing death saying, "Oh come on, cheer up anyway." The song has now become a standard, which is great.'

Life of Brian ranks high in the Python universe. Cleese says, 'That's our masterpiece. That's what I'd like to be judged by in the future.' Gilliam agrees, 'I think it's my favourite, for all of its flaws. It's dealing with really funny things, intelligent things. I think it's number one. *Holy Grail* probably goes two.' And Palin adds, 'I think it really holds up almost all the way through. I would say it's the most satisfactory of all the films we made. I think *Holy Grail* and *Meaning of Life* have some terrifically funny and much more odd and surreal moments, but *Brian* has a thought going through it; it holds together as a drama, it has a great unity to it. It actually holds together as a sort of philosophy, if you like, as well.'

It was no real surprise when *Life of Brian* scored big with the public. And within the film industry, eyebrows were raised at how naturally George Harrison and, in particular, his business partner Denis O'Brien, took to film-making. John Goldstone says of this unlikely initiation in the world of film production, 'I think they had fun on *Brian*, it was a real challenge. Both began to realise how interesting film-making can be.'

Intended as merely a glorious one-off, *Monty Python's Life of Brian* instead became the foundation stone of a company that was to find itself, reluctantly perhaps, at the forefront of the renaissance of British film production in the 1980s. Gilliam says, 'So it was Python, Denis and George, that was the company, that was HandMade. Then Denis said, "We need a logo." So I went away and quickly devised a logo. And we were off.'

It was to be some ride.

CHAPTER 2

THE BEATLE AND THE BANKER

Eric Idle fondly refers to George Harrison and Denis O'Brien as 'Bialystock and Bloom', the characters played by Zero Mostel and Gene Wilder in the hit comedy *The Producers*. Michael Palin called them 'among the most retiring film magnates in the world. They make Howard Hughes look like Jeffrey Archer. To look at them, you'd think they'd just had a pretty good year running a rubber goods shop instead of a film company.'

Harrison and O'Brien really were among the most unlikely movie entrepreneurs the industry had ever seen. Yet, incredibly, their partnership seemed to work. What strange alchemy was at play here.

George Harrison had already dipped his toe into the murky shallows of the movie business as a performer in those classic Sixties Beatles films. Richard Lester, who directed both *A Hard Day's Night* and *Help!*, once told this author that Harrison might well have carved out some kind of future career as an actor. 'On balance, I would say the person that was the most accurate of all The Beatles in terms of "give him a line and he will get the right elements in it without trying too hard" was George. In *A Hard Day's Night*, if you watch George he just gets his lines right. Paul is

25

all over the place, and John, sometimes it's wonderful and sometimes it's thrown away too much. George was just so wonderfully accurate.'

The famous Apple Corps Ltd, The Beatles' own company which managed their finances and was also intended to fund worthy causes – the '"non-happening" of the late Sixties', Harrison once joked: 'Come all ye faithful, and we'll give you all our money' – also had a film division and one of the first recipients was George's mate, the then struggling and largely unknown John Hurt. Harrison saw Hurt in the play *Little Malcolm and his Struggle Against the Eunuchs* and thought, Let's do this as a movie! Noble indeed. 'But we didn't even get a distribution deal,' Harrison recalled years later. 'It was very depressing.' *Little Malcolm* was Harrison's first venture into film production and enough to put one off the movie business for life.

Like so many of his generation, George Harrison fell in love with cinema not so much because of the movies themselves but the actual physical act of going to see them. He remembers the first picture he ever saw, aged four – *Bambi*, and particularly recalls 'the horror of the forest on fire'. Entering those majestic picture palaces was an event, not just another night out. 'I spent most of my schooldays in the cinema,' he told *Time Out* in 1988. 'In Liverpool in the late Forties and early Fifties there were all these fabulous art deco cinemas with marble floors and goldfish in the foyer and a nice glow with the lights and just to go there was a turn-on.' In the mid-Eighties, Harrison wrote an article in his local newspaper attacking Henley Council's plan to demolish the Old Regal cinema in the town's high street and replace it with a supermarket. He won his campaign.

As for Denis O'Brien, a graduate of Washington University Law School and the Faculté de Droit in Paris, he was a gifted accountant, business adviser and lawyer. Between 1967 and 1969 he practised Law in Paris before moving into merchant banking in London with Rothschilds. Subsequently, he went solo as a consultant, establishing a reputation for himself as a very tough operator indeed. A very intelligent man, almost a Wall Street banker type, he knew his way around the financial and legal communities on both sides of the Atlantic. He was also a keen sailing enthusiast with a passion for owning yachts … *expensive* yachts.

Both men were to a large degree naïve in the way of movie enterprise, their amateur status reflected in the name they chose to christen their fledgling company – HandMade. Actor Denis Quilley thought it was a name that perfectly complemented their ethos, their attitude. 'The very title HandMade is very endearing, as opposed to machine-turned.'

The name actually started out as a bit of a joke. Harrison had recently visited Wookey Hole in Somerset and been intrigued by its historic paper mill. Unable to resist buying a few rolls, he noticed an unusual watermark – 'British Handmade Paper'. 'I said, "Let's call our company British HandMade Films," ' Harrison told the *Sunday Times* magazine in 1983. 'But when we went to register it, we were told, "You can't call it British!" You can only call things British if everybody is on strike the whole time and it's making huge losses. So we said, "Sod it – we'll just call it HandMade Films." '

The man Eric Idle dubs 'the strange O'Brien' was first introduced to George Harrison by Peter Sellers, whose own life was a cracked montage of surreal episodes. The year was 1973, not long after the dissolution of The Beatles. Denis O'Brien was a man of Cleese-like vertical proportions, bespectacled and the owner of a laugh reminiscent of a hyena having an orgasm. Gilliam says of him, 'Denis was tall, I mean *really* tall, but with a very small head. All of his extremities were tiny – tiny head, tiny hands and tiny feet – and this big, long body in between.'

O'Brien's first brush with showbusiness came in 1971 when Peter Sellers, at the suggestion of wife number three Miranda Quarry, hired the American to put his increasingly desperate financial situation in order. Subsequently, O'Brien became Sellers' business adviser, agent and lawyer, negotiating film deals on his behalf, notably the last few *Pink Panther* vehicles, until an acrimonious split in 1977.

Sellers had known Harrison since the heady days of Beatlemania and, by the early Seventies, was very much under the influence of the musician's Eastern-style philosophy. He habitually wore kaftans, practised yoga and took to chanting. Sellers informed Harrison how O'Brien had rescued his professional affairs and suggested he may be the man to sort out his own finances after the costly and messy collapse of Apple Corps Ltd.

The two men met in Los Angeles and, despite their contrasting personalities – O'Brien decisive and forceful, Harrison vague and retiring – rapport was instant. 'George is an absolutely extraordinary individual,' O'Brien said in 1988. 'When we met, some kind of synergy occurred between two opposites. George was very centred and I walked away from that meeting thinking, This is the most powerful person I've met in my life. I'd do anything for this guy.'

As for Harrison, he was quietly impressed with O'Brien's financial acumen and prudence and had no qualms in hiring him as his business manager. Within a year, O'Brien was handling all Harrison's financial and tax affairs. Gilliam observes, 'The way I was told it, the reason Denis had actually got George was that he showed him that there was all this money out there that had never been collected from all the songs and records. So Denis set up an operation to collect the royalties from all over the world, and suddenly George was in the money again.' A handy situation to be in when the Python's *Life of Brian* begging bowl came round.

Harrison was by no means the first rock star to bail out Python. John Goldstone confirms, 'The film industry didn't really recognise the potential of Python as a crossover from television to film. It was always Python's ambition to make movies. When they did *Holy Grail*, the budget was, I think, £150,000 and even that was not available to be raised in normal areas so we had to put this consortium of backers together, these rock 'n' rollers – Led Zeppelin, Pink Floyd and Jethro Tull.' A beneficial arrangement, being artists themselves, the rock stars granted Python the same freedom they themselves would have wanted. Similarly, Harrison and O'Brien barely interfered in the production of *Life of Brian*. 'We could not have made this film anywhere in the world with as much artistic control as we had with George and Denis,' Cleese said at the time.

O'Brien's company, EuroAtlantic Ltd, resided at 26 Cadogan Square, just off Sloane Street in London's fashionable Belgravia area. Set up in the early Seventies by O'Brien to look after the business affairs of Sellers, Harrison and other lesser-known clients, it was a small management company employing (as it continued to do so throughout the HandMade years) lawyers and accountants, basically financially adroit people who could give sound business advice, with Denis ensconced at the top.

To raise the necessary funds to get the Python movie launched, O'Brien put up as surety his business premises, while Harrison did likewise with Friar Park, his ornate Victorian mansion in Henley-on-

Thames that had been his home since 1970. They showed remarkable courage, but it also displayed utter naïveté on their part because nobody, then or now, finances a movie in the way Harrison and O'Brien financed *Life of Brian*. O'Brien himself would, in retrospect, call the move 'absolute insanity'. If some rich benefactor is willing personally to bankroll your movie, any producer worth his salt would scream, 'No!' Conventional wisdom would be to get some distribution deals in place first; don't make the movie before you've got yourself a distributor otherwise what you could see for your money is absolutely nothing, except five cans of celluloid (scrap value about ten quid), and if no punter will pay to see light shone through them, then you're well and truly buggered. But if you've done the stupid thing and made a hit, you've got the best thing possible, a finished film that distributors would fight like dogs over a bone for, leaving you to ratchet up the deal and make a fortune. This is precisely what happened with *Life of Brian*. It was a colossal piece of beginner's luck.

Just how many people knew about this mad gamble is unclear, though it couldn't have been very many if Terry Jones himself, the director of *Brian*, was left in the dark over it. 'I didn't really like to think about how much money was on the line. I know Denis was incredibly nervous when we were editing the film, and once or twice I had lunch with Denis and I could see he was terribly twitchy, hoping things were going to work and I was just keeping cool about it. I only learnt years later from George that to raise the money he'd put his house on the line and Denis had put the premises of his offices up as collateral. So if I'd known that, I would have been a lot more worried about the outcome of the thing, but at the time I just thought, Oh, they've all got tons of money and it's all right. I'm glad I didn't know.'

Like Harrison, O'Brien was a big Python fan. He loved the *Brian* script but there did follow days of hard thinking before finally agreeing to rubber stamp so risky a bail-out proposal; after all, his knowledge of the film industry was seriously lacking. Goldstone's perspective was that 'Denis didn't have a great experience of the whole range of the film business. Because he managed Peter Sellers he had a certain amount of experience in terms of performance contracts and so on, but I think the whole gamut of production and distribution, he admitted that he didn't know a huge amount but was willing to learn. I told him about the EMI situation, that we had a structure of a deal there, and he said, "Well, OK, I'll do the same deal." So we took the draft contract that we got from EMI and handed it over to him to adapt for his own company which was EuroAtlantic. What O'Brien knew he would have to do was structure the deal in a way that would be tax-effective for George and that what would have to happen would be something in the nature of a partnership that would enable George to off-set the investment in *Brian* against his ongoing income from other sources, and that it would need to be a separate entity from EuroAtlantic. So the idea was to set up a new entity and they came up with HandMade. There was no talk about doing anything else, it was just this one film.'

Once all the financial and legal matters were laid to rest, filming was allowed to proceed. Then, of course, Python went and spoilt it all by making *Life of Brian* a global smash hit. Idle says, 'I think one of the real problems was when *Brian* started to make money. It was a classic Bialystock and Bloom ... George and Denis really were like the classic *Producers*. This is not supposed to make money, it was a tax write-off. After that, I think Denis saw the potential tax advantages of losing money in the film industry.'

Eric Idle had, in fact, been the first Python to experience a face-to-face encounter with O'Brien. 'I met him once when I was hanging out with George and he had this model of a beach development thing he was trying to set up in the Seychelles shortly before it was taken over by an armed coup.' Palin, too, met O'Brien through Harrison and was rather taken with him. 'He seemed very affable, always laughing in a slightly manic way, and I thought, Well, that's a good sign. He and George seemed such an unlikely pair, like some sitcom might have been written about the two of them, the rather straight international lawyer with fingers in pies around the world, and George there trying to be just the pal of the Pythons. I can remember thinking, because Denis wore quite well-cut suits, that our money was safe.'

But it was Harrison and not O'Brien who made the first significant HandMade appointment, that of Ray Cooper, a musician and old mate from the late Sixties. Cooper remembers, 'I was about to start a two-man tour of Russia in 1979 with Elton John, and George and his wife Olivia came to visit me many times, and George would bring me reports of what was going on with *Life of Brian*. One day he said, "It looks like maybe I've got a film company on my hands. What are you doing after you've finished this?" I said, "I don't know." And he said, "Well, you used to be an actor, you know about these theatre people, let's see what we can do. Let's work together." It was as naïve as that.'

Cooper hadn't been so much an actor as a spear carrier, albeit alongside the likes of Laurence Olivier, Derek Jacobi and Albert Finney and on the august stages of the RSC and the National Theatre. But he'd carried his spear in exalted company, nonetheless, and hadn't earned much money doing it, either. 'So in the evenings after performances, I would shoot around to the jazz clubs to make an extra few bob or just literally to play, because I loved performing, it was what I was born to do, I think. My dear mother, who was from a very working-class background, with no support mechanisms, had managed to secure me a musical background. From the age of five or even less, I was stuck playing a piano and, by the age of 12, I was an incredibly adequate reader of most of the dots that you could put in front of me, something which was to be very rich in its rewards later on.'

However, the smoky cellar rooms of the London jazz club scene of the mid-Sixties were unfortunately littered with pianists, so Cooper found himself gravitating instead towards playing percussion instruments out of instinct, for survival's sake. 'Music was taking over from my spear-carrying activity; I was actually earning more money, and I was still performing. And once you got into that jazz circuit, they were the core of the session musicians in those days, those were the guys that were on The Beatles' and the Rolling Stones' sessions. So I moved into session work where, with a modicum of talent but a great deal of luck, I managed to become quite successful and worked with The Beatles ... and that's when I first met George.'

Now one of the country's top session musicians, Cooper met another figure who was to loom large in his life – Elton John. 'I was in Elton's band from the early Seventies through to '76 when he retired on stage at Wembley, much to the shock of his band, but certainly his management, and the world generally. He was very depressed and he just made a shock announcement on stage; that was it, this was the last performance. So I became briefly an independent record producer. And there was my association with George. Also, I worked on John Lennon stuff, with Paul McCartney and Ringo, but my mate, one-on one, was always George. Why did we become such close friends? I think an understanding of some form of path that we were both on. He was generous in his heart … seeing someone with a like spirit and helping them on that path.'

After working with Elton John on his comeback tour in London and Russia, Cooper returned to acting, filming *Popeye* in Malta for Robert Altman. It was on his return that he found himself employed at Cadogan Square and an integral part of the HandMade set-up as Head of Production. 'That, in my day, was literally in the old producer's sense of development. You saw something, you saw a book, you had a coffee with someone and you wrote some notes on the back of a fag packet, that was your storyline and you developed it and then you put it into production. For me, this was a dream coming true, because there are maybe two art forms left now that have the celebration of bringing all the arts together and film is one of them, and opera is the other one, because you get writing, dance sometimes, music, design, everything, whereas in the other forms, something's missing, if not several component parts. So it was wonderfully embracing having all those great minds, to be sitting at a desk listening to those ideas churning around which end up on the screen.'

Cooper also had special responsibility for creative control on advertising material. But most importantly of all he was George Harrison's eyes and ears at Cadogan Square, responsible for reading the many scripts that poured into HandMade, a job Harrison hated doing. 'I know I can rely on Ray being sensitive to the artistic side of things,' Harrison told *Film Comment* in 1988. 'There's always a conflict between the "business", what people see as the brutal business aspect, and the "artistic" side. Since I've been an artist and have Ray there all the time, it eases the problem a bit.' The irony of being a Beatle and the person who derided the money men with lines like 'What do they know?' and now being in that position himself, of being 'the money', never left Harrison. Indeed, it amused him greatly. 'I can see it from both sides now.'

The general perception of HandMade from the very beginning was that it was a straightforward partnership between Harrison/O'Brien and

Monty Python. It was one of The Beatles joining up with the *enfant terribles* of British comedy to make movies. These bonds were forged even closer when it was suggested O'Brien also become Python's manager. Idle says, 'I said to the other Pythons, "This guy's good, he knows what he's doing … why don't we get Denis to be our manager? He's professional, EuroAtlantic looks rather superb." So I was really responsible for taking us into Denis's management in the first place.' And the other Pythons didn't need much persuading on the matter. Goldstone recalls, 'There was a feeling that Denis could sort out their affairs in a way that their current management couldn't. They were all rather taken by Denis's style and ability to really do things.'

To clarify and handle the financial affairs of Python's money and to have in-house expertise that could deal with all the various business aspects that such a merger entailed, O'Brien hired Steve Abbott, a chartered accountant who'd recently qualified from Price Waterhouse. 'At the time,' Abbott comments, 'the Python group was represented by Anne Henshaw [now Anne James], but as individuals they all had their own separate business managers, agents and accountants. Certainly some of them had top-class accountants looking after their affairs. The big problem was that some of them didn't and, spectacularly, Graham Chapman was financially managed by a company which collapsed. So, if you like, the six spokes of the wheel sometimes didn't co-ordinate because, by the late Seventies, with the exception of John and *Fawlty Towers*, Python really dominated the income of all of them, because of the success of the films it was the predominant factor in their companies. And clearly Denis's plan to have them all under one roof made a lot of sense, no question of that, in terms of dovetailing deals, just for tax efficiency as much as anything else. So I suspect even the ones who had their affairs completely up to date, they all recognised it made a lot of sense. There was certainly no sense amongst any of them that they hated being processed in this way.'

A huge Python fan while at Cambridge, Abbott's ambition was always to work in the entertainment business rather than the stuffy confines of city institutions and, for a while, toyed with a career in music. EMI were particularly keen to snare his services. 'I was relieving my boredom while being at a major accounting firm by going to a lot of punk gigs and I met a lot of the bands and some of them were thick, and it's like, the music's great but if I have to sit down and do someone's tax return, do I want someone who's puking lager all over me? I didn't know the Pythons personally but I'd read interviews and I thought, Well, at least they're sort of intelligent and erudite and maybe they'd be nice guys to work with. I think the reason I got the job working for Denis was that I had the balls or stupidity, however you look at it, to arrange the interview with him on the day my exam results came out, so in order to sell myself to them I was able to point out that I had a high pass rate because I had no relevant experience at all. I'd been doing major international company's finances, I'd never seen film budgets or record royalty statements or anything like that. So, on the day I legally became a chartered accountant I walked out on Price Waterhouse where I'd trained and walked into a job with Denis O'Brien. This was in November 1979, the week that *Life of Brian* opened in Britain.'

Abbott had also grown up loving The Beatles and never got over the buzz of working under Harrison. 'He was just like an ordinary bloke, just very nice. I never had any responsibility for George's business affairs; my professional worry as I spent more time in that office was that he was signing documents he didn't properly understand. He clearly completely trusted Denis and the team at EuroAtlantic. George would go into financial and legal arrangements and, I suspect, at the time would ask Denis if they were all right, or ask the questions of Denis. I never really witnessed that, but it was a worry of mine. I encouraged the Pythons to ask questions about anything, particularly if I sent stuff out to them, and be comfortable. And certainly after I left HandMade, I would always say to my clients, "I want you to sign this document but first of all read it and ask me any questions before you do," and I always suspected that that wasn't the case with George in those days. But if you look at it from his point of view, who the hell do you trust, if you're paying?'

Harrison made no bones about the fact that he hated the business side of movies, all that wheeling and dealing, or, indeed, that he knew next to nothing about it. 'Making films is sort of a hobby for me,' he once said. 'I can't let it become too serious, otherwise it'd become work.' Having got himself out of that star rat race once, he wasn't about to get back on the same treadmill. The Apple group fiasco, which saw The Beatles locked in legal battles for years, had taught him one salutary lesson – someone with weight and experience was needed at the helm otherwise things could quickly get out of control. Going out making deals was never going to suit Harrison; that was solely the domain of O'Brien. That Harrison was perfectly happy for O'Brien to be, as he put it, 'the business person', was a decision that could have proved financially costly.

HandMade as a film-making entity did not then exist. Cadogan Square was basically full of people working for EuroAtlantic and running various things like George Harrison's publishing catalogue and his house in Henley. Cooper remembers, 'The office was Dark Horse records and all that sort of stuff and HandMade squeezed in. HandMade had a little office, and then it got bigger. The key personnel in the beginning were obviously Denis, this sort of jolly giant, wonderful, you thought at that point, genius banker and lawyer, what a marvellous combination; George, who was not present in the office but would come in every so often, was always reported to, I'd go and see him; there was Derek Taylor who was The Beatles' publicist and a dear friend. He was a wonderful man, a wit, an incredibly intelligent man who supported everybody. Then myself, the Pythons and a lawyer. So it was an interesting team, a fairly weird and wonderful mix, and it worked. And what a glorious, wonderful innocence there was to it all.'

As far as Abbott was concerned, his wages were paid by EuroAtlantic and, although he might be asked if someone had a technical question concerning Harrison's affairs, 99 per cent of his efforts were devoted to looking after the Pythons and their finances. 'It was very friendly at Cadogan Square, very happy. All I'd been subjected to in three years at Price Waterhouse, because our clients were so massive, was seeing big multinationals and people who were bored. People's idea of fun was getting up to japes by the coffee machine. It was very, very intimate at EuroAtlantic. There were maybe eight to ten staff, no more than a dozen maximum, there wasn't enough room. As for Denis, there was such awe of him by people in the office. Everybody in the building was like, Denis was God.'

And it was O'Brien rather than Harrison who caught the film-making bug big time, so it wasn't long before he began to bask in the glow of *Life of Brian*'s success. Idle recalls, 'So now he's a film producer and he's got friends in Hollywood saying, "Hey, I like your movie." And he says, "Yeah, I'm a film producer now." One of his friends was John Calley, who was head of Warner Brothers at the time, and Denis wanted to show him that he could be a film producer, too; it was like, my dick's as big as yours, and so there was ego involved. I think George went with it; he felt it was a good thing to be sponsoring people's dreams, he's always had that sort of Apple desire to help other people. George was a very good man like that.'

Harrison took justified pride and enjoyment from his involvement in *Life of Brian*. Like Denis, he'd found it a stimulating challenge that had proved satisfactory on both a personal and monetary level. But even this early on in their relationship, a clear defining line was emerging between how George would operate within the framework of HandMade as opposed to Denis. In spite of his closeness and fondness for the Pythons, Harrison paid only the briefest of set visits during the making of *Brian*, one that was remembered by Terry Gilliam. 'He was down in Tunisia just for a few days. George never interfered. On *Time Bandits* he came on the set once, I think. He just sort of let us get on with it. He's smart. With any creative things you make your choices at the beginning, you choose the right people, then you've got to trust them generally.'

It was Denis who was much more involved in the actual production side of it, while at the same time happy, for the moment, to play backseat driver to producer John Goldstone, conscious that such matters were presently beyond his scope of experience and that the film was safely under control. Goldstone comments, 'I guess this is something that didn't happen in the later films. I didn't work with Denis again, but he'd clearly felt he'd learnt a lot and therefore could apply that learning to other people's films.' Often with disastrous consequences.

O'Brien was a willing convert to the wheeler-dealer world of film finance, spurred on by the realisation that if he financed a picture himself and then sold it territory by territory, sometimes flying out personally to countries to arrange local deals, he could potentially do better than if he went to just a single major distributor to handle worldwide sales. This part of the business truly fascinated and captured O'Brien from the off, appealing as it did to the born banker in him, this whole gambit of separating off parts of the globe, of bedding down individual deals. So having taken the risk in the first place over *Brian*, through Harrison's money and protecting the possible losses by a very clever tax shelter scheme, he'd then negotiated killer distribution deals which, when the Python movie became a hit, started yielding money in untold quantities. John Goldstone also played his part by introducing O'Brien to those distributors he'd entered into business with on *Holy Grail*, contacts that were to prove invaluable. The experienced film producer had nothing but admiration for his *modus operandi*: 'Denis did an awful lot himself, he was a deft negotiator. He did have experience of the music business and began to see that there were similarities and even applied some of his knowledge of music deals to the film deals which made them more interesting.'

So what started life as a one-off rescue bid now metamorphosed into something bigger, and while Harrison was certainly happy to go along with it, O'Brien was the real driving force behind the launch of HandMade. Abbott says, 'It all came from Denis, that's the way it was run, it was all very autocratic. It was the money, I'm sure. It was the tax deal more than anything; he's always had a good nose for money, Denis. George was absolutely straightforward in this; from his point of view, it was nothing more than wanting to help his mates out. From Denis's point of view, it became a very clever tax deal which worked; there was a good tax write-off from it. And it worked for George's tax planning ... at that time he was paying tax at a maximum rate of 98 per cent, so tax shelter was important. It was also possibly the fact that Denis's management company could get new and established clients. It brought into the fold a very quiet Beatle, who was basically the *raison d'être* of that company in Cadogan Square, and all the Pythons, and suddenly there was energy and activity. More to the point, it's like a printing factory for pound notes ... you've got this film that's just unstoppably making money. Denis was good at business, he could make shit-loads of money, and I'm sure what drove him at the beginning was the ability to make money and the tax advantages of making British films. I don't think he had a love for celluloid. I think he was what he was trained to be, an investment banker.'

It seemed a cosy and potentially lucrative arrangement. O'Brien had the Pythons under his wing, both as a group entity and as individual performers, giving HandMade the potential of churning out the occasional Python project, plus movies that might star one or more of the team, as well as other product to keep the whole enterprise ticking over. It looked like the start of something great, and for the Pythons maybe the chance to get back at an industry who had ignored their admittedly small but important contribution to UK cinema. Cleese observes, 'The British film business is quite selective about what it recognises as the British film business. It never treated the Pythons as though they were any part of it. Maybe it was because we didn't go to all the dinners. But we were always regarded as some sort of slightly separate group, and I never quite understood that.' Gilliam agrees that 'Python comedy is always a second-rate art. Alexander Walker did a book on British cinema in the Seventies and Python was a footnote, *that's all we were*! When I go to Brussels, people there say Python *was* British cinema in the Seventies. In a way it's good that we're treated like shit because it keeps us angry. If we were accepted, we would just get like John and we'd make films like *Fierce Creatures*.'

And it was Gilliam who was the first to exploit the new situation, which was no great surprise to Idle. 'Gilliam's never slow to seize an opportunity to get money.' A partner in the emerging HandMade company, Gilliam was way ahead of the other Pythons in grasping the fact that, in the shape of Harrison and O'Brien, here was access to the cash he needed to become the kind of film-maker he'd always wanted to be. All that was missing was the right idea.

CHAPTER 3

MIDGETS AND VILLAINS

Ever since *Jabberwocky*, Terry Gilliam had a vision, bleak and Orwellian, of a pen-pusher's Utopia. He christened the script *The Ministry* before changing his mind and calling it *Brazil*: 'After *Life of Brian*, we just started talking about projects and I was trying to sell Denis on *Brazil* and he didn't have any understanding at all of what I was trying to do there.' So out of sheer frustration that his pet project was going nowhere fast, Gilliam sat down with the sole intention of making a movie that at least had a chance of being financed, and one that the whole family could enjoy. But it was to be the antithesis of your average children's film, a return to the Brothers Grimm and the darker world of fantasy. In other words, a kid's film with fangs!

The idea for *Time Bandits* was born over the course of one brainstorming weekend in November 1979. Gilliam says, 'I wanted to do this whole film from a kid's point of view, making a child the hero. But I didn't think that a kid could carry a whole movie, so I decided to put a gang around him, people the same height, and off it went, it just sort of grew from that.' Gilliam loved the notion of this rapscallion band of midgets from heaven who'd been part of creation, toiling away in the tree

39

and shrubbery department, thoroughly pissed off with their lot and turning to crime. Stealing a map of the universe that pinpoints all the various rips in the fabric of time and space with the intention of jetting between centuries to loot the art treasures of history, they crash-land inside the twentieth-century bedroom of an 11-year-old boy called Kevin and take him on a series of adventures, meeting the likes of Napoleon, Robin Hood, Agamemnon and the Devil himself.

O'Brien was entranced by the idea, no doubt impressed by Gilliam's enthusiastic pitch in which he not only described the plot but acted the whole thing out, too. It was a 'go' project. Next, Gilliam recruited one of his Python colleagues to help with the scripting chores. Michael Palin recalls, 'He came round to the house one afternoon with this bit of paper and said, "Look, this is it, *Time Bandits*. Do you want to write it?" So that's how it started. I really liked the idea of another collaboration with Terry. I'd enjoyed doing *Jabberwocky* and I do admire him and his work. He's got a wonderful imagination, Terry, an ability to get it out of his head and on to film. I really admire that. And I think the scale of how he wants to do things is matched by an intelligence that runs through it as well, and there aren't many people quite like that.'

It was going to be a race, though, with less than two months to complete the script as plans were already under way to shoot during the summer of 1980. But there was one minor problem. Palin said to O'Brien, 'I can't start on the script for another month because I'm doing a *Great Railway Journeys* series for the BBC,' which elicited the response, 'What! A *Great Railway Journey*? Michael, I love railroads, too but, I mean, a railway journey for the BBC? This is a Hollywood movie we're about to make.'

Getting finance, however, proved impossible. O'Brien took the finished screenplay to Los Angeles but nobody wanted to know. 'Who the hell *is* Terry Gilliam, anyway?' seemed to be the Hollywood reasoning. Palin comments, 'You look back and *Time Bandits* was very successful but, at the time, very few people were falling over themselves to do Terry Gilliam films. Terry had made *Jabberwocky*, which was a marvellous film, but a dark and unusual film. So *Time Bandits* was quite a risk.' In the end, Harrison and O'Brien decided to back it totally themselves, again mortgaging the office in Cadogan Square to raise the required $5 million.

In the Python universe, Palin had written most of his material in conjunction with Terry Jones. The pair also collaborated on the successful *Ripping Yarns* comedy series for the BBC. So it was largely a new experience writing with Gilliam, one that Palin found pleasurably stimulating. Together, they made a formidable creative team with Gilliam's more darkly surreal humour nicely counterbalanced by Palin's more affably absurd approach. 'Terry's into fantasy more,' observes Palin, 'and I'm slightly more realistic in that I like writing real, rounded, three-dimensional characters. I wouldn't write about horses going through wardrobes in a child's bedroom because I wouldn't know quite how you do that, but Terry does because he's not afraid of the potential of cinema in any way; he will test himself all the time with wonderful and inventive visual effects which he would just throw in, and I wouldn't have done that … you have to know what you can get away with.'

With the main story already planned out by Gilliam, this left only the dialogue to be worked out and for the characters to have flesh put on their bones. 'It was like writing a series of small playlets within the framework that Terry had created,' Palin adds. 'I had to create as succinctly as possible a whole raft of different historical characters who only had maybe ten minutes to establish themselves. And also to create characters for the Time Bandits themselves, their relationship with the boy and the fact that they weren't a kooky little bunch of dwarfs. We didn't want that at all; we wanted them all to be quite disagreeable, argumentative, as bad tempered as anyone else.'

When it came to describing the character of Agamemnon, the stage direction simply read: '*The Greek warrior removes his helmet, revealing himself to be none other than Sean Connery, or an actor of equal but cheaper stature.*' It was largely put in as a joke. Gilliam says, 'We'd no idea we'd ever manage to get Sean. You wanted somebody who was a big surprise and a major star in what we thought was this small, little movie. The shock value of somebody as big as James Bond, Sean Connery, was what we were after. I just couldn't think of anyone else who had the qualities Connery has. Agamemnon had to be a hero, a king and he also had to be a father figure to the boy. We wanted a hero and Connery's a hero.'

With his eye firmly on the international box office, O'Brien took Gilliam's stage direction literally and set out to snare Connery at any cost. He caught up with him on a golf course. Luck was on O'Brien's side as

Connery happened to be a big Python fan and was both intrigued by the idea and sympathetic to HandMade's struggle to find backing. The Hollywood star recalls, 'I was amazed that Terry Gilliam had such a problem raising only five million. I did the picture for nothing but a piece of the gross.'

Gilliam was gobsmacked when O'Brien called him up with the news that Connery was on board and the director's first encounter with the superstar at London's Grosvenor Hotel remains vivid to this day. 'When you first meet Sean, he's overwhelming; he's the only star that I've ever met who is as big as he appears on screen. He's actually more intimidating and more impressive in real life. He's just like this great mountain, a giant. And he doesn't suffer fools at all. I wouldn't ever want to cross Sean. All he's got to do is growl at you for a minute and you're reduced to quivering jelly.'

But the casting of Connery also created the first of numerous flash points between Gilliam and O'Brien that later were to reach volcanic proportions. Gilliam's perspective was, 'Denis gets full credit for Connery being in the film, that was his great casting contribution. But the deal that Denis was going to do with Sean was for not much money up front but this huge gross percentage which was going to come out of my percentage. So if it had been done, Sean would've been collecting all this money and I would never get it because it would always go to Sean first. And this was my manager who was doing this deal! I thought, This is great! Luckily, Anne James, who was running the Python office before and became our manager afterwards, spotted this one and said, "Terry, don't do it." Denis's job as my manager was to look after me, but he seemed at times more interested in looking after Connery at that point; there's a future in Sean, who knows if there's a future in me? Anyway, that got resolved.'

The only proviso to Connery signing was that all his scenes had to be shot during a brief break in late May before work started on his main picture of the year, *Outland*. This pushed forward the schedule drastically, leaving Gilliam to organise costumes, props, a skeleton crew and the Time Bandits themselves all in double-quick time. The dwarf auditions were held at the Neal's Yard offices that Gilliam and Palin shared in London's Covent Garden. Gilliam recalls, 'We used to have these two old banana warehouses, Georgian buildings, very small with incredibly steep stairs going up to the first floor where the office was and these little guys would come up for auditions. You'd hear, clunk, clunk, and a little head would appear at the bottom of the door.'

With dwarf actors fairly thin on the ground, Gilliam succeeded in assembling a highly talented troupe that included David Rappaport, who'd worked on television and subsequently appeared with Sean Connery in Richard Lester's *Cuba*, and Kenny Baker (the man inside *Star Wars*' R2D2), part of a vaudevillian-style double-act with fellow cast member Jack Purvis. Gilliam credits Palin with breathing life into the various dwarf personas, achieved more often than not by imbuing them with the real-life characteristics of the actor. Gilliam says, 'Randal, played by Rappaport, was always the leader. Strutter, who was the lieutenant, was always bitching and moaning but he didn't really have the stuff to be the leader; he'd stab you in the back if he had a chance. Fidget was Kenny Baker, we made him the cute one, the one that everybody liked, but in a sense that's the way he is, so we were definitely using their real characters in some sense. Jack Purvis was in many ways the most heroic of the guys; there was something about Jack that was always the strongest and the best and so he became that character. Og is the stupid one and Vermin is, well, just vermin, really. So it was a combination of having some characters that were rather well established in the writing, and the others just grew out of who they were.'

The whole notion of casting a film with dwarfs came from Gilliam's memories of growing up in the San Fernando valley where a circus used to roll into town each year and local kids would find odd-job work with them. 'One year, I did the freak show tent so I got to see all these extraordinary people sitting around being ordinary and it really fascinated me, so that stuck with me. I just love the idea of taking guys that are small and treating them like heroes, treating them like Alan Ladd, almost as tall as Alan Ladd, I think he was about three inches taller than those guys. That's what the joy of doing it was and giving these guys a chance to get out of their fucking Womble costumes and R2D2 tin cans and be people. And they all rose to the occasion, they were all brilliant.'

As May arrived, Gilliam found himself up a mountain in Morocco, it was 120°F and his young male lead Craig Warnock, chosen from hundreds of applicants to play Kevin, had not only never made a film before but faced with acting opposite James Bond had completely frozen. It was panic time. Gilliam, who hadn't directed since *Jabberwocky* four years earlier and was still to a large degree learning his craft, was lumbered with pages of elaborate storyboards that were proving impossible to film. It was Connery who saved the day.

'Listen,' he said, pulling Gilliam to one side. 'Here's what you do. Shoot my stuff first, get me out of the way and then you can have all the time you need with the kid.'

Gilliam heeded Connery's advice, admitting later that he wouldn't have got through the Moroccan shoot without his encouragement. He came away from the experience impressed by the Scot's professionalism and down-to-earth persona. 'There was no starriness about Sean, he was just one of the people working on the film. He was totally at ease with everybody, there was no sense of hierarchy. When we made *Time Bandits*, it was a time when his career was going through a bad patch. Also, I think he was feeling guilty that he hadn't been maybe the father he should have been to his son, that this was a chance for him to be a surrogate father to the young boy.'

With an unknown adolescent leading player, backed up by a myriad of anonymous midgets, the film was seen as something of a gamble so it was decided to play safe and cast 'name' actors in the historical roles. Palin had written the part of Robin Hood with himself in mind, but it was O'Brien's idea to bring in John Cleese. Indeed, O'Brien desperately wanted all of the Pythons to be in the film. Palin remembers that 'Terry didn't want *Time Bandits* to be a Python film. You see, *Jabberwocky* had been called a Python film and the other Python members were quite touchy about that, Eric especially and rightly so, because it wasn't a Python film. And as *Time Bandits* was not intended to be written by the rest of the Pythons, the idea of having all the group in it would have added real confusion. I don't think Denis ever quite understood that, that there was a feeling within Python that it was very important that only Python films should be given the Python name, that is when you had everyone in them. But they wanted John in the film; this was all financial, it's about money and John's still the most tempting Python to investors, so we adapted the Robin Hood part for John. I wasn't annoyed, it wasn't a central role; I gave away a role which I know I could have done but John I think did it better in the end. It then meant I had to write myself the part with Shelley Duvall. We just invented this pair of star-crossed lovers. Denis insisted that I should be in it, and any other friends of Terry that were around, so Shelley Duvall was around and these two characters were very quickly cobbled together.'

Cleese himself, who'd found the script 'a very funny piece of writing', was oblivious to these backstage machinations. 'I was only slightly discomfited to discover, several months later, what no one had told me at the time, which was that Michael had written that part for himself. I really had not known this. I think Denis applied a bit of pressure to Michael; obviously Denis was looking for my reasonably well-known name, and Michael consequently had to play another part which wasn't as good as Robin Hood.'

Cleese's entire appearance in Lincoln green tights runs to just five minutes and he was only on location in Epping Forest (standing in for Sherwood) for two days, '... which is about, as far as I'm concerned, the ideal amount of time to film for. You know, the first day's fun and then you get bored at tea-time on the second day. I've never particularly loved the process of filming, it's so slow. But I got on well with Gilliam and liked the people that I was working with, including dear David Rappaport. And I got fascinated by how quickly one adapted to the fact that these guys were midgets. It seemed very strange for a few hours and by the second day you were just sitting chatting to them. It sounds condescending, but in one's own mind they'd just become like anyone else. It didn't take very long.'

Miles away from the dashing brawn of Errol Flynn, this Robin Hood is frightfully polite and well spoken, seemingly oblivious of his grime-ridden surroundings and the Bruegel-esque peasantry, based as it was on the Duke of Kent. Cleese explains, 'I remembered that utterly meaningless procedure by which, before football matches, the Duke of Kent or somebody similar would appear from a tunnel and shake hands with all the players. It always struck me as the most extraordinary ritual, the complete futility of that walking up and down thing, you know, are you looking forward to the match, those sorts of questions. It was like the fact they used to sing 'Abide with Me' at the Cup Final. When I asked why, somebody said, "It's the Queen Mother's favourite song." I remember thinking, I didn't know the Queen Mother was playing in the Cup Final, or indeed refereeing it. It's one of those extraordinary manifestations of British traditional behaviour that leaves one almost reeling in an attempt to understand its significance.'

However good Cleese is as Robin Hood, and he is good, his decision to appear in the film was not altogether an altruistic one. Steve Abbott observes that 'there was no question that *Time Bandits* was basically sold to John Cleese as a financial thing. He was sold the Robin Hood part as something that was tax efficient. It was my first major professional clash with Denis because he used a financial report I'd prepared for John without me being there, he used my figures, my report, to persuade John to do a film for tax reasons. And there's nothing wrong with that; Denis was playing to his strength, he was good at tax planning.'

After Connery and Cleese were snared, the rest of the cast fell conveniently into place. As Mr and Mrs Ogre, a seafaring husband and wife cannibal team, it was hoped to pair Peter Vaughn with Katherine Helmond. Gilliam notes that 'the studios had no interest in Katherine because she was a TV star in *Soap* – that doesn't count – and so I settled on Ruth Gordon, but she managed to break her leg on a Clint Eastwood movie, so she was out and I got Katherine.' In came Ian Holm, complete with cod-French accent, as a height-conscious Napoleon, and Ralph Richardson as God, played like a fusty old boarding-school headmaster. Great casting, and dear Ralph took it all oh so seriously, marking out his lines in red ink and occasionally saying, with absolute assurance, 'God wouldn't say that.'

'Suddenly out of the blue getting people like Sean Connery and Ralph Richardson, just wonderful,' says Michael Palin. 'All these wonderful people I never thought I'd ever write anything for. It was quite a challenge to get things right for them, but Richardson rewrote most of his scenes, in a sort of gentlemanly ruthless way. I tried to get Richardson to do one of the *Ripping Yarns* because I thought he was such a funny, quirky actor. I think the God we created for him was probably from my school days, a 1950s post-imperial God, a bit cheesed off with the way history had gone.'

With Richardson installed as God, the only question remaining was: who should play the Prince of Darkness? 'Originally, I offered the Devil to Jonathan Pryce,' says Gilliam, 'but he obliged to take a very large shilling from another film that went nowhere rather than the penny we were offering.' Instead, Gilliam cast David Warner, whose wildly pantomimic personification of evil is the film's scene-stealer.

Time Bandits was a successful, if highly pressurised, shoot. Some rewriting did go on, mainly to combat problems that arose during filming, like ideas being too costly or difficult to realise. Gilliam referred to the script as being organic, forever trying to keep up with the production. The biggest casualty was a lengthy sequence that preceded the dwarfs entry to the Devil's Fortress of Ultimate Darkness. Gilliam explains, 'The gang had escaped from a giant and were trying to get their bearings when suddenly this tendril wraps around Og and drags him into this cave. Inside, the bandits find these two desiccated old women knitting away and this tendril is in fact a bit of their yarn. What they're knitting are huge spider webs all over the place and the spider webs are full of young, good-looking knights in shining armour, pretty boys that they're keeping stored for their use. And under their great broad skirts they have eight feet and they scuttle along the floor. They're just sitting there looking for new boyfriends and our gang have to escape. So we shot that scene, and it's a really good scene, but it's gone now, destroyed, it doesn't exist anywhere. I've got one bad Polaroid of it, that's all.'

Other fascinating missing scenes included Kevin waking up at night to find his bedroom flooded with water and a pirate ship sailing through his window, and the bandits in twenty-second-century London. 'They rob a bank and it's a silly thing where they're too short, the bank teller can't see them,' Gilliam observes. 'It was a silly sequence and we cut it out before we shot.'

Gilliam, though, still regrets losing the spider women but by then he had insufficient money to shoot the two linking scenes that had been written to go either side of it. That left the problem of how to get the dwarfs into the Fortress of Ultimate Darkness. 'We had to make a quantum leap. How do we get from A to B as quickly as possible. The answer is, you're there already, you just can't see it, it's an invisible barrier.' A new scene was hurriedly written in which the bandits, lost and disorganised, turn on Randal who, in defence, hurls a skull at them, shattering the invisible barrier and thus leading the way ahead. It was a brilliant piece of improvising that reflected what was really happening amongst the actors who'd all been on a 'hate David Rappaport' campaign for weeks. Gilliam remembers, 'That scene is about those characters and so we made Dave Rappaport that little shit, which was what everybody felt. So in that scene if you look at them, they really aren't acting any more, they're really going to get the fucker.'

Throughout filming, Rappaport had built up huge resentment between himself and the other dwarf actors by not wishing to be associated with them. 'Rappaport saw himself as different from the rest of the gang, because he wasn't a dwarf, he was a great actor,' Gilliam says. 'I said, "No, no. Dave, you're a really wonderful 4ft 1in actor; you've got to put the two things together, you cannot separate one from the other, Dave." He was actually different from the rest, he wouldn't sit with them. If it was lunch, he'd be near John Cleese, with the "actors".'

Perhaps the biggest moment of desperation came as filming drew to a close and Gilliam realised he didn't have an ending. Connery was limited to just 14 days on the film, for tax reasons, and his time had already been used up. This was pretty bad luck as Agamemnon was due to take a central role in the climactic Good v Evil battle, dying the kind of hero's death reserved only for A-list stars. Gilliam was stumped. Then it came to him — since he couldn't kill Agamemnon, why not snuff out one of the midgets? 'So I said, "Let's kill the cute one." And so we killed Fidget. And the good thing about Fidget dying is that Kenny Baker and Jack Purvis were a stand-up comic duo, so I thought, Kill the guy's partner and you've got something going. That led to a great emotional scene with Purvis as Wally raging against the Devil.'

Next, Gilliam was reminded of something Connery said at their initial meeting, a desire to return in the film's final moments as a fireman who rescues Kevin from his burning home: 'So I got Sean the one day he was back in the country … I think he was seeing his accountant … and he had like a couple of hours in between meetings. We got him over to Lee International studios in Wembley and put him in a fireman's outfit. All I had was a fire truck as a bit of a set and we got two shots of him, one of putting the boy down and then another getting into the cabin, looking back and winking.' It was a nice final touch.

The making of *Time Bandits* turned out to be the phoney war; the real blood and guts began once the film entered the editing stage. Gilliam says, 'Denis started interfering. His skill was that he was brilliant at economical jugglings, but this is always the problem with anybody from the financial or executive side of film-making, they think they're creative, too. I mean, they're creative in their area, which is the stuff we can't do, but somehow they can't seem to ever stop at that. Denis doesn't understand the other part of the process. But that's when they all come in, during post-production; not just Denis, because now there's an object, a finite thing, you can see it, you can have an opinion about it, everybody can have an opinion about it, then the question is, is their opinion more useful, more interesting, more correct than the film-maker's opinion?'

The first ripples of discontent surfaced when O'Brien insisted that Gilliam change the film's ending where Kevin's mother and father are killed. 'You can't blow up parents at the end of a children's film!' exploded O'Brien. Gilliam stood his ground. 'That's the whole point. No one's done it before.' But O'Brien was insistent. 'It'll alienate the audience.' Gilliam was ready for that one. 'The audience is kids and every kid has this fantasy about getting rid of his parents.' To solve the argument, a special screening for a bunch of youngsters was arranged and the first one out, a particularly precocious five-year-old boy, was asked what his favourite moment of the film was. 'The parents being blown up!' He whooped with delight.

The next battleground was over the music. O'Brien wanted to pepper *Time Bandits* with a batch of new George Harrison compositions, plus what Gilliam describes as 'Heigh Ho' songs that would render the work like some warped version of *Snow White and the Seven Dwarfs*. Ray Cooper had been drafted in to help supervise the score. 'I'd never met Ray before,' Gilliam says. 'I think his main function was to try to convince me to put a lot of these songs all over the film so it was a musical. Ray and I agreed within the first two or three minutes that this was a bad idea, this was not what the film was trying to do.'

The two men formed a solid friendship from that moment. 'We sort of got joined at the hip at that point,' says Cooper. 'And so far I've been a part of every one of his films, which is a great privilege. He's a very masterly, interesting, crazy person to be around, manic and wonderful, always that spark is electrifying. And *Time Bandits* with Michael Palin writing, the two of them together, I wish they would do that again, it was a stroke of genius. All of Terry's innovation, animation techniques, everything he'd learnt came to full fruition for *Time Bandits*, and therefore for HandMade, which then was on a real wave.'

The pressure of post-production meetings between Gilliam and

O'Brien reached a head one afternoon at Ray Cooper's home when Gilliam completely lost his rag, seized a print of the film with one hand and with a nail in the other barked into O'Brien's face, 'Here's this nail, here's the negative. I'm going to rip it down the middle, 'cos I made it, I can destroy it!' Gilliam had become utterly exasperated by this stage with O'Brien's behaviour, always seemingly on his back about the film, bringing up a succession of problems. 'We had huge fights,' remembers Gilliam. 'It just became like bashing a head against a brick wall, but I was the brick wall and he was the head, that was the stupid thing. I kept saying, "No, don't go there, Denis." And he'd go – Wham! "Stop it, Denis." And eventually I started screaming at him, "You're a fucking idiot, Denis. I've told you time and time again your brains are bashed out all over this wall that I am and you won't stop." That was the first time that I was aware of his pig-headedness, how he couldn't back off. When I get possessive and protective of my films, George can see it and Ray, OK, just step back, there's no way of dealing with Terry at this point, let it rest for a day or two. Denis could never do that, he just was convinced of his own rightness all the time – so was I, but I think my credentials were a little bit better in that area. He doesn't actually understand how an artist works. George and Ray do, they've been there.'

It's striking how Gilliam refused to budge on anything with O'Brien over *Time Bandits*, even eliciting mild exasperation from one of his most ardent admirers, George Harrison, who told the director, 'You remind me of John Lennon, you're so difficult, so bolshie. Can't you just compromise?' It was the thing that Gilliam was most proud of that Harrison ever said to him. Harrison's other major critique over that incident took the form of his one and only song for *Time Bandits*, which plays over the end titles. Gilliam remembers, 'What I discovered after the event was that that song is George's notes to me about my attitude on the film. On the lyric, there's something about apologies. He felt I owed Denis and him some apologies because I was so unbending in the way I approached things. It's really funny because I enjoyed listening to the song but at the time I had no idea it was George writing his notes to me.' Some of the lyrics read '*Greedy feeling, wheeling dealing. Losing what you won. See the dream come undone*,' and most revealingly, '*... all you owe is apologies.*'

Eric Idle actually believes that some of the gloss came off the

HandMade wagon for Harrison as a direct result of *Time Bandit*'s turbulent post-production. 'I think George fell out of love with it when he made *Time Bandits* because he just realised what Gilliam was really like. You try to discuss a budget with Terry Gilliam, it's kind of ridiculous. Terry is completely mono, he's taken several businesses out of existence. Several companies have fallen victim to the Gilliam piracy.'

Palin, too, is a little critical of his Python colleague in the inflexible approach he took on that film. 'I think Terry is very keen to get things exactly the way he wants them. I'm much more prepared to sort of duck and dive, to weave around a system which I know is never going to be perfect. You've got to be able to deal with people, you've got to make a little deal here, step back there, go forward there and decide how you are actually going to get to do the work you want to do.'

When their relationship had irretrievably broken down, Gilliam's parting shot to O'Brien was a gift of two small brass balls. 'Denis had been spending so much time in LA he'd developed all these habits – "Put your balls on the table" – that sort of macho talk. One Christmas after *Time Bandits*, I felt nice for a moment and had these two brass balls made and put them into a beautiful box. I actually made the lining of the box crushed velvet and a little brass label that hung there and said "For putting on the table". And I sent them to Denis. And he sent it back saying, "I think you'll need these more than I do." He didn't get the joke or accept the thing and I thought, This is stupid.'

The ultimate cost of Gilliam's spats with O'Brien over *Time Bandits* was that it turned out to be the only film he ever directed for HandMade. A major regret, because in many respects Gilliam was the archetype HandMade director. His childlike exuberance for the film-making process encapsulated what HandMade initially stood for – films made by artists, individuals, not corporations, not committees. Gilliam's attitude towards cinema at that time was almost to treat it as if it were a cottage industry, some eccentric hobby one pottered about doing in a garden shed on weekends.

This was especially true of his approach to special effects. Certainly he was out to prove such magical feats and images could be achieved for little money as opposed to the millions spent on, say, *Star Wars*. The madcap space-ship sequence in *Life of Brian*, for example, was shot on a shoestring in his Neal's Yard office. Months later, Gilliam actually bumped into George Lucas who raved about it. 'Yeah. OK. We did it for a fiver,' Gilliam replied nonchalantly.

It's ironic that, in recent times, Gilliam has become best known for his profligacy rather than his artistry, mainly due to the budgetary problems incurred on *The Adventures of Baron Munchausen*. Back in the era of *Time Bandits*, he spoke passionately about a desire to steer away from computers, to fiddle about physically with the celluloid himself, to feel his fingerprints literally on the work, so that his movies were, in a revealing quote, 'more handmade than other films'. The loss of Gilliam as a director to O'Brien and Harrison and to HandMade Films was great indeed.

Despite all the post-production headaches, Gilliam delivered a hugely original, visually imaginative feast with *Time Bandits*. Part historical comedy, part fantasy, part knockabout farce, all for $5 million at a time when other films were spending several times as much with far less to show for it. His desire to bridge the gap between live action and the surreal nature and inventiveness of his animation had been spectacularly achieved in a movie that was not only a landmark for HandMade but for the director himself.

When it opened in London on 16 July 1981 against stiff opposition from the latest Bond opus *For Your Eyes Only* and *Raiders of the Lost Ark*, reviews were positive. 'It is, without doubt, the most thoroughly satisfying, frightening, comical, even educational children's film in years,' raved the *Sunday Times*. 'Fantasy film-making of the highest order. I doubt whether we will see imagination of such staggering brilliance on the screen again for a long while to come,' reported *Starburst*. But, surprisingly, *Time Bandits* underperformed at the UK box office and the blame was laid squarely at the door of O'Brien. Gilliam asserts, 'He marketed it in England like the next Python film. And this is the thing that Denis kept doing. *Life of Brian* went out and was marketed in a certain way and he did the exact same thing with *Time Bandits*. I said, "It's not Python, it's a kids' film, you've got to sell it differently." He didn't do it. It was like he'd learn the wrong lessons, he couldn't distinguish why you can't do *Time Bandits* like *Life of Brian*. They're different animals.'

Gilliam was determined the same mistake wouldn't be repeated in America. But first they had to sell it over there and no one wanted to know. Gilliam recalls, 'I don't know whether Denis was asking too much money for it or just the studios didn't get it ... it could have been a combination of both. In the end, he went to Avco-Embassy, which was the miniest of the majors, or the majorist of the minis, offering them a deal where they would pay nothing for the film but we would use their distribution system. Denis and George also had to guarantee $5 million on prints and advertising.'

The deal struck with Avco was unprecedented and highly innovative in the way it was structured. Steve Abbott notes that 'Denis negotiated the most killer deal imaginable, I mean, *the* killer deal. In order to make Avco make the deal, he did the outrageous step of putting up money for prints and advertising – no one did this at the time – took the most enormous risk, and when it came in, he made fortunes from it.'

HandMade, not Avco-Embassy, also controlled how the film was campaigned ahead of its November opening. Gilliam designed the release poster himself but ran into trouble over the content of the TV trailers. He was astonished to learn they weren't allowed to show dwarfs, 'because people don't like dwarfs,' Gilliam was reliably informed by the publicity people, to which he angrily retorted, 'They're *not* dwarfs, *they're Time Bandits*!!' He adds, 'That campaign got into a big battle because there had been a recent film called *Under the Rainbow* about the making of *The Wizard of Oz* starring Chevy Chase, and because it bombed they blamed the dwarfs!'

Gilliam instead came up with the inspired notion of carrying out three separate ad campaigns, one for the Python fans, one for the kids and one for the family audience. It worked a treat as *Time Bandits* went straight to the top of the box-office charts, raking in an impressive $6.5 million in its first three days. Its performance was remarkable, despite *Time* magazine's prediction that it would befuddle moviegoers and not earn a dime, a view not shared by the majority of US critics who heaped praise on the film. The *LA Herald Examiner* proclaimed, 'Deserves to be called a classic', while the *LA Times* wrote, 'One of the great fantasy-fulfilment adventure films.' '*The Wizard of Oz* of the '80s,' said *US* magazine.

During its first month, *Time Bandits* was taking almost $1 million a day and, by January 1982, still resided in the Top 20 earners. It was an achievement nobody had anticipated. Palin remembers, 'That was the best time I remember with HandMade, with Denis ringing me when the returns came in. We were all completely amazed that it was doing so well in America. We were all fairly buoyant about it.' To this day, it remains Gilliam's most successful film in terms of box office, and for a time it was the highest-earning British comedy film ever made until a certain *A Fish Called Wanda*. 'That bastard Cleese!' grumbles Gilliam.

Not surprisingly, there was talk of a sequel. The public's appetite for one was definitely there, but Gilliam wasn't interested, keen to move on to the next project, intent on using the success of *Time Bandits* to get *Brazil* off the ground. Today, though, he still harbours a tinge of regret for not fully exploiting its popularity. 'The pity is that we didn't take advantage of the merchandising possibilities and do games and toys. I think Denis was talking about doing an animated television series, but we didn't want that. It was partly our fault, we were such purists then; a film is a film, we didn't want to be like George Lucas and market all this stuff. We were fools, basically, because there are so many things you can do with *Time Bandits*.'

HandMade were on a roll. Their first two movies had met not only with critical plaudits but had also proven financial hits. Praise, too, was being heaped upon the company. *Stills* magazine described HandMade as 'the brightest new star in the faded firmament of British film production'. Harrison, not surprisingly, was singled out personally, hailed almost as the saviour of British cinema, a label he'd rather have lived without. 'Newspapers keep saying I'm saving the British film industry,' he complained to the *Sunday Times* in 1983. 'I can't deal with that. It's as though I sat down and said, "The next thing I'm going to do is save the film industry!" I'm far too humble these days to think of saving anything – I can't even save myself.'

More staggering was the fact that *Brian* and *Bandits* had been so popular in the American market, usually a graveyard for British movies, especially comedies. Abbott suggests, 'Denis was a beginner in terms of film who just had the most amazing chunk of beginner's luck with *Life of Brian*. Though the first film I produced was *A Fish Called Wanda*, so talk about beginners and beginner's luck! And then, lo and behold, he did it again with *Time Bandits*. Just amazing.'

O'Brien's growing confidence manifested itself in the setting up of a distribution arm to HandMade in September 1980 and the appointment of Alfred Jarratt, formerly of CIC, then one of the UK's biggest distributors, as its Managing Director. It made plain sense to everyone connected with the firm. Ray Cooper observed, 'After *Time Bandits*, Denis sensed quite rightly that we should really be distributing our own films. It was probably to do with collection of monies, being in control of financial reportage, really. If you're distributing yourself, you have more control.'

Jarratt's first act was to hire Brian Shingles, who'd worked with Jarratt years before at CIC. Shingles was to play an important part in HandMade's history; brought in during the company's golden early days, he would also be witness to its tragic and catastrophic end. 'Brian became a stalwart of HandMade,' Cooper says. 'He was so important and has been overlooked many times. He's a passionate film person and he was in charge of literally getting the films into the cinemas; he was in charge of those cans of films. An incredible man.'

As Alfie Jarratt himself had still to clean out his desk over at CIC, Shingles was left to arrive for work at a practically deserted office. He remembers, 'I got there in October 1980 and, in effect, HandMade didn't really exist at that point. There was EuroAtlantic, Harrison's music, all in Cadogan Square. I went to the first floor which was going to be the HandMade offices, and I was the only one there and I thought, I don't know if I like this, actually, because there was not much I could do except get the office set up, the distribution side, as far as just the very basic elements, because there was no staff. I'd been hired to do distribution and be office manager and I thought, Well, I can't manage an office because there's nothing here. And then Alfie came with the rest of the staff a few weeks later.'

Jarratt was a big gun in the industry. At CIC, he'd marketed *Jaws* and was also responsible for picking up *Life of Brian*, so he arrived at HandMade with a definite reputation. Shingles says of that time, 'But I don't think they realised what they took on when they brought Alfie in, every other word was "fucking this, fucking that". His language was rich. What was funny was that EuroAtlantic were like nothing I'd ever experienced. The film industry is quite down-to-earth and here are these lovely offices in Cadogan Square, the EuroAtlantic staff speak very well, there's a lawyer with his upper-crust English, and there's Denis looking like a businessman and a banker, and there's myself just very casual in comparison. I thought, This isn't the same atmosphere, this is not what I'm used to, I feel really like a fish out of water. And then Alfie came in saying, "… fucking this, bastards, cunts …" all this. And he used to shout, he used to lose his temper, he was a bit of a bully in that respect. I don't think Denis and the rest of the company realised this about Alfie; this image they wanted for HandMade was going to be severely undermined by Alfie. And when he was in a bad mood and he had the windows open, they used to say that Denis and everyone else could hear him two flights above when he was ranting. Alfie was a real character.'

In addition to handling films produced in-house by HandMade for domestic as well as for worldwide distribution and marketing, Jarratt and Shingles were also given a free hand to acquire other movies from outside sources for distribution. But with *Life of Brian* already released and *Time Bandits* not yet complete, they didn't have two spools of film to rub together.

Again, it was Eric Idle who emerged as saviour. In November 1980, he was asked by Helen Mirren to attend a London film festival showing of a violent mobster picture she'd made with Bob Hoskins that was facing traumatic difficulties; nobody wanted to release it. It was called *The Long Good Friday*. Idle says, 'I loved the movie and I thought, 'This is a hit.' So I phoned up Denis O'Brien and I said, "Denis, put your money down here, you'll have a hit film, my boy." And he did and, as a mark of his gratitude, he sent me absolutely nothing, and I think flat forgot about it. So I never got any credit for *The Long Good Friday*, but the producer and director wrote me a nice letter saying thank you very much and Bob was always very thankful. But it was a fantastic film. I was happy to help out.'

Made back in the summer of 1979 and financed by showbiz kingpin Lew Grade, the problems started after the film was in the can and director John Mackenzie had taken a five-day break in the sun to wind down and recharge after a strenuous shoot. 'When I got back,' explains Mackenzie, 'our producer, Barry Hanson, said there had been a little bit of trouble over the film. Grade's company owned it and didn't want to put it out as a film at all; they wanted it cut down to 80 minutes and sold to television. I said, "Well, that's ridiculous, what absolute nonsense, we just can't let them do that." And he said, "Well, you know they're my bosses." I said, "Barry, it's not going to happen." He said, "Well, as a matter of fact, they've done it." I nearly hit him in the middle of Wardour Street.' The battle for *The Long Good Friday* had begun.

Everyone who'd worked on the film felt betrayed by the actions of suited money men who displayed no faith in what they'd achieved, preferring to recoup the budget with a swift sale to television. A cinema release would have entailed costly ad campaigns, paying for prints and so on, and was a gamble no one at Grade's organisation was prepared to take. Barry Hanson adds, 'They also wanted to make it marketable for American TV. They pulled in this old white-haired editor who afterwards looked as though he'd had a heart seizure by watching it. He was brought in to actually carve the thing to shreds. They were determined not to release it as a film, quite the contrary, they were going to kill it.'

Mackenzie was in no doubt that the film's subplot concerning Irish terrorists had Grade's people running scared. 'You can't let the IRA win,' he was told, to which the film-maker replied, 'You want a gangster to win?' He goes on to explain, 'Lew Grade thought it was an IRA publicity film and unpatriotic. He was a bit frightened that a few bombs would go off in his cinemas and it's very difficult to argue with that sort of paranoia. Actually, the IRA liked it so why should they bomb us? But our film wasn't pro-IRA, no way, because I hate the idea of bombing. I don't hate the IRA, but I hate the things they did, bombing innocent people, I just do not condone that at all.'

The real breakthrough came when *Friday* was screened as part of a Mackenzie retrospective at the 1980 Edinburgh Film Festival. Critics were bowled over and poured public scorn over the decision not to give it a deserved theatrical run. In a wasteland of home-grown movies, critics saw *Friday* as affirmation that there was still talent and vitality left in British commercial film-making.

Encouraged by the reaction, Barry Hanson stole the film from the cutting room and started parading it around the industry, even flying with it to the States. 'I went to Paramount and showed it to Jeff Katzenberg and, I think, Don Simpson. They liked it but didn't want to pick it up for domestic America. I showed it to a few other people in LA then brought the thing back. Pressure was mounting, everybody was saying they ought to put it out as a film because, by this time, I'd made sure as many people as possible had seen it.'

And yet the executives at Grade Central (or 'that shower of bastards' as Mackenzie refers to them) remained intractable. There was nothing left now but for everyone involved – from Hanson, Mackenzie and writer Barrie Keefe, to Hoskins and Mirren – to make public pleas for finance to buy their own film back from Grade. It was a race against time; ITV were already scheduling it for a prime-time slot early in the new year. The asking price was £1 million. Hanson took a full-page ad out in *Screen International*, the UK's equivalent of *Variety*, packed with glowing notices (notable amongst them David Puttnam's belief that *Friday* was 'the outstanding post-war British gangster movie') plus his office phone number begging prospective buyers to get in touch. Both Rank and EMI toyed briefly with the idea of taking it on but ultimately passed. After that, nothing.

The mood was dark in the *Friday* camp. Convinced that Grade had finally managed to smother their film, some began contemplating the most extreme measures. Barrie Keefe recalls, 'Just before Christmas, we were all sitting in our office in Carnaby Street. It was getting dark and there was a Salvation Army band outside playing carols. The film looked dead in the water; I never thought the bloody thing was ever going to see the light of day. And there was Bob Hoskins with a bottle of vodka and two poodles on his lap he'd bought as Christmas presents for someone. He said, "Wait a minute. There's four of us here … I know a geezer who, for £10,000, that's only £2,500 each, he'd wipe him out." It was one of those mad moments, you think, my God, I can pick up the *Daily Mirror* tomorrow and see Lord Grade's been wiped out. And Barry Hanson said, "Hang on, Bob, you know it's a big family, another one would pop up." He said, "All right then, five grand each." There was a lot of silliness 'cos of exhaustion. That was at the absolute lowest of the low.'

Worse was to come when it was decreed that Hoskins's voice would be indecipherable to American ears so was completely re-dubbed by another actor. 'The whole thing was unbelievable,' fumes Mackenzie. 'You know, the business is full of tasteless idiots. Bob was totally incensed, it's the worst thing you can do to an actor. So the fight was on.' Hoskins decided to sue. As the trial date approached, an impressive array of famous names, Alec Guinness among them, agreed to testify that what Grade's people were doing was tantamount to a prostitution of Hoskin's acting ability. Sensing things were getting out of hand, Mackenzie set up a face-to-face meeting with Grade's right-hand man, Jack Gill.

'I remember it was the day before Christmas,' Mackenzie recalls. 'It was snowing. I went to his office and said, "This is going to look bad for you, it's rotten for us, and the film's going to suffer." But he was adamant the case was going ahead. I said, "Well, here's who's going to be the witnesses against you." And I read the list and he went pale, he went white. I said, "That will look extremely bad … you'll be castigated. Now the simple answer is, we have someone who will buy the film and then everyone will be off the hook." And that did it, we got the film back.'

Still babies in the industry, HandMade displayed more understanding of what constituted a hit movie than the dinosaurs over at Grade Central. Mackenzie's perspective was that 'the Pythons liked it and Denis O'Brien saw that he could make a killing with it. George Harrison hated it, but Denis was running the thing. George was sort of a backseater, he didn't really know what they'd bought; it was only later when George saw it he was quite upset, he thought it was too violent, but by that time it was a big success so he just accepted it.'

HandMade's offer of £700,000 to buy the film was funded, ironically, from the profits of *Life of Brian*, the film Lord Grade's brother Lord Delfont so famously turned his back on. Together, these two siblings really were the Cannon and Ball of the British film industry. They represented the old guard, HandMade the new.

Barry Hanson claims the whole débâcle over *The Long Good Friday* was the fault not of Lord Grade but his lieutenant Jack Gill. 'Grade was wrongly painted as the villain,' Hanson asserts. 'It was Jack Gill, he hated it. When we were negotiating to buy back the film, we had a joke with the lawyers. Gill always put his name on his television programmes, "Jack Gill Presents", and the lawyers said, "I think in your case it's Jack Gill resents to present." But I suppose Lew did have ultimate responsibility in what was going on with it. But all this was going on in the face of his bloody company collapsing, when he was making bloated blockbusters like *Raise the Titanic*. Lew never saw our film until right at the end because they kept it from him and, of course, he liked it, thought it was a very well-made film, but by then the die had been cast as to what would become of it. I think it was a pity that Lew didn't see it earlier and didn't have any opportunity to get behind it.'

During the HandMade negotiations, Hanson had no contact

whatsoever with Harrison; his dealings were principally with O'Brien. 'Denis was a bit bizarre, I suppose,' Hanson adds, 'but he was straight with us, he honoured the deal I had with the Grade people and we were grateful for what he did. I haven't had a cost statement from him for 20 years, which we should have done. Not a word about what it did and what happened to it. And we didn't have a video deal. It was the beginning of the video boom and I remember going back to him and saying he ought to honour that as being non-theatrical, but he wouldn't have it. And I do know they sold it to EMI for quite a lot of money.' HandMade also left the *Friday* team in the dark in terms of how things were performing in the overseas market. Hanson for one even had to pay for the air fare to attend the New York opening of his own movie!

*　　*　　*

Like so many British gangster movies, the influences of *The Long Good Friday* are traceable back to the Kray twins. Writer Barrie Keefe, born and bred in London's East End, remembers as a 17-year-old pissing in the smelly urinal of the Krays' local pub in Bethnal Green when Ronnie walked in. 'He turned and said to me, "What do you think of this?" Knowing he was gay, my heart was sinking. What am I supposed to look at? I thought he meant his cock. I was terrified. What it was was a gun, and he was saying stuff like, "It's got a good feel, ain't it?" ' It was the start of Keefe's lifelong fascination with gangsters.

The Easter weekend of 1977 – Barrie Keefe is at home, bored. The phone rings. On the other end is Barry Hanson, a producer with Thames Television, wondering how Keefe is getting on with the television thriller he'd asked him to write. Not very well, as it turns out. It was during dinner some months earlier that both men had come up with the notion of making a London gangland TV film. Keefe says, 'Barry commissioned it there and then. It was gonna be called *The Last Gangster Show*. There was no story or anything, it was just like, let's do a British gangster movie, because there weren't many around at the time.'

Keefe drove around the East End and the Isle of Dogs looking for inspiration and found it in the shape of the new Docklands. Keefe hated what he saw, a once-proud area stripped of its vibrancy by yuppie developers, and out of that anger grew the first seeds of his story. What if some entrepreneurial villain tried to muscle in on Canary Wharf? The central character of Harold Shand began taking shape.

That evening, Keefe met up with a friend for a drink. 'We ended up in a totally Irish pub somewhere in North London. The band on stage played rebel songs and, at one point, got a Union Jack and set fire to it. When the collection bucket came round my mate was wise to this and whispered, "Don't say anything, keep your voice down," 'cos I had a Cockney accent.'

Keefe couldn't help thinking this was like the good old/bad old days of the Krays; it was pure villainy, nothing short of a protection racket. A major strand of the film's plot, terrorism versus gangsterism, had presented itself. Keefe called Hanson with his idea. 'Write it!' the producer bellowed down the line. 'Just get at that typewriter and fucking write it.' Keefe knuckled down and pounded out a first draft in four days. He called it *The Paddy Factor*, Scotland Yard lingo for crimes that can't be explained so are put down to the IRA.

Despite its shortcomings, soon to be exposed, what this initial script had going for it was an exceptional central character, Harold Shand. Born out of Keefe's desire to write a part for James Cagney 'if he'd been a Cockney', Shand is a gangster extraordinaire, a sort of Cockney Corleone who charms a visiting Mafia big-shot while at the same time protecting his patch from marauding IRA mobsters. The general consensus was that there was only one man capable of bringing Shand to glorious life, a relatively unknown actor who'd recently scored big on TV in Denis Potter's *Pennies from Heaven* – Bob Hoskins.

Hoskins was tracked down to the London Hospital for Tropical Diseases where a 27ft-long tapeworm was preparing to emerge from his backside. Mackenzie says, 'Bob now says it was 35ft or something ... it gets longer every time I hear that story. He'd just done *Zulu Dawn*, a terrible film, I'm told, but he was very committed to it, and he was very committed to Africa. Bob gets very intense about causes and he commits himself to them, but only for a time, but he does so wholeheartedly, which is lovely and it's very refreshing and you go along with it. So he went out there to South Africa and he decided he wanted to live like the natives. "I'm not living in a fucking hotel," he said. So he lived in a hut. They gave him a hut and a telephone, and that's how he got the tapeworm.'

The procedure was a delicate one; the worm had to be removed foot by foot and a nurse warned the visitors not to over-excite her patient as the worm might snap, leaving poor Bob to endure the whole 'birth' again. Keefe adds, 'But telling Bob not to get excited is like telling Ian Paisley in full flight not to mention the Troubles.' Sure enough, as Hoskins listened to the pitch it was difficult to restrain him, having instantly connected with Harold Shand. 'The gang could call him "H",' he declared, before suggesting the film be called *H*. Leaping out of bed, creative juices flowing, Hoskins demonstrated how the poster should look, a dominant H, like a crucifix, with Shand nailed to it.

Thanking Bob for his thought-provoking suggestions, Keefe and Hanson left. However implausible the crucifix idea, it reminded Keefe of one gruesome story from his days as a journalist. He recalls, 'I had to go and see someone in hospital that had been found crucified to a warehouse floor. That was the punishment if you overstepped in someone else's territory. I asked him, the holes in his palms quite visible, how it happened and he said, "Listen, son, put it down as a do-it-yourself accident. And I'd keep your fucking mouth shut." ' A not dissimilar incident eventually found its way into the film.

Like Keefe, Hoskins had been brought up in a tough London neighbourhood, Finsbury Park, and knew his fair share of dodgy characters. Anxious to base Shand on authentic heavies and not be a crude caricature, Hoskins casually hung out with some of these bygone rogues. Most were flattered that an actor wanted to be like them. 'Well, look at this little feller here, wants to be a gangster!' they'd playfully jibe. There was even employment to be had for a lucky few on the film as extras or technical advisers. Mackenzie observes, 'They were quite an interesting lot. Barrie Keefe also knew quite a few, actually, because he'd been a journalist in the East End and had an "in" to that world. They were only on set for certain scenes. The big one is where the gang all get tooled up with guns and Bob tells them as they go off, "Be discreet." Well, those were all crooks and criminals who knew what the hell they were doing.'

This 'underworld' presence ensured the film contained what Keefe calls 'the smell of authenticity'. Certainly, the crew made full use of the free advice on offer, as well as Mackenzie. 'They'd say, "John, not that I've ever done it, but if you're gonna stab someone you wouldn't do it like that." '

During one scene, Hoskins was in full flight, arms flaying about and mouth on overdrive. One of the cons quietly took him aside and said, 'Look, you don't have to shout. They know who you are, so why are you shouting?' It's the understatement that makes it work. Keefe agrees. 'The thing I noticed when I was moving around in that kind of environment, in the background, just listening, was when anyone was making a threat, and I did hear a message go out to hit someone, they speak very quietly. There's no "Get that fucking cunt!" Rather, it's "Well, this is definitely out of order, I think he needs a bit of a seeing to." It's so quiet and that's the real menace.'

Hanson meanwhile was having no joy in hawking the script around. Thames were the first to turn it down, followed by Euston, makers of *The Sweeney* and *Minder*. Luck intervened when Hanson was given a budget of just under £1 million by Charles Denton, Managing Director of Black Lion Films, run by Lew Grade, with the intention of turning *The Long Good Friday* into a feature film. Next, John Mackenzie was hired and read the script. 'It was pretty awful, a bit theatrical and self-consciously tweedy funny, almost like a *Carry On*, which was totally wrong because we wanted it to be real, but with irony. The essence of the story was there, but it needed an awful lot doing to it.'

Pre-production began in earnest at an office acquired in London's famous Carnaby Street. Mackenzie remembers it as 'a dreadful place, above a shop that sold tatty old jeans and belted out music all day'. The meetings there were intoxicating, producing what Hanson called 'high-octane creativity', with ideas being volleyed around between writer, producer and director. Hoskins was also heavily involved, particularly in terms of dialogue, bringing with him as he did the Cockney vernacular. He was responsible for the classic line where Shand, hearing of a fallen comrade's body being taken to the morgue concealed in an ice cream van, says, 'There's a lot of dignity in that, ain't there? Going out like a raspberry ripple.' Bob's help did in the end, though, prove something of a strain. Keefe explains, 'Bob doesn't have ideas, he has visions. He's so creative and has such an energy level. He has a different idea every five minutes. Film is a collaborative process, but we had to send him away because he was too inspired. Barry said to him, "You've got to get a sun tan and look fit for this part." So they sent him on holiday to Greece. It was just an excuse to get him out of the fucking office for a bit. We had visions of him running up and down mountains but he came back with about an extra stone in weight.'

Keefe's thankless task was to pool everyone's ideas and make them work on paper, building up his original 50-minute TV script to nearly two hours in length for the cinema. Once Hoskins locked him in the office overnight, posting two packets of fags through the letterbox to keep him going.

Keefe wanted his story to move at a rate of knots, pepper it with his characteristically abrasive dialogue and be visually gripping. 'In other films I've seen, you often just get people sitting around tables talking, so I tried to think of imaginative places to put them, like in the abattoir scene. That dialogue with the gang bosses could have been sitting around the table. I think if you're going to see a film, it's got to be something exciting and visual, 'cos you don't remember the dialogue so much, you remember what you see.'

Shand's interrogation of a cache of villains strung up on meat hooks is perhaps *Friday*'s dominant image. Mackenzie recalls, 'Originally, they were captured in a truck and tied up, that's all. Then we decided to take them to an abattoir, we thought it would be great … but was it hell, it was dreadful!' Mackenzie's idea was to wheel them in on the overhead rails upside down, just like meat carcasses, which presented its own special problem. 'It was a nightmare. The guys were wired so they wouldn't drop on their heads, but we couldn't leave them hanging upside down, especially the bigger guys … one of them started to faint, you know, all their guts drop. So we devised a scheme whereby we kept their legs tied but in between takes ladders were put underneath them and someone would get up and they would be held up and then lowered for the shot. There were quite a few stuntmen in there, and a few cons, too.'

By the close of pre-production, eight separate scripts existed and Mackenzie resorted to laying all the copies on the office floor and cherry-picking what was best from each one. Crucially, it was Mackenzie's decision to build up the role of the IRA. 'For me, that was the theme of the film, really, it was committed terrorist versus capitalist thug and which wins. I thought that was a very interesting theme because it had never been done before and it gave extra weight to what was a gangster film. We weren't trying to praise terrorism, but it was that these people were committed to their cause and not just to wealth and the glorification of themselves, which was what Harold Shand was all about.'

But that left a big problem over the film's title. Hanson liked *The Paddy Factor*; Mackenzie hated it. 'You're giving the fucking plot away,' Mackenzie argued. 'We're not supposed to know it's the IRA.' It's only as the film unravels that Shand learns his empire is under threat not from usurping local gangsters but Irish provos. The subsequent search for a suitable replacement title became something of a *bête noir*, with Hoskins again being the main culprit. Every few days he seemed to have a new title – *Harold's Kingdom*, *Havoc*, *Citadel of Blood* and *Diabolical Liberty*, after one of Shand's infamous expressions. 'It was crazy,' admits Keefe. And it was in desperation that Mackenzie suddenly said, 'We've got to have a fucking working title.'

With the story taking place over Easter, Mackenzie juggled with the words Good Friday, then, remembering the Philip Marlowe story *The Long Goodbye*, cleverly merged the two together coming up with *The Long Good Friday*: 'I said, "Let's just use that." So I wrote it on the clapperboard and it sort of stuck, although people kept coming up with new ones. Bob would say, "I've got another title." I said, pointing at the clapperboard, "That's the title!" '

Thoughts now reverted to casting. For the Mafia big-shot Anthony Franciosa, a tough Italian-American actor, was hired. Mackenzie recalls, 'But we didn't know at that stage he was badly into the drug scene. After three days on the set, somebody gave him the latest script and he said, "You mean it's changed?" And we said, "Well, yeah, yours was a very early edition." He said, "I've learnt it all. I'm not a good studier and I could never learn any more words." So he took off and went back home.' A replacement had to be found ... fast. Eddie Constantine, no stranger to the gangster milieu having starred in the cult movie *Alphaville*, was flown over from Paris. Mackenzie believes 'he's actually not great in the film because he couldn't remember the words, so we staggered through it, really. But he looks the part, he had this classic gangster look.'

Way down the cast, indeed he doesn't even get to say a line, is one Pierce Brosnan. In only his second film, the future 007 plays an Irish hitman. Mackenzie remembers, 'Pierce came from my casting director. I didn't know him at all. I said, "Let's not go for conventional ideas of what IRA guys are like." We had to have this business of him being a sex trap for this guy at the beginning, so we needed someone who looked good.'

Mackenzie later directed Brosnan in one of his best pre-Bond roles as the Russian terrorist Michael Caine hunts down in *The Fourth Protocol*, but very nearly killed him shooting *Friday*'s climactic scene where he holds Hoskins at gunpoint in a car. 'That was quite dangerous. Normally, you'd do some of that stuff on back projection in the studio but we just couldn't afford any of that so we had to do it for real with the cameraman in the car, Pierce right next to him and I had to drive. We even had the sound man in the car … unbelievable … people were in the boot, wires everywhere.'

From day one, Mackenzie knew how he wanted his film to end, on a big close-up of Hoskins in the back of this car as he comes to realise he's being driven to his death, his face a map of contrasting emotions, arrogance, rage, fear, resignation and finally a begrudging admiration for his opponents. 'So I had to drive the damn car and direct Bob in the rear-view mirror. We came out of the Savoy, turned left into the Strand and headed towards Trafalgar Square. It's quite difficult to drive the car and not only watch the actor but cue him. I mean, I was acting with him in a sense, so it's very difficult to take your eye off him, so we nearly crashed. Somehow, magically the Strand was emptyish in front of us, it was about one or two in the morning. But as I got more enthralled with Bob the less I looked down. I thought, Christ, he's doing it, he's absolutely terrific, and I got so involved this fucking bus just missed us because by that time I was hitting Trafalgar Square. Anyway, it didn't hit us, thank God. I could have killed them all.'

Besides Hoskins, the most important role to get right was Victoria, Shand's posh bit of skirt. As originally written, Victoria was your traditional gangster's moll, not very bright (in Hanson's words, 'a pea-brained tart') who says nothing throughout the movie until the end when she smiles revealing a gob full of bad teeth. 'I can't sustain a film with that!' argued Mackenzie, who visualised the character as being much more than an appendage with tits to Mr Big, but strong and effective in her own right. The actress he had in mind was Helen Mirren. 'I always thought she was terrific, a class actress. She was well known but hadn't done much in the way of films. I went to see her, had a long conversation and we sold her on the idea. She was very keen on some sort of film part, she could see that it had a lot of potential.'

Like Mackenzie, Mirren's take on Victoria was to turn her almost into

Shand's equal, a woman of power and influence. Keefe set about drastically rewriting the part to fit this new vision. Mackenzie remembers, 'I did have a few tussles with Helen, but never in the sense of making her the little lady at the sink because the whole idea was Victoria wouldn't be like that. But, of course, she wanted more, she wanted to be Harold Shand really, she wanted to go out there shooting people. She tends to be that when you see her in those *Prime Suspect* telly things; she's a bit of a ball-crusher with the boys. I used the word "acolyte" once and she hated it. Maybe I was being too artsy-fartsy. It was in the scene when he's in the shower. Maybe I got a bit carried away with it, I saw it as a symbolic thing, him being cleansed for battle. And I said, "Bring in his clothes and put them on the bed and burn all the old clothes … I want to make it almost like a Greek thing where you're a sort of goddess or maybe you're the acolyte." "*Acolyte!*" she said. "Fuck," I said, "wrong word, why did I say it?" We had a big fight over that. She eventually did it, but she tried not to and got very silly saying that it made her subservient. "I've never made a cup of tea for a man," she said, or something like that. She's a fucking liar, I mean now she does nothing but make cups of tea for her husband!'

The chemistry between Hoskins and Mirren is undeniable and the actress's contribution to the film must not be underestimated. Keefe had written a love scene. Both are terrified of the IRA coming and out of fear springs sex. But Mackenzie was loath to do it. 'I didn't want to see them lash around the floor. I said, "It's going to spoil it, let's keep the bedroom out of it, or imply it's there rather than have lashings of saliva and all that shit." Helen agreed totally, which surprised me 'cos I thought she would maybe want that 'cos she likes to show that she's a bit of a sex goddess. We thought of other things to do and then she said, "I just think it would be great for once we see fear, that she's frightened, wouldn't she be frightened?" And I said, "She'd be scared shitless, we all would." She said, "Well, I think I should just break down and cry." And I said, "What a great idea." Now if I'd suggested it she would have said, "I never cry! The man will cry." It was a great idea and it worked beautifully: it made her so human, not weak at all.'

As the start date loomed, poor Barrie Keefe was still thumping away on his typewriter churning out new scenes. 'It was such an endurance test doing that film. By the time I'd typed the end, I think on the Sunday night and filming started on the Monday, I was so knackered. I lost a stone-and-a-half in weight from start to finish and slept for two days when it was all over.' Remarkably, *The Long Good Friday* remains Keefe's first and only filmed cinema screenplay. It was a pressurised shoot, eight weeks during the fine British summer of 1979, but joyously harmonious. Many who worked on the film have spoken of it being one of the happiest they'd been on.

Mackenzie, who earned the nickname 'Frenzy Mackenzie', aimed for a film of high style with everything done out on location, much of it around Docklands. Shand's yacht, hired according to Hanson from a business type who'd just had the dubious distinction of being kicked out of Idi Amin's Uganda, was moored at Canary Wharf where today the huge skyscraper stands. Then it was just an open dock with a tatty little shed down one side. Though a building site, you could smell in the air that development and rampant capitalism was coming. In this respect, *Friday* was a very prescient film. The Tories had just swept into power and Shand, the old-fashioned crook-turned-capitalist, was keen to embrace the ruthless free market ideals of the onrushing 1980s. His scheme to set up a semi-legit international consortium to redevelop Docklands using Mafia money made him the bastard offspring of Al Capone and Margaret Thatcher. 'He was definitely a proponent of Thacherism,' Mackenzie suggests. 'He had the local councillor in his back pocket, which was sort of shades of what was happening with Docklands. There was an awful lot of *baksheesh* going on. But you felt that entrepreneurial stuff, this mobster extolling the cultural values of London. Maybe Thatcher was inspired by him!'

The Long Good Friday opened in London during February 1981, notching up record-breaking business in some cinemas. It wasn't long before touts were operating in the West End selling tickets for double the face value and, later, even bootleg videos, the dubious quality of which appalled Mackenzie. It was a hit, no doubt due to the near universal critical response. 'The first British thriller to even approach the crackling vitality of the classic Hollywood gangster movies,' said the *Daily Mail*.

Hoskins was especially singled out for praise. 'Not since Edward G Robinson has a character actor dominated a thriller,' wrote the *Sunday Times*. Going on to win the *Evening Standard* award for Best Actor and also nominated for a BAFTA, Hoskins was catapulted into the big time becoming one of Britain's biggest film stars in the 'Eighties. Keefe remembers with fondness an occasion when he phoned Hoskins up about something soon after the actor had taken off in Hollywood and getting the reply, 'What you don't seem to realise, Barrie, is now I'm in a different stratosphere.'

Hoskins is a revelation as Harold Shand, blasting through every scene like an Exocet missile, bragging that his gang is 'the best organisation since Hitler put a Swastika on his jockstrap'. Keefe notes, 'It's Bob Hoskins's film, he gives an absolutely spellbinding performance. I think it's down to Bob why the film is respected as it is.' Brimming with Cockney flamboyance, Hoskins manages the bravura achievement of making this thug funny, menacing and tragic. Quite a feat. The shifts from maudlin sentiment to bestial ferocity are fearsome. It's a facet one suspects that lies not altogether too deep under the surface of the real man. Keefe observes, 'Bob's very funny, also he can be very dangerous. He's got black eyes and when he stares at you he never takes his eyes off you. I would hate to cross him.'

Amidst the joyousness of the film's homegrown success, there was tragedy. While *The Long Good Friday* played to packed houses, Keefe's wife lay dying of cancer in a London hospital. 'I never saw the film in the cinema until the 2000 re-release. It was heartbreaking, a sad time in my life. The night of the London première I took a video machine to the hospital and a bottle of champagne and we watched it together in the hospital ward.'

Despite scoring big in the UK, remaining in the London top ten for 14 weeks, American distributors were reluctant to take a risk on the film. After several months of intense wrangling, a deal was struck again with Avco-Embassy, who'd done so well out of *Time Bandits*. Again, Avco took no risk whatsoever with the film; all promotional costs were guaranteed by HandMade, who also supervised all creativity by way of posters, trailers, etc. It was essential to O'Brien that *Friday* be sold as a mainstream international movie, after the other distributors had dismissed it as fodder for the art houses. It was an amicable arrangement, although Hanson remembers Avco voicing disquiet that O'Brien wasn't prepared to go the extra mile of stumping up cash for television advertising which, in the end, may have been responsible for its restricted release.

Friday's New York opening in April 1982 was not far removed from its London début in that it met with glowing notices. Renowned critic Judith Crist described it as 'the best gangster movie since *The Godfather*' and *US* magazine enrolled Hoskins into the movie's 'most illustrious rogues gallery, a criminal roster that includes Edward G Robinson's *Little Caesar* and James Cagney's *Public Enemy*'. The American public appeared less enthused, however, and Mackenzie puts that down to several factors – the language problem (US prints came complete with a glossary of Cockney terms and their translation – i.e. 'grass': a stool pigeon rather than the stuff you smoke), poor distribution (it didn't play beyond a few big cities) and simply failing to get the joke. Mackenzie believes, 'They didn't get the humour because of the old business of irony. I think the Americans are better at it now but in those days you either had a serious film or you had a jokey film, and you can't mix them up. The public enjoyed it, but enjoyed it just as a thriller, they didn't get the laughs.'

CHAPTER 4

PYTHON'S LAST HURRAH

It's been called the Woodstock of Monty Python and, over four intoxicating nights in September 1980, they ruled Hollywood. Python were the talk of the town, chased by groupies, seen at all the best parties, driven around in limos and generally grovelled over. It was an inspired notion getting the lads to perform what was essentially a 'greatest hits' package of sketches at one of America's premier stadiums, the Hollywood Bowl. What better way to exploit the rising tide of cult excitement over Python in the US? 'I thought it sounded like fun and when I got to Los Angeles,' John Cleese says, 'and it was, I think, only the second time I'd ever been there, and the previous time was for an overnight, because I'd always avoided the city because I knew I wouldn't like it. In fact, what I did like was the weather, the fact that it was sunny every day. It was immensely cheery and we were staying in a very nice hotel and we were all kind of in the prime of life.'

But could a bunch of British comics fill so massive an outdoor auditorium that in the summer months was home to the Los Angeles Philharmonic and had over the years played host to the likes of Sinatra, Streisand, Garland and even The Beatles? Michael Palin observes, 'The interesting thing about the Bowl was that it's actually designed to take 17,000 people, I think that's the maximum. These concrete terraces go right up the hill in front of the stage and they sort of reduced the size by bringing ornamental trees down the steps, and the trees came nearer and nearer, it was a bit like *Macbeth*, the forest coming to Dunsinane. We filled up about a third of the area, we got crowds of around 7,000 people, which I suppose is quite a lot.'

Although there were no plans to produce a theatrical-release movie, the Pythons decided, for posterity's sake, to commit the event to celluloid. Neither Gilliam nor Jones took up the challenge of the director's seat; the rigours of performing live were deemed difficult enough without the added burden of directorial duties. 'So we got someone else called Terry,' Palin says, 'because only people called Terry are allowed to direct Python films.'

Terry Hughes's relationship with the Pythons dates back to the 1960s when he was at the BBC producing and directing *The Two Ronnies* and, later, *Ripping Yarns*. Although he subsequently moved to America, communication channels with the Pythons remained open. 'They were coming over and knew I was in LA and told Denis O'Brien, who then approached me to see if I was available to do the directing. Denis was very much the executive producer, a funny man, he was involved in the early days of budgeting, whether we were going to shoot on film or on tape. We ended up shooting it on high-definition tape and then it was transferred to film. Of course, I was thrilled to have the chance to work with the Pythons again. I remember we all met for a rehearsal on the stage of the Hollywood Bowl one glorious sunny afternoon, and everybody was kind of hysterical about the silliness that we were all there standing on a stage in Hollywood. It was quite giddy.'

As early as 1970, the Pythons had begun transferring their television material to the live stage, culminating in highly successful shows in London's Theatre Royal, Drury Lane, in 1974 and a long season at the City Centre, New York in 1976 where the group were treated with almost Beatle-esque reverence. Carol Cleveland recalls, 'We had an amazing reception at the airport, camera crews and everything. And the first time we came out of the stage door there were hundreds of screaming fans outside. That was the moment we really thought, God, we're big here. Michael Palin, who is and always has been the shyest of the lot, he was the first one to step out of the stage door and suddenly – Wow! And this girl rushed forward and literally threw herself at Michael, swooning in his arms, near fainted away. And I'll always remember Michael's face when he's holding this girl and looking at us, like, "What do I do?" After that we couldn't go out the stage door, we used a car, but when they'd see the car we'd have hundreds of fans chasing us up Fifth Avenue. And it was the same in Hollywood.'

If not more so. In Hollywood, the group were fêted as mega celebrities, each sketch line worshipped as if it were a lyric penned by Lennon or Dylan. 'The show was very similar to a rock concert,' Terry Hughes says. 'They knew all the words, they'd join in. I don't think the Pythons knew it was going to have the kind of enthusiastic response it did. They were hopeful it would, but I think they were amazed at the vocal enthusiasm of the audience. I remember at one point they laughed at something that John Cleese said and he walked to the front of the stage and said, "That's a fucking straight line!" '

The phenomena of Python's live performances assuming the mantle of rock gigs wasn't new; it had first emerged at the New York concerts, taking the group totally by surprise. Cleveland says, 'Those New York shows really were like a rock concert because they were screaming and yelling all the time, they weren't listening. So we were a little bit better prepared by the time we got to the Hollywood Bowl, but it was an incredible experience. I have to say I think that was really the pinnacle of my career. We did our best to fool them because they seemed to know every word to every sketch before you opened your mouth. On the second night, we were about to do the travel agent sketch and, of course, as soon as they saw me and all the travel posters they immediately knew what sketch it was and were prepared for the first line which is me, when Eric walks over and I just look up at him from doing my nails and say, "Oh hello, would you like to come upstairs?" So we're just about to go on and Eric said, "Carol, don't say that, say such and such." So I went out and there was this big "Whoa" of recognition and I open my mouth and say, "Hello, would you like a blow-job?" And there was this stunned silence, 7,000 people suddenly silent. And then you heard all this muttering and then – Whoosh! – it exploded.'

In direct contrast to the television series, the Hollywood Bowl and

New York gigs allowed the Pythons far greater freedom to improvise; in a way it was like a return to their university revue days. Cleveland agrees. 'It was very disciplined when we did the BBC shows. A lot of people ask how much of that was improvised and, of course, none of it was, it was all scripted, it's just because we didn't over-rehearse the material. And it was very disciplined in the studio because we had a limited time to record the shows. But when we did the stage shows and we had this extraordinary reaction from people, we could have a lot more fun and there was an awful lot of larking about then, there was a lot of improvising. I think all the guys really probably enjoyed the stage shows more than anything else, it seems to me, looking back on it.'

Every night, the Hollywood Bowl played host to a carnival atmosphere; clumps of the audience would arrive dressed as Mr Gumpy, complete with trademark white hanky on their heads, and assorted other Python characters. Palin remembers, 'Because it was open air, it was delightful to perform there because you weren't in an enclosed, overheated theatre, you could see the stars and the moon and the sun setting over in the distance from the stage. There was a nice balmy feeling of people out there enjoying themselves with their picnics and whatever, which is something you just wouldn't get in an enclosed theatre. The four shows were very enjoyable to do and everybody had a great time and felt this was the way to do it because we'd just come together for that one solo outing, it wasn't part of a long tour.'

Cleese also recalls those nights with great fondness. 'We had a good time, the crowds were so friendly. It was a wonderful atmosphere. And we'd got used to playing to American audiences at that stage and it had been pretty similar at Drury Lane when we'd done the big London show that there's not a great deal of nervousness or stress in playing in front of such friendly audiences.'

So popular were the Hollywood shows that every night the Pythons were obliged to do at least ten minutes of curtain calls, such was the response. 'The audience would go mad,' Cleveland says, 'throwing all these things on the stage, flowers and all the girls' home-baked cookies, little presents of various descriptions, their knickers. Eventually, we'd have enough of these curtain calls, right bugger that, we want a drink, so we'd make our way down to the VIP tent, and they'd still be there, they wouldn't leave, even though we put a big sign up on the screen – PISS OFF – they were still there thinking we're gonna come back and do more.'

There was also the comfort of working with familiar faces which made for a calm and easy-going environment, plus the realisation that perhaps the group were performing at the peak of their powers. Many fans place the Hollywood Bowl as the greatest of their various stage appearances. Terry Hughes remembers, 'It was a wonderful experience because the audience had never seen the show before. You had all these West Coast college students who'd been starved of seeing Python live because they had done the concerts in New York, so there were people dying to see them. The concerts were all sold out. And it was just so magical to be working with a bunch of friends, never knowing whether they'd get back together again to do anything else after that.'

The large student contingent might also explain why the fragrance of the air sometimes fell on the wacky backy-side. Terry Jones recalls, 'Having to walk out in the crowd at one point to do the albatross sketch with John and you'd get pretty high because there was so much marijuana being smoked.'

Beside the heavy student presence, Python also found themselves the hottest ticket in town among celebrities who would arrive backstage loaded with congratulations and exclusive party invites. 'It was our little bit of Hollywood fame,' Palin says. 'It was all a bit of a new world for most of us and it was nice to be sort of cosseted.' For a brief period, the Pythons were part of the superficial showbiz buzz of LA, rubbing shoulders with fellow comedians Steve Martin and Robin Williams and rock 'n' roll fans Harry Nilson, Joni Mitchell and Mick Jagger. Harrison was also there but this time couldn't be tempted on to the stage as he had been for the 'Lumberjack Song' during one of the New York shows. 'Steve Martin actually gave a party in our honour,' Cleveland adds. 'He had the most amazing house which was all white, everything was white, the outside and the inside, every room was white, all the furniture was white, everything was white. I remember this vast living room and there was nothing in it save for this white carpet and a couple of big white leather sofas, and there was nothing else except his few works of art and in the centre of the room was this extraordinary wooden sculpture which went up to the ceiling. So it wasn't very much like a home, it was like walking into an art gallery. And he had a pool, obviously. And I remember Michael – it was always Michael – who got this, he was sitting at the edge of the pool sort of just dabbling his feet in the water and these little would-be starlets were skipping about in the briefest of bikinis, shrieking as they do, and one of them, obviously dying to get attention, jumped in the pool in front of Michael and when she came up out of the water her bikini top had slipped off. She came straight up in front of Michael, and Michael, again not knowing what to do with himself, just turned bright red.'

Hollywood is a great town to be a winner in. Nowhere in the world is success more honoured or valued, even less sneered at. After their triumph at the Bowl, America opened up for the Pythons as never before. While some stayed to try and carve out new careers Stateside, others resisted, and always would do, the corrupting lure of Tinsel Town. Palin admits, 'I myself rather mistrust LA. It's very seductive and people are very pleasant, but it's like sort of water through your fingers, you just don't know quite where you are; people will tell you wonderful things one day and the next day not return your calls, it's quite a tough place. I like a city you can walk around in, I like the seasons, so there's two reasons why I wouldn't like to be in LA for long. So I never considered staying out there. I like the combination of being able to produce the material in London and then go to America and enjoy the fleshpots and the success of something that we'd carefully crafted together on our own terms back in England, that seemed to be the best way for it to work. But to go out to Hollywood and produce programmes on Hollywood's terms, I think, would have been the end of Python fairly quickly. I did some *Saturday Night Live*s but Eric was the pioneer there. Eric moved quite easily amongst the American showbiz aristocracy, was prepared to spend some time with them and build his life around America much more than the rest of us did. Although John, of course, was married to an American … married to three Americans!'

Palin's gentle hostility towards Los Angeles didn't stop him from passing on sound advice to others undecided about whether to give Hollywood a go or return to the relatively secure bosom of blighty. Cleveland remembers, 'Michael said to me one day, "Carol, you really ought to think about staying here for a bit. The show is huge and several people have spoken to me about you. I think you'd be wise to stay here for a bit." And, indeed, I should have done. I should have grabbed my chance and it's one of my major regrets that I didn't. But I had to come back to England to finish a touring play for Bill Kenwright. So there I was, after having all this star treatment in Hollywood, and I came back to this awful theatre in Crewe and this little bed and breakfast and I thought, God, a week ago I was a Hollywood star, what's this all about? Yes, I probably made a big mistake there; but there you go.'

On a technical level, the Hollywood shows had been proficiently executed. The facilities at the Bowl were impressive, with the added luxury of two 40ft x 60ft TV projection screens erected on either side of the stage so folk right at the back could see just as well as those sitting in the front row. But because of the sheer vastness of the auditorium, everyone knew that the night would live or die on the reliability of the equipment involved. Cleese says, 'It was a bit scary because, with screens that big and radio mikes, you're in terrible, terrible trouble if anything goes wrong. I mean, if your mike packs up you're dead, nothing you can do about it, and the technology at that time wasn't anything like what it is now. I remember on the British stage tour in 1973 the mikes did pack up a few times.'

Luckily, there were no major glitches and filming passed off smoothly. Hughes says, 'I wasn't given a free hand in as much as it was a fairly formally structured piece, much of it they had done before, there was an existing structure to it. It wasn't, in my opinion, my job to reinvent the wheel in this case; my job was to capture the essence of the show. We were there four nights and we shot each night. We had, I think, six or seven cameras. Then John stayed on in California and I did a rough cut and he and I worked together fine-tuning it. John was both free and willing to stay on in the States for a while. It was amicable and great; we saw everything the same way and had an overall vision of what it should be, it dictated itself. I don't remember any moments of disagreement about what we should or shouldn't be doing.'

For Cleese, it was a whole new experience. 'I'd spent a lot of time in the editing room on *Fawlty Towers* but I'd never really spent much time editing a Python thing before because that was what Terry Jones would normally do. So I spent two weeks editing it with Terry Hughes, who's become a great friend.'

However personally satisfying the whole Hollywood Bowl experience had been, the after-effects were to prove traumatic. The Pythons had been promised a fee of $1 million for their Hollywood appearances but some time after the event it was with horror that they learnt their money had been more or less used up elsewhere, not a penny remained. The offer to play the Bowl was on the table prior to O'Brien becoming Python's manager but, once responsibilities for the group became his, Denis sidelined the show's original organiser to take personal charge himself. Gilliam observes, 'Denis started meddling, completely wrongfooted everybody working on it, and wasted money. I said, "That was our money, Denis. Where do you get off just spending it?" And his attitude was he was our manager, that's what he did, he was looking after our best interests. He tried to be paternalistic all the time, which with Python particularly you cannot do. And I found at that point, this is it, Denis just can't draw the line between anything. His money was never our money, but our money was always available to be his.'

It was around this time that Gilliam first warned George Harrison that perhaps O'Brien wasn't the financial genius he seemed. But Harrison shook his head. He had complete faith in his business partner, and even when Eric Idle began voicing similar concerns, he wouldn't listen. Harrison couldn't, or didn't want to, believe it.

One plan for the Pythons to get back the missing money was unorthodox to say the least. 'We were in Jamaica,' says Eric Idle, 'and Denis owed us that million dollars from the Hollywood Bowl and we were writing *The Meaning of Life*. We had a meeting about what to do about Denis and I came up with a brilliant plan. I said, "We'll just steal his yacht." And everybody said, "Yeah, what a great idea, we'll just go on board, they're not going to stop us, we'll get on board, take the yacht and then we'll have the yacht." John vetoed it because he's a lawyer and he said, "This is piracy." So we were kind of disappointed.'

The Pythons now found themselves in the incredible position of having to release the film of their Hollywood Bowl concert to cinemas in order to get back the money they were owed in the first place. 'That was the one thing we didn't want to do,' states Gilliam. 'Right from the beginning we said, "No way" – we'll record the stuff, probably thinking that we would release it on video at some time, or maybe it would go on television, but never as a film. The last thing we wanted was it to be a film, but it was the only way we could actually get any money out of the process. We were very purist about what film was and what television was, particularly Terry Jones and I were always fighting to make our films look like films.'

And unfortunately *Monty Python Live at the Hollywood Bowl* looks exactly like what it is, a filmed stage show, raw round the edges, with none of the finesse of *Life of Brian* or *Holy Grail*. Jones says, 'I feel it's a bit dull, the actual filming of it. I think Terry Hughes is a very good director, but for me it was very dully shot. They got these high-definition cameras but they just sort of set them up in three places and shot the scenes as if you were shooting a TV show. I would have shot it more like a pop show, I'd have had it all hand-held. We had a little bit of that but, in my view, not enough. I think the whole feeling of the show would've been better if they'd been less keen on just shooting the sketches clean and rather just got in there with the audience and shot from the wings a bit more.'

Still, *Monty Python Live at the Hollywood Bowl* remains the only celluloid record of a live Python stage show, so in that context must be viewed as some kind of priceless cultural document. Palin's view is, 'While being actually quite successful in the sense that it's enjoyable – there's some good performances and it's got a nice bouncy feel to it – it's still not considered mainstream Python,' and that probably explains why *Hollywood Bowl* was never theatrically released in Britain, only in America where it surfaced during the summer of 1982.

That whole fiasco forced the Pythons to stop and radically reassess what they wanted from O'Brien and his position as their manager, although some of the more, shall we say, 'liberal' members of the group were either genuinely unaware of the financial shenanigans behind Hollywood Bowl or have simply chosen to erase the entire episode from their memory. Cleese claims, 'I genuinely don't remember it. I tend not to remember stuff from business meetings. When I go in the meeting, I listen reasonably carefully and I understand it and I make any decision that is necessary and it's probably a reasonably sensible decision, but two days later I can't remember it. It has no interest to me.' And Palin admits, 'I'm quite slow on things sort of financial. Providing the show gets done, that's the main thing. I never felt that we were being spectacularly ripped off.'

Yet Steve Abbott, whose job it was to look after Python's financial interests, is adamant that it was the muck-up over *Hollywood Bowl* that precipitated the eventual split between Python and O'Brien. 'There's no question that Denis, as Python's manager but without consulting them, made arrangements for the financing, making and selling of the film and didn't let the Pythons know. That was it in terms of the group and Denis, the trust was never there again. The *Hollywood Bowl* was at the end of September 1980 and we'd all gone by May 1981, so over that winter the writing was on the wall. So, without their knowledge, Denis had invested money that was otherwise due to Python in that film and, in order to get back what was theirs in the first place, they had to release the *Hollywood Bowl* movie to unlock what was their money.'

Then something else happened, surreal in the extreme and fairly indicative of the fragile relations that now existed between the two camps. Idle says, 'I had warned George Harrison about something. I don't know why I got this inkling but I warned him about Denis and he got wind of the fact that I'd said something about him and he became furious. I think the worry for Denis was that I was such good friends with George that he might listen. Anyway, Denis went nuts and came up to where I was living and fired me from Monty Python, which was hilarious. I laughed and laughed. It was like, "Yeah, fuck off." So I was out of HandMade, suddenly I was not a member, not represented by Denis and blacklisted.'

The news of Idle's dismissal quickly filtered back to London where it was greeted first with disbelief and then utter dismay. Abbott remembers, 'I came to work one Monday morning and everyone was looking like there'd been a death in the family. "What's the matter?" I asked. "Denis has terminated Eric." Those are the exact words I was greeted with that Monday morning, and obviously it affected me since Eric was my client within the organisation. The board members of EuroAtlantic gave me this news. I said, "What do you mean?" "Oh, they had a big row and Denis has fired Eric." I said, "Just a minute, we're the management company, he's the client." I now know this kind of thing happens; in Hollywood, lawyers and agents get rid of their clients if they're not making enough money, but for me this was a concept that I just couldn't get my head round. I said, "It isn't for Denis to terminate Eric. Eric can fire us but we can't fire Eric, he isn't our employee, he isn't working for us." They patched it up … within a month Eric had come back, but it was never the same again. That was very, very odd. It speaks volumes as to how Denis wanted to operate as a manager. If he had phoned me up that day and said I'm thinking of terminating Eric, I'd have just laughed in his face ... the words "tail" and "dog" leap to mind here.'

By this time, Abbott was deeply suspicious of the way O'Brien conducted himself in his professional and business dealings and how he'd surrounded himself with a network of loyal staff who acted almost as a barrier that could be difficult to penetrate. 'I used to go mad at the office because Denis would swan in and it was like, "Yes ... no," and I would say to the other professionals there, "Just a minute, we've got to discuss this," and they'd be like, "No, we'll take these papers up and get Denis to OK them and sign them," and I'd say, "Look, I know about these things, I can answer any questions, let me go and discuss it." This kind of thing was always going on. Certainly the people that were there before me were always incredibly deferential and protective of Denis. He had close confidants and very loyal people around him and Denis trusted them all to protect him, to put a ring around him.'

These were professional concerns, but from a personal standpoint Abbott found the HandMade office a genial and fun working environment. 'There were kind of rituals on Thursday when George Harrison's staff got paid; there was always a communal lunch at the pub. And on everybody's birthday, there was no question, a little party was always laid on. People would really make an effort, it didn't matter how busy you were, if a deal had to be closed or whatever, people would get together. The staff were very happy. The only thing that made me unhappy or people who ended up leaving were professional worries rather than levels of comfort there or money, as they paid well, very generous Christmas bonuses. It was a very good atmosphere, people were genuinely friendly.'

O'Brien had another, more pertinent reason for feeling particularly aggrieved with Eric Idle, namely, the actor's veto of a recent business plan. 'Denis had this huge deal with a company and he wanted to sell the world rights to Python,' reveals Idle, 'and we were all going to get shares in this company. Well, if we'd done that he would have had control of the Python income. Everybody said "Yes" and I said "No". We always had this veto and I said "No". I just thought it's wrong to do this, it's a bad mistake businesswise. And so I went away and he couldn't get through what he wanted and then when I came back everybody had also changed their minds, which is often what happened in Python, and it was slung out. So Denis had a bit of a grievance with me. Then everybody just in their own way felt that Denis was going out of control.'

Among the first to reach such a conclusion was John Cleese. Famously into analysis, the reading and measuring of people's characters, he understood to a large degree, perhaps more than any other Python, just what made O'Brien tick. 'I always rather liked Denis but I realised that he tended to operate in a way that was, I thought, technically a little bit paranoid. It was as though you were either family or you weren't family. And if you were family he would do an enormous amount for you, but he wouldn't tell you much about what he was doing for you, he wanted to be Dad and he wanted to present you with good news and lovely surprises so you would say, "Oh Denis, that's wonderful." But you weren't really allowed to ask what he was up to or how it was done.

'Denis is basically a money man and he would come to us with offers. He would say, "This company will pay you so much money to do this," and we'd say, "Yes, Denis, that's wonderful but it's just not something we want to do." We were literally a group that were unmanageable, in the sense that we didn't really want to be managed. And I think after a time he found us frustrating. And we became increasingly worried as we began to realise that we really couldn't get much information and suddenly we were being asked to sign forms and bits of paper and we would say, "Well, what is this company?" and he'd tell us the name of the company.' However when the Pythons questioned him about who the directors of these companies were, they cannot recall ever being given an answer. 'And we're not the fastest or smartest bunch of people businesswise' continues Cleese, 'but we began to realise fairly soon that this simply wasn't a satisfactory arrangement.'

The others, too, were finding O'Brien's methods, particularly when it came to money and his employment of tax shelters, a mite disturbing. Jones confides, 'I enjoyed Denis's sort of high finance input, he injected a feeling of excitement into things, into what we were doing. The only thing that alarmed one, he'd be doing all these incredibly complicated routes where the money was going and it would all be scribbled down on a piece of paper and then thrown away, he said so there'd be no trail kind of thing. And I had this slight feeling of being a little bit at sea. These weren't simple at all, when it came to Denis's finances, they were wonderfully convoluted and "tax-effective" I think is the word. So there was this feeling of not being in control of one's own destiny.'

It was all a little too mystifying. Idle remembers, 'Denis had all these labyrinths of companies overseas in Guernsey and places like that.' Again Idle cannot remember ever being told who the directors of these companies were. 'We wanted to be above board and with Denis … his response was always "Trust me".'

Well, that trust was rapidly diminishing, a view shared by Python accountant Steve Abbott who was privy to the complicated money strategies employed by O'Brien that included all sorts of antics that, although fairly prevalent in the industry, hovered around the line that made it legal. 'After working there for a while, I started seeing more and more of the picture and I didn't want any part of it. It reached such a silly stage. For me, this was an issue, my feelings were pretty strongly known. To this day, I've got information in my head that could nail a lot of people.'

Of particular concern was O'Brien's complex latticework of companies. Although shareholders in EuroAtlantic, the very fact that the Pythons were being kept in the dark about so many of the money decisions was really starting to hit home. 'We began to get worried about how our money was going to be used and invested,' says Palin. 'Basically, it was very complicated and involved these offshore companies and none of us really understood it. I think we just looked at it and said, "We don't want it this way." It came down to a lack of confidence in EuroAtlantic.'

Many of these companies had been in operation for some years prior to the formation of HandMade and were invariably situated in tax-efficient areas of the globe like Guernsey, Luxembourg, Holland and Panama. Abbott suggests, 'The biggest mistake Denis possibly made with me is that, as a treat, several members of the office, myself included, were invited out to Guernsey for lots of board meetings of these off-shore companies and suddenly, I'm not daft, suddenly – Wow! I think that was probably not long before I left.'

The Guernsey office was small – tiny, in fact – with a permanent staff of just two. Brian Shingles recalls, 'Everyone knew about the Guernsey office, but what its function was, who knows? Nobody really questioned it because it seemed the whole set-up was geared to look after George's affairs, make HandMade films and do whatever else was necessary, so it didn't seem so strange. Lots of companies go offshore, but how labyrinthine it was, no one realised.'

Someone Ray Cooper has described as 'one of the most influential women in film in England and Europe' began her career in that office in Guernsey. Her name was Wendy Palmer, a New Zealander not long in London with a degree in marketing and finance who was doing temp accounting work when an agency sent her along to HandMade.

'The funny thing was,' Palmer says, 'because the parent company was called EuroAtlantic, the temp agency had thought they were an oil company, so I'd gone along to Cadogan Square thinking I was going to work for an oil company and there I was working for a movie company.' Her first impressions of O'Brien were of a charming and smooth individual, very professional and business-like. 'But extremely small feet for a very tall man, which I always found quite disconcerting.'

Palmer's job was to look at all the films, particularly the big ones that were earning a lot of money – *Life of Brian* and *Time Bandits* – and to evaluate the royalty statements and chase up the payments. 'And it was extraordinary because no one had really been doing it and in the first month I brought in like a million-and-a-half dollars. Then they offered me a permanent job as an accountant and I was like, "Thank you but no thank you, that's not really what I'm intending to do." And they said, "Well, what are you intending to do?" and I said, "Well, marketing is my thing," and they said, "Oh, that's all right, stick around, do a bit more of the royalty accounting and then we're going to need somebody doing marketing for us and then you can do it." And that was basically it; I was 22, and it was kind of like all my dreams come true. I loved film but I never thought I'd be able ever to work in it, and they virtually plucked me off the street and gave me a career. And what an amazing thing to happen.'

After a six-month stint in London, Palmer was siphoned off to the Guernsey office in mid-'82. 'I was there for 15 months, too long, I couldn't stand it after a bit. It was just me and a PA. That office had been going for some time because of the various Dutch tax structures and the offshore management. And there were all the Peter Sellers files still around.'

Going on to establish herself as one of the leading female figures in the British film industry, it was here where Wendy Palmer learnt her trade, sat in that tiny office in Guernsey just reading the files, soaking everything up, like an actor learning his craft in Rep. Crucially, too, she is numbered among a select band of witnesses who have an intimate knowledge of just what went on out there. 'It was totally labyrinthine. There were companies after companies. No one ever got the whole picture, that was how Denis managed it, so that even those people that were very directly involved in those structures, the lawyers and the accountants, they only ever got bits of the picture, they never really got the whole thing. You couldn't even see whether it was black, white or grey, it was really impossible to untangle. It was clever the way he kept everybody just with little bits of it … not stupid, Denis. But they did save a lot of tax, especially on those Python movies because they were so successful, they did save huge amounts of tax. He saved George a lot of tax, too, because all George's tax structure was out of there. But I never got a sense that it was really illegal; there might have been things that happened that were borderline, and maybe it was worse than that, it probably did get very grey at points, but a lot of companies run those offshore things. It was about tax efficiency as much as anything. I think that especially the creative people around HandMade were more fascinated by it than they really needed to be; it was not any reinventing of the wheel or anything illegal, it was just complex, labyrinthine and tax efficient.'

It wasn't just the tax schemes that sent alarm bells ringing within the Python camp. Other aspects of the HandMade set-up were beginning to disillusion them. Jones says, 'My worry with HandMade was always that the tail would wag the dog. It was after about a year of Denis's management, which was great in many ways, very dynamic, but it was going into his office at EuroAtlantic, these very smart offices, and going into these separate rooms where you had like a dozen people working for us and Denis was showing off saying, "Look, they're all working on your things," accountants and lawyers, all that stuff, and I was thinking, My God, have we got to generate enough income to support this enterprise? I just don't think anyone in the Python team wanted to be saddled with overheads like this. I didn't want to feel that we had to keep working in order to generate money to keep an office going. So I started getting a bit itchy about this and began making noises that we ought to get out.'

HandMade's new distribution arm was also a cause for concern. Since its inception, only films of dubious quality like horror flicks *Venom* and *The*

Burning had been brought in. Flunking at the box office, they'd brought not one iota of distinction to the company and their exploitative nature had reflected badly upon Monty Python, who Joe Public saw as being very much integrally linked with the HandMade brand name. Gilliam reveals, 'Python left because HandMade were setting up this distribution arm and buying in shit films that were going to go up under our banner. I mean, it's understandable if you've got a distribution arm you've got to have product coming through, but we had no control over what was being bought. So we decided, that's it, that's when we split. Literally. We just walked away from it; it wasn't like we were bought out, we just walked away, that's what Python does. We never took anything, we just said, "Goodbye." But I was pissed off they kept my logo. I wanted to take my logo with me.'

In the spring of 1981, less than two years after the triumph of *Life of Brian*, a meeting of the Pythons was called. Idle recalls, 'We went away to a hotel and had sort of a two- or three-day conference about what we felt and where it was going. At that point, they all decided they wanted to leave and then John was wonderful because he said, "Well, look, O'Brien is a bit of a ..." John knew what type he was, I think "a narcissist", and said, "We can't just leave, we have to make it look like it's his idea." So it was very carefully and cleverly orchestrated so that Denis was sort of grateful we left. And I don't think he ever knew that. It was brilliant, it was the application of intelligence and analytical methods, because John knew what type he was. He was the only one into analysis in those days, and he knew how he would behave and react and how to get away and get what we wanted without making Denis look foolish.'

The shock of Python's departure was acute and resonated throughout the whole company, like a stroke. It was also largely unexpected, the disintegrating trust between Python and O'Brien took place behind closed doors, away from the general staff, detectable only to the keenest of observers. 'What I didn't personally realise,' Ray Cooper says, 'when you join Denis in any shape or form it was total and he couldn't take questioning. I should have seen the red light; maybe I didn't want to at that point because life was looking sweet. He was a very intelligent man but secretly I realised later there was an arrogance about him and the Pythons as fantastically intelligent men ... they're not going to sit back and say, "OK, take our lives, run with it," they'd never been managed in that sense.

It was, "Hang on, can we see the contract?" and Denis was like, "You don't trust me." One thing you couldn't do was express that. But I was busy, there was half an ear cocked to what was going on. And I think that was the reason why, early one Monday morning, the Python filing cabinets were literally on the pavement outside Cadogan Square and Python split, rather ignominiously.'

Contrary to Eric Idle's view that Cleese's expertise had enabled the Pythons to leave with O'Brien's blessing, Abbott saw things quite differently. 'I think Denis was stunned when anybody resigned from his office and he was certainly stunned with the Pythons. He was staggered when it happened. I don't think he could believe it. I wasn't at the meeting but the Pythons have told me since, just stunned disbelief, even when they said, "But, Denis, you used our money." You see, in his mind, he thought he was doing everything for their joint best interest.'

Unfortunately for Denis, there was another shock waiting for him in the wings. The Pythons wanted Steve Abbott to go with them. Cleese says, 'When we split with Denis, we said, "Look, Steve knows all our affairs, can he come with us and look after us." I'd always thought that was OK, but I subsequently heard that I don't think Denis was very pleased about it.' Something of an understatement. O'Brien had, in fact, pleaded with the accountant to stay on with HandMade.

'Everyone was very polite, right to the end,' Abbott recalls. 'On my final day, which was the Friday, Denis said, "Steve, the Pythons and I had a meeting last night, there's a job for you here, whatever you want to do, get more involved in the films, whatever. They're going to ask you to go with them." Everything was done politely. At lunchtime, I went to see him and said, "Look, the only reason I came here was I wanted to work with the Pythons. I've developed a relationship with them. I've been utterly professional about everything I've done and I'd like to go with them." And I was kicked out of my office an hour later. Denis couldn't believe it. I mean, he promised me anything I wanted to do to stay. He couldn't believe people would want to leave the family. It took the Pythons and myself about the best part of six to nine months to work out the divorce. But we did.'

It was a divorce further complicated by the fact that the Pythons were in the process of setting up a new film project. What was ultimately to become their last ever feature, *The Meaning of Life*, ironically came about at the instigation of Denis O'Brien himself. 'When *Life of Brian* was very successful,' John Cleese states, 'Denis invited us down to this beautiful island of his, Fisher Island, only about 12 people on it and two golf courses, it was distinctly very rich. He flew us down by helicopter and we had some meetings and he said something which remains to this day one of the most extraordinary things that anyone in a suit has ever said to me, which was that if we made another film again fairly soon, none of us would ever need to work again. And I've always desired not to work and just be able to chase my tail and do things that amuse me as opposed to doing things for money which are almost invariably less interesting. So we all pricked up our ears and thought we would do *Meaning of Life* as a result.'

It turned out to be a poor decision to plunge headlong into another Python movie before everyone was really ready. Cleese continues, '*Meaning of Life* was as frustrating an experience as *Brian* was a satisfying one because we could never ever quite figure out what the movie was about and we just spent immense amounts of time writing material without ever having any sense of a real theme. I thought it was bordering on a waste of time at one stage. We then decided to make one big effort and to go off to the West Indies again. But after a couple of days, we were getting nowhere and I said to the others, "I have a plan. Let's forget about this work and have a really nice 12 days in the sun and then go back to England and tell everyone that we flogged ourselves to death, codgered our brains, burnt the midnight oil and generally strained ourselves and produced nothing that we liked." And I practically sold the idea to the group. And the next morning, that bloody man Jones was there saying, "Well, you know, I really, I really think …" And he'd worked out this order overnight that made quite a lot of sense; even I had to agree that maybe it was worth doing a bit more work. He'd put the various material we had into quite a good shape, and we worked on that shape and that was the film we eventually made.'

But this was to be a film the Pythons were determined that Denis O'Brien would have no part in whatsoever. 'We didn't do *Meaning of Life* for HandMade,' says Michael Palin, 'because certain of the Pythons didn't have faith in Denis at all. I think the notion of doing the film with HandMade came up at a meeting and was dismissed almost instantly.'

After the success of *Brian*, Python were big box office and in the enviable position of being able to broker a deal with just about any of the major studios. When Universal came in with an offer of $8 million to make the film, Python took it, much to the private chagrin of Messrs Harrison and O'Brien, although publicly both men put on a philosophical front. 'We never had a contract with Python to say that you must stick with us for ever and ever,' Harrison informed the *Sunday Times* in 1983. 'If I can help someone like Gilliam, with his eccentricities which border on genius, I will, subject to Denis putting it on a realistic basis so that we don't go bankrupt inside six months.'

Python's 'defection' to a Hollywood studio was a massive set-back for everyone at Cadogan Square. '*The Meaning of Life*, that was a blow them going to Universal for that,' believes Shingles. 'We fully expected that *Meaning of Life* would have been a HandMade film, had the situation been different.'

Some of the staff could at least take quiet satisfaction from the fact that the end result was nowhere near in the same league as the venerated *Brian*. Cleese suggests, 'I think *Life* has got some absolutely terrific things in it, but also some really not very good material and I thought it was a shame to go back to a sketch format film, like our first. It didn't add up to much, I felt. And I found the filming, unlike Tunisia on *Brian*, a terrible grind. I remember towards the end of it I felt very tired and quite depressed. I didn't enjoy a lot of it very much. Individual bits, yes. But I've never enjoyed the filming process very much, there has to be something special about it like Tunisian sun to get you up at 6.00am.'

The reason why it was essential that Python broke all ties with HandMade prior to cameras rolling on *Meaning of Life* – ironic, given O'Brien's sphere of expertise – was purely for reasons of tax. Abbott explains, 'Why the split had to happen in 1981 was that they'd set aside 1982 to make the next Python film. And this really pissed Eric Idle off that they only made movies in World Cup years because he liked watching football. They did *Holy Grail* in '74, *Brian* was shot in '78 and, fuck me, they were going to do *Life* in '82 and Eric was really angry about it. Anyway, if Python had stayed within HandMade, the financial and tax structure would have had them completely meshed in the EuroAtlantic–HandMade group of companies and it would have been very hard to extricate them from it. As it was, when we left in '81 it took a long, long time; contracts had to be reversed, flows of money had to be untangled, service contracts had to be redone, and so on. If that film had gone through the HandMade apparatus, it would have been hard to untangle, so it really had to happen pretty quickly. It was essential that *Meaning of Life* was not a HandMade film. It had to come to an end before then.'

Abbott now became responsible, along with Anne James, for the business and financial management of Python, and his first priority was to repatriate contracts and sums of money on their behalf, determined that everything should be above board and beyond reproach. 'I must be the only person in this line of business who, as a selling point to potential clients said, if you come with me you'll pay more tax. But that's what I did and all the Pythons agreed to do it. I spoke to them all individually. Denis's way of tax dealing so bewildered someone like Terry Jones. I remember a conversation I had with him the first year after HandMade. He was directing *Meaning of Life* and he phoned me one day and said, "There's a real problem, we can't do one of the sequences. I think we should do it in England ... the best way to do it would be to make it in England." So I said, "Well, make the fucking film in England." And he said, "But then we won't be abroad, you'll need us to go abroad for tax." I said, "Terry, you've been around Denis O'Brien too long, you know ... what the fuck are you talking about? You do the film where you have to do it and I'll take care of the contracts, but even if you have to do every film for the rest of your life in England and the tax rate's 99 per cent and you could make them in France and the tax rate will be 1 per cent, what are you going to do? Are you going to make films to suit the tax man or are you going to make films that you want made?"

'He'd been so bewildered by Denis, and he was apologising to me, the director of a movie is coming to some guy who is a fucking accountant to apologise that he wants to shoot a sequence of a film in England. Terry was completely bewildered by dotted line drawings of where money flowed, and so it was great to be able to disabuse him of this myth, take as good care as I could of his companies, but everything's fair, everything's traceable, everything's in this country, everything is back under your control. It was a question of, yes, you pay your bloody tax, nothing wrong with that.'

Python's split with HandMade also had a profound effect upon George

Harrison. Not just a happy and willing supporter of their collective and individual talents but a huge fan, too, it must have been a painful personal wrench to see them go. Not as emotionally unhinged about it as O'Brien, Harrison was actually fairly pragmatic about their decision to leave. 'Well, do what you want to do,' is how Michael Palin remembers him reacting to the news. It seems that he was almost resigned to it happening, having by this time understood how the group operated, his fan's eye view of them corrupted pretty early on in the messiest of ways. Gilliam says, 'When we did *Life of Brian*, there was one meeting that George came to. We'd done the first or second cut of the film and we'd looked at it. It's funny, it's like if you're a fan of The Beatles you want to feel that The Beatles all worked wonderfully well together, an ideal working relationship, and George came to this meeting of us talking about what to do with the film and I could just see his eyes getting wider and his disappointment getting greater 'cos none of us seemed to agree on anything and it was not clear at all how we were going to salvage this fucking mess. And I think it was the last time he ever came to a meeting ... he just didn't want to see this side of Python.'

Harrison remained on good terms with the group, with some more than others, like Idle and Palin. To the rest, he always remained a distant figure. Cleese admits, 'I think I probably met George about four or five times. I got the impression that he was a very low-key guy. I remember I went down once to Henley with him and had a very pleasant dinner, sitting opposite Barrie Sheen for the entire evening without having the slightest idea who Barrie Sheen was. He just seemed a very nice guy. In the end, I said to George, "Who was that nice guy?" and he said, "That's Barrie Sheen!" I said, "Who's he?" and he said, "Only the motorbike world champion."'

But the Pythons' vanishing did leave a gaping hole in Harrison's ambitions, his vision of what he wanted HandMade to be, a small film-making entity with the Pythons at the heart of its output. 'I've a feeling George would liked to have done Python films,' Palin thinks, 'films suggested by the Pythons, that's what he enjoyed. Getting *Life of Brian* done, he probably hoped that would be the start of a number of Python movies, and probably he was a bit hurt by the fact that we didn't do *Meaning of Life* for HandMade.'

This notion of HandMade as a sort of creative head office for Python film projects appealed to other group members, too. Gilliam thinks, 'If Denis had been smarter and just kept Python and then we could just bring in the odd other film to keep it going, it could have been fantastic. If he had just stayed back. The group was always great at looking at each other's scripts and things, or in the case of *Time Bandits* John coming in and doing a part. We could have continued to do that kind of work. But I think, in the end, it probably would have collapsed because even Prominent Features, which we set up as our own operation, doesn't work. We don't work that way, there's too much internecine warfare going on.'

Maybe Python as a working unit is simply unmanageable, whether by O'Brien or anyone else, they're free spirits and thinkers who won't allow their wings to be clipped. John Goldstone believes, 'Python was always a unique and independent group of people, very strong ideas about things, on having complete control over what they were doing. And the fact there were six of them, to actually handle six people that have got such different characters, ambitions and needs was pretty difficult to take on. It wasn't like taking on a band who somehow act more as an entity. I think, in the end, it was just probably too much for Denis to cope with.'

The Pythons themselves recognise this, that the situation at HandMade was untenable almost from the beginning. Jones suggests, 'In the end, I felt Denis was too active, that really Python didn't want somebody who was going to come up with projects and push us into doing things. All we needed was somebody who would react to us ... we wanted somebody who was rather more reactive than active.' And John Cleese adds, 'Denis was prepared to be very protective and very generous to you if you were "family", as he called it, but I was always a little worried even at that stage about how tough he was being with people who weren't family. And once we began to realise that the price of being family was that he had to be daddy and we had to be the children, it became obvious that it wasn't going to work, because none of us would want to work like that, we'd want a more equal relationship.'

And what a shame. Handled properly, HandMade and Python might well have co-existed, perhaps not harmoniously but certainly to the mutual benefit of both parties. But O'Brien was always dreaming up various master plans and mega deals for the group to exploit and they just weren't interested. 'Denis was always too keen to push ahead,' Idle says, 'there's a fine line between leadership and enabling people who are creative to go ahead. I think, in a sense, he was responsible for the Pythons not making many more films because he tried to get not only a Python film every four years, because we said, "Look, it's every four years, if you just leave it be," but he would try to get individual films in the middle which was like trying to get individual albums while you're trying to get a Beatles album out. It destroys the point of having a group work.' And Palin adds, 'No one bought Python, and I think Denis felt perhaps he could and this was the mistake he made.'

Despite Python leaving the HandMade stable, O'Brien knew what side his bread was buttered and continued to court members of the team to make films for him. His dealings, however, with Steve Abbott were less than cordial. Although no longer with HandMade, Abbott continued returning to Cadogan Square, in his professional capacity as Python's accountant, sometimes even making the odd trip over to Guernsey, to look at the books and files pertaining to *Life of Brian* and other Python/HandMade-related films. He was always made to feel incredibly welcome by the office staff. There was no hostility whatsoever, although such visits were always carefully arranged to coincide with O'Brien's absence from the country. 'Denis didn't speak to me for years. I remember John Cleese said to me, "It's just like in *The Godfather* when Brando says, 'Never, ever go to anyone outside the family.' " Well, Denis sees you as having left the family." Denis is the only person to this day that's actually cut me off in public. I was going to a screening and he and Alfie Jarratt jumped out of a cab and Alfie, even though we'd only crossed over for like six weeks, greeted me like a long-lost son. And I said, "Hello, Denis," and held out my hand, and he just looked the other way and walked off, and that's not happened to me before or since. I don't think he could forgive what he saw as a betrayal, sort of moving on to the other side.'

CHAPTER 5

A VERY BRITISH INSTITUTION

HandMade as a film company was unlike any other then operating in the British film industry. For starters, its headquarters wasn't an office per se, but a tall and narrow, brown crenellated house in a predominantly residential square. Hardly filmic. And it was situated in Knightsbridge at a time when every one of its competitors and contemporaries were based around the coffee bar and sexpot environs of Soho or Wardour Street. It's position, no doubt, contributed greatly to the team spirit within the office, the fact that they weren't among a cluster of a dozen or so other film companies. It was interesting, certainly provocative, and very clever except it became too estranged in many ways. Brian Shingles comments, 'HandMade did its own thing fairly quietly and I always wished we banged the drum more. But that wasn't Denis's way and that fitted in with the image of Cadogan Square, away from Wardour Street, we weren't part of that, and I think that probably didn't help because you're not one of the boys. And I don't know that George would've wanted to have been in Wardour Street anyway.'

Unlike Goldcrest, the nearest competitor to HandMade, then headed by a much more spirited and vocal leader in the guise of David Puttnam,

O'Brien deliberately generated an air of semi-anonymity, not so much blowing his own trumpet as not even owning one. HandMade, for example, failed to exploit sufficiently the terrific success of *Time Bandits* or their own part in it to the degree that, say, Goldcrest did with *Chariots of Fire*. This despite the Gilliam fantasy taking more money at the US box office. It was *Chariots of Fire* that won the propaganda war and was very much seen as the great white hope of the British film industry, even if Goldcrest needed Hollywood backing to get it made, while *Time Bandits* was funded by English pounds. Ray Cooper observed, 'We pulled back while Puttnam was out front waving the banner.'

Even worse, O'Brien and Harrison (especially) were almost invisible as figureheads when they should have been much more front-of-house, more visibly representative of the company. Instead, they rarely, if ever, consented even to giving press interviews. Such behaviour inevitably led to accusations of aloofness and a fuzzy, nondescript public profile that even this early on produced mumblings of disquiet from leading HandMade figures. Shingles says, 'We were so low key, that used to be very galling because you had Goldcrest in the trade papers every week. It was Goldcrest this, Goldcrest that, David Puttnam was the saviour of the world, and you used to feel that somehow we were being left behind. And you had the Palace boys starting up who were mavericks – Nick Powell and Stephen Woolley – they were personalities, they had a profile, and they were always in the trades. And Denis said, "No, we don't want to be like that, we just want to get on with our thing, doing what we do best, keeping a low profile. People will recognise us for what we are." It was so galling. You'd say "HandMade" and people would say, "Oh, is that the George Harrison thing?" And you'd say, "Yes." And they'd go, "Oh, you haven't done much, have you?" That used to be really frustrating.'

What HandMade did have, though, was a great logo and O'Brien exploited it to the full. Wendy Palmer remembers, 'The HandMade logo was on everything. Denis was a master in many ways, nothing could go out without a logo on it. That logo was plastered everywhere. I guess more could have been done in publicity terms, but we didn't really need to with hindsight. We were always a bit elusive, a bit of an enigma. No one really knew what went on or how it went on. That added to its mystique.'

As you entered the actual HandMade building in Cadogan Square, through the double doors, your eyes fell immediately upon the lift, the famous lift. One scarcely used the staircase, which was immaculately polished every day. The HandMade lift is fondly remembered by those who frequented the office, chiefly because of its size, or lack of size. It was tiny. Michael Palin observed wryly, 'HandMade has the only lift in the world which has a maximum occupancy of one-and-a-half people, or four children. You wonder why Denis didn't like to do co-productions? It was because he couldn't get anyone else into the lift.'

HandMade shared the building with EuroAtlantic and the offices of Dark Horse, Harrison's own record label. 'EuroAtlantic was like the parent company,' according to Shingles. 'It used to operate Denis's companies and also oversee George's interests. Initially, there was no cross-fertilisation, it was two distinct companies, there was a clear divide between them and us. They used to get the perks at that point and we never did. Denis would always say, "We're all one family, really," and we said, "Well, that's not quite right." But that did change later on, the company became much more involved between the two and we were just part of one big, happy family and never thought of ourselves as separate entities.'

The building itself was like a rabbit warren inside, haphazardly broken up into numerous offices, some remarkably small. In the rarefied upper echelons was Denis O'Brien's comfortably upholstered office, with its views across rooftops of apartments and offices bustling for space behind Harrods. His office was serviced by *the lift*, but only if one was in possession of a certain key, without which there was no access. Cooper says, 'We had meetings twice a week, early in the morning, in this boardroom at the top. Not quite the top because that was the penthouse where Denis actually lived, but as far as you could go as a normal mortal, unless invited or given the key. The boardroom was very elegant, this huge Regency table, and we would have our creative discussions there.'

Denis was particularly fond of this table and had let it be known within the office that it was a Chippendale. 'The irony was that, later, when everything had to get sold off, it turned out it was a fake,' remembers Wendy Palmer. 'And Denis was just so freaked out about this table, if he came in and there was a coffee cup on it without a mat underneath he'd get totally freaked out. And I remember Bruce Robinson used to get on that table and dance. I kid you not.'

On another occasion, during a birthday celebration, the table was all laid out with food and it collapsed under the weight. Shingles says, 'Denis wasn't there so we had to get French polishers in to fix it and, of course, things never look the same afterwards and Denis came back and he looked at the table while we were talking, and he looked, and everyone just carried on as though nothing had happened. I don't know if he ever found out.'

Anyone unfamiliar with the layout of O'Brien's office might never have guessed that there was a secret door, a panelled door, designed to blend in with the wall. It opened to reveal stairs leading up to his private apartment, his UK residence when he wasn't gallivanting around the globe doing deals or luxuriating on his private yacht. The suite perfectly complemented O'Brien's cultivated lifestyle. Cooper recalls, 'It was beautiful ... beautiful furniture and books everywhere. Very tasteful.' Here, indeed, was a man of elegance and style, not averse to ranting at members of his own staff who lent too heavily back on his prized antique chairs. He was also particularly proud of his own special store of expensive claret, each bottle carrying its own number. This air of culture also extended to his appearance. 'Denis was very elegant,' Ray Cooper confirms. 'Bow-tie. Originally bearded, which was his token to being slightly left of field.'

When he was there, O'Brien was very much a nine-to-five figure. Even when he was out of the country, which was often (one colleague joked that O'Brien was the only person he knew who suffered from jetlag going from one holiday to another), he'd remain in touch with the office; his presence was always felt. In charge during his absences would be his secretary, Corrina Howard. Palmer believes, 'You can't really look at Corrina without looking at Denis. She kept everything together.'

Harrison couldn't have been more different. Although he retained a private office, with a permanent assistant attending to his affairs, he was scarcely seen at Cadogan Square. When he did come in, he might pop his head round a few doors to say 'Hi' and catch up on industry gossip. He also made the effort to attend the odd office party or lunch. At Christmas, everyone got gifts from him, or if he had a new album release he enjoyed handing out free copies. But, as a rule, he rarely socialised with HandMade staff, some of whom he wouldn't even have recognised if he passed them on the street. Cooper says, 'George didn't want to come in; he had me there and I would go out to his house and we would talk scripts. I'd tell him stories and he'd agree them. He would come in every so often, but normally he wouldn't come in because he didn't want that position, and I don't blame him … he didn't want to be the businessman or the ogre, he wanted to help people do what they wanted to do. And I think that was the whole aspect of The Beatles anyway, Apple Corps, the shop, many things that were about, naïvely and innocently, just trying to help people, enable people.'

For Harrison, the last thing he wanted out of HandMade was an office job. 'I never intended to be David Puttnam,' he once said. Because O'Brien and Ray Cooper were there to keep him informed of any developments and about current projects, he felt his presence wasn't really required. Happy to take a back seat, involving himself only as much as he wanted to, Harrison had perhaps finally managed to find the perfect balance between showbusiness and personal peace and quiet. But his absence, particularly on the publicity front, was seen by some as handicapping the company. 'Everyone used to say it was "George the recluse",' says Shingles. 'He certainly wasn't high-profile, he wouldn't be seen at premières. I wish George had been more involved because distributors used to say, "Will George come and do publicity for us … will George do this?" And we'd say, "He's very busy." And, in the end, we'd stop passing on requests to George because you knew the answer, it was almost academic, so why ask? But it would have been very beneficial.'

Besides Ray Cooper, another old friend from Harrison's past, Derek Taylor, who'd been The Beatles' publicist, also had an office at HandMade during these dangerous and wonderful early years – 'the glory days' as Terry Gilliam refers to them today. 'There was a kind of wonderful *avant garde*ness in the beginning,' Cooper recalls. 'But suddenly there was a clean-up, the whole thing started to change. Derek Taylor left very early on, he saw the writing on the wall a long time ago. Unfortunately, what started to happen was HandMade got bigger; suddenly Dark Horse was getting smaller and George's little bit of the office. We ended up taking the whole thing over.'

With money pouring in from *Life of Brian* and *Time Bandits*, HandMade's expansion was inevitable, though O'Brien took pains not to lose the family atmosphere that he had done so much to engender and which made working in the office so special. Shingles says, 'Most of the staff would agree it was unique. You were protected, not molly-coddled, but we were protected and it gave rise to lots of eccentricities, people behaved how you would never see people behave in any other walk of life. It really remained a small company and you fed off each other and you behaved ridiculously. That was why it was so unique. At that point, we had a wonderful time. You can never recapture it.' Shingles recalls one memorable winter's afternoon when the staff enjoyed a massive snowball fight ... inside the office building!

This uniqueness was felt almost immediately by new recruit Hilary Davies who arrived at HandMade from Warner Brothers. She arrived initially as a secretary, but would stay on for 15 years. 'It really was like being part of a big family, because there was only 20 people maybe at that stage, it grew a bit afterwards, but it was never massive, so that's what made for a really nice atmosphere. I thought it was wonderful. I really enjoyed going to work. And you either came and you liked it and you stayed, or you came, didn't like it and left pretty quickly. You were either one or the other. Everybody really got on and they were just very committed to their work. It was total commitment from everybody. We all loved the films that we were working on, even the ones that didn't turn out so well ... in the end you had an affection for them.'

Because Hilary had studied languages at university, she eventually wound up at distribution and marketing, attending film festivals and markets around the world, notably Cannes. And it was in the area of distribution where potential dangers concerning HandMade's burgeoning ambitions first manifested themselves. Getting bigger inevitably means larger overheads, then you have to keep making films or buy in product from elsewhere to get your overheads down. A lull in production immediately following *Time Bandits* meant there was a void out there which had to be filled by something.

Unfortunately, of all the clapped-out, turgid rubbish floating around in 1981, HandMade had the distinction of picking up possibly the worst three for distribution. *Tattoo* featured ex-Bond actress Maud Adams and was about a mad tattooist who kidnaps a beautiful girl and paints her body before forcing her to have sex. *Venom* was one of those so-bad-it's-laughable British thrillers that centred around an escaped snake inside a house full of stereotypes. One's tedium is saved only by the exceptional moment where the reptile wanders up the inside trouser leg of Oliver Reed and bites into his knackers. Lastly, *The Burning* was a repellent *Friday the Thirteenth* rip-off remarkable only for being the first film from Harvey Weinstein's soon to be behemoth Miramax.

How could any company survive such a trio of releases? Cooper suggests, 'As an acquiring force and an independent company, uniquely independent in those days, we were up against the majors, so they had all the great work. We didn't have the money, even HandMade didn't have the money at that stage to buy in the best films, so we were dealing with stuff like *Venom* and *The Burning*. Awful. It was a big mistake.'

The Burning actually should have been a money-spinner, arriving as it did during the great censorship and video nasty debate, but HandMade got cold feet over it and toned down the ad campaign to such an extent that the film failed to find its target audience.

Inside HandMade there was much vocal disquiet about the film choices being made and it was Alfie Jarratt who began feeling the pressure. At CIC, he'd ridden on a wave of successive hits but now found the clout he once wielded all but wiped out. There was a sense of him being marginalised and frustrated that he wasn't able to achieve at HandMade what he'd wanted to. He'd regularly saunter off to the famous White Elephant restaurant at lunchtime to meet up with old film mates like Bernie Delfont, but back at the office he seemed to have lost the will to fight his corner. Shingles' view was that 'it became increasingly tense between Alfie and EuroAtlantic. Denis's view of HandMade was to be a classy production/distribution outfit and Alfie didn't fit the bill in a way – he was aggressive, the old school, and the films let everyone down badly. In the end, they realised it just wasn't working and Alfie went.' Not long after his dismissal, Alfie Jarratt died.

In November 1982, surprising no one, HandMade announced they were to wind down the distribution end of its operation. It had been a bold experiment that had dreadfully backfired. Although the company intended to continue distributing its own movies wherever possible, no longer would it seek to buy in films from other sources.

But the whole distribution débâcle hadn't been a total waste of time. According to Cooper, '*Venom* with Klaus Kinski and Susan George baring her tits yet again, bless her heart – and magnificent they are always to see – was a piece of nonsense, really. But one good thing did come out of it. Michael Kamen wrote the score for that movie and I heard it and some other music that he'd done. At the time, I was moonlighting on *Brazil*. One of the jobs I always had was to help Terry Gilliam through the music side of post-production. So I heard the *Venom* soundtrack which was interesting and realised this was a man who had a sense of space, but his film career was going nowhere. I said to Terry, "I think I've found a composer for you. He's unknown but I think you should meet him." I brought him along to see a rough cut of *Brazil* and Michael's mouth dropped open, and we sat with Michael week after week pulling out of Michael what he didn't know he had in him. And that launched his career because when Steven Spielberg saw *Brazil*, he wanted the composer and Michael's career never looked back.'

In between his assignments on '80s Hollywood blockbusters like the *Lethal Weapon* and *Die Hard* series, Kamen perhaps felt duty-bound to return periodically to HandMade, becoming almost their composer-in-residence, scoring *Mona Lisa*, *Shanghai Surprise*, *The Raggedy Rawney* and *Cold Dog Soup*.

It was during the course of the next two years that HandMade's reputation for making low-budget, short-schedule, mass-release films, using British financing, was forged. *Scrubbers* was in many ways an odd choice for HandMade's first post-*Time Bandits* film. It remained out of kilter with everything they subsequently produced and is the company's sole dip into unadorned social realism. It was also one of their most fraught productions and left veteran producer Don Boyd still spitting venom at the name of Denis O'Brien and HandMade 20 years later.

From its earliest days, *Scrubbers* was stigmatised as the female *Scum*, a largely unfair comparison, although it did hail from the same makers of the highly controversial Roy Minton drama, banned by the BBC, about the injustices in a boy's Borstal which shocked the nation and forced the government of the day into positive action. Don Boyd asserts, '*Scum* changed the law ... it really was groundbreaking in that sense. There were questions in Parliament and the Home Office completely overhauled the Borstal system after the release of that film.'

Returning from America having produced John Schlesinger's

elephantine farce *Honky Tonk Freeway*, Boyd faced massive pressure to make a *Scum* follow-up. He resisted. Then the idea cropped up that perhaps it would work if the same uncompromising study was done but this time focusing upon the turbulent life at a girl's Borstal, viewed mainly through its effect on two very different young women. It was Boyd's assistant who came up with the inspired notion of bringing in Mai Zetterling as director.

Still fondly remembered as an actress, notably her sex kitten role alongside Peter Sellers in *Only Two Can Play*, Mai, now 58, had moved into directing feature films and acclaimed television documentaries in her native Scandinavia. When the idea of *Scrubbers* was mooted, she bit almost immediately and set about totally rewriting a provisional script penned by Roy Minton, who was eventually paid off, though retains a screen credit.

Getting such a difficult project financed proved relatively straightforward. Boyd had various money offers on the table but HandMade stood out as the best option. They had a good reputation, he felt, and the Python connection was another plus. A meeting was arranged at Cadogan Square. As far as Boyd was concerned, 'The HandMade office was very odd because you would go in downstairs and there was this strange area where you hung around until they let you go into this tiny, horribly claustrophobic lift which took you into an area that could have easily been a residential apartment. I always felt there was this rather greasy, ingratiating atmosphere there. It was a slight, crusty, old world feeling combined with a sense of secrecy. You knew, of course, that if anybody was unwelcome they wouldn't get up into that lift.'

Once the financial aspect was sorted (*Scrubbers* was allotted a restrictive but fair budget of around £600,000), Boyd sought from O'Brien reassurances that his own company, Boyd's Co, would not become subservient or gobbled up by the mightier HandMade. 'Denis explained to me the system he had, he said he was very keen with George Harrison to give a big boost to the British cinema. I told him the film was set up to be a Boyd's Co production, we had funds attached to it and that we had a separate identity, that we were a production company that made movies, successful ones, and we didn't see how this was going to work into the HandMade set-up. And he managed to convince me, very cunningly, that Boyd's Co wouldn't be emasculated if I was to produce the film personally.'

This was agreed and the contract was signed, a punitive contract that, in hindsight, Boyd wouldn't have touched with a barge pole. Basically, it was a case of, if the film comes in on budget then you'll earn your money. But Boyd sensed O'Brien's real intention was to undermine his position as producer and manipulate the project away from Boyd's Co completely. There were mind games going on, childish in nature, such as sending a thank you gift of wine to every member of the crew except him. 'Denis was terrible during the shooting and George Harrison wasn't any better. It was all very familiar to me because I'd just been for three years in Hollywood and I knew how the games were played. The politics of film-making is just complete bullshit. Denis kept playing this weird sort of paternalistic game as well. Although we were supplicant he made you feel that you were part of a little family that he was going to be involved with and look forward to nurturing. It was all complete nonsense because at the same time whenever there was an opportunity businesswise to marginalise what I represented, he would take that opportunity, so I always felt very combative with him. And he would always say, "Now look, Don, don't feel like that. I'm on your side." He made me feel that I could be part of the family and then at the stage where it was clear he was getting his way, then I was suddenly an orphan.'

Deeply distracted by the strange dichotomy which existed between the two companies and the personalities involved, Mai Zetterling approached the project with impassioned energy nevertheless, hoping to touch the public's conscience. Spending some three months on research, Mai spoke with social workers and ex-Borstal girls, aware that the background to the film needed to be totally authentic. Directing for the first time in the English language, she also worked extremely closely with her largely inexperienced cast, including the young Kathy Burke and Robbie Coltrane. He recalls, 'I was almost the only male in the cast, and the girls forgot I was there after a while and started talking like they were alone, which was quite an eye-opener. Mai wandered about with a bullwhip and was very funny, and, of course, I bored her to death asking her about all her films as an actress, which was fascinating. I also met Kathy Burke, she must have been a teenager then, and fearless. At times it felt like the real thing, a lot of the girls had done time and began treating me like a screw, so the dynamic was there. I was asked to be suggestive with a vacuum flask, if I remember right, so no change there.'

It must also have helped that Mai was a woman. It's debatable whether a male director could have pulled off such a project quite so effectively. Boyd believes, 'Mai had the sensitivity to deal with a woman's issue in a sociological context. She also had an individual take on life and I felt the film needed that to separate it from *Scum*. It shouldn't have been a female *Scum*, it had to be something that had its own identity.'

But being a woman in a prodigiously male-orientated industry fostered its own unique set of problems, notably with the assistant director who resented Mai's exalted position. Boyd observes, 'To demonstrate the degree of antipathy between Roger, the AD, and Mai, Roger had baked a special cake which was presented to Mai at the end of wrap party. It was in the shape of a penis and testicles and that was his present to her, indicating what she had represented to him, which was a man. He didn't understand that she would be offended by that and she was deeply offended by it. He thought it was a funny way of saying, "Look, you've won your spurs, you're one of us," and Mai was saying, "No, I'm not one of you and, by the way, I didn't want to be one of you at all." It was the worst thing he could have possibly done. Poor Roger, he later fell off a cliff in Turkey, killed himself directing a commercial.'

Scrubbers went before the cameras in February 1982 on location at Holloway Sanatorium in Surrey, a one-time insane asylum where Nijinsky met his end in 1950 having become a raving lunatic and where Tony Hancock was once a patient. This oppressive and rambling gothic edifice, derelict for two years, housed both the production offices and the studio where makeshift sets, based on photographic material from various women's prisons, were authentically reproduced. The makers wanted everything fantastically close to real life, from the clothes to the interchange of dialogue. O'Brien fretted over whether all the slang words might render the film too colloquial and ruin its chances of playing overseas. He also despised the amount of foul language used. Mai herself feared the swearing might condemn her film to an X rating, but still believed the way these kids spoke couldn't be softened. The *Daily Star* branded the Borstal girls 'the most loutish and foul-mouthed ever to appear on a cinema screen'. In the end, *Scrubbers* was granted an AA certificate (today a 15) by censor James Ferman who hoped this unflinching view of Borstal life would be a salutary lesson for teenagers on the cusp of a life in crime.

Amid the ongoing tensions between Boyd and O'Brien, Ray Cooper was a beacon of sanity. Boyd says, 'When there were times when Denis caused problems with me, Ray was a good person to talk to. I used him really as my buffer with Denis. He was a little bit enigmatic, I couldn't quite understand what his agenda was, but what I loved about him was his romantic intellect, he had a very romantic view of what cinema could be like. He was very much on the side of the artist and his relationship with George made it difficult for Denis to be the bully boy all the time. We always knew that if we had a big problem we could go to Ray to help us out. He was a very important go-between in getting Denis to understand that, if you didn't have Mai's vision, the film wasn't going to be anything, it was just going to be a mess.'

Ray Cooper was *Scrubbers'* most ardent supporter within HandMade and editorially important, too, having contributed comments as the script was being fashioned. Now, during shooting, he made sure never to be absent from the set and was a constant source of encouragement to Mai particularly. 'I had a wonderful time with Mai, she was a joy to work with. It was actually the first time I did a little bit of direction. There were a couple of scenes which Mai very politely said, "Well, you do that one," which was very sweet. It was wonderful, there was an energy there. I suppose because we were paying for it ourselves, we didn't have anyone looking over our shoulder.'

As for George Harrison, he was the most distant of figures, scarcely having any dealings with the film, attending only the one production meeting. 'I remember George appearing on the set at the beginning,' Boyd says, 'coming over to me and saying, "What are you doing here?" And I said, "I'm the producer of this film." And he said, "Well, I thought I was the producer." I said, "George, it's your money. What do you think I've been doing over these last few weeks?" Apart from that, I didn't have a lot of dealings with George. I knew he was a figurehead that we could manipulate through Ray Cooper up to a point. George seemed happy to be the sleeping partner in all this. He wasn't involved editorially at all. He approved the script but he wasn't involved in any of the contracts or any of the financial arrangements; that seemed to be left entirely to Denis.'

As on *Time Bandits*, it was when the film was in the can that the real problems started. 'We brought the film in on budget,' Boyd adds, 'it came in without any extra shooting whatsoever. And when we were editing it, we were left alone until really near the end, which is a very familiar technique of lots of executives, and then Denis jumped in and said, "Right, I'm now going to be involved in the finalising of it." '

O'Brien wanted *Scrubbers* shorter and less violent, to sanitise it, basically. He even tried to play Boyd and Mai off each other, which didn't work. Though, finally, Mai realised that she had to ingratiate O'Brien, after all he was going to be the film's future, not Boyd, and more or less in the end got the cut she wanted.

As for Boyd, he became *persona non grata* and was ditched completely, barred even from attending test screenings of his own movie. 'Once, essentially, Denis got out of me what he most wanted, which was the creative and producing input that made the film what it is, I was written entirely out of it and, to this day, I've never had a statement from them. I've never had any money. I never got my fee. I never heard another word. I produced an important film and I didn't earn anything from it and neither did my company. Once everything had been paid out, our involvement actually cost us money.'

Even marketing and distribution decisions were taken without input from Boyd's Co. Any suggestions that were put forward went unheeded. 'Denis just wanted me out of the picture,' says Boyd, 'because he didn't want any of the glory to go in any direction other than to him or HandMade. We wanted to put on the posters, "From the producers of *Scum*", but HandMade didn't want any of that. It was a big mistake, a very stupid mistake, it would have made it much more commercial and made me wonder how commercial Denis wanted it to be, whether he wanted it to just disappear.'

Upon its release in November 1982, *Scrubbers* was met with generally warm notices. 'This is a more powerful, compassionate movie than *Scum*, made with passion, blazingly well acted and it troubles the conscience, which is no bad thing,' wrote the *Daily Mail*. The *Guardian* said, 'It is an impeccably liberal scream against the system which still manages enough crowd-pleasing tactics to keep the customers happy.' Of course, there were detractors. 'Alternately overplayed and trivialised, pile-driving and prurient,' slammed the *Financial Times*. The *Western Mail* found Zetterling undecided about how she wanted *Scrubbers* to work. 'In the end, it falls uneasily between campaigning documentary and sloppy melodrama.'

After opening the London Film Festival, *Scrubbers* played in a few West End venues and sporadically round the country before disappearing from the public gaze, rarely surfacing since. Boyd's feeling is that 'it was very frustrating to think that a film that was well reviewed, that we put so much work into, should have had such a tiny release and just marginalised entirely by HandMade, especially as HandMade then went on to proclaim all kinds of important things for the British film industry. Denis didn't really back it properly and I just felt he had a strange agenda in relation to it. I don't think he liked the film and just decided to write it off. And, of course, that seemed to suit the tax arrangements. We just felt we were the also-rans that Denis didn't want to back and certainly didn't want to acknowledge because of the ambiguity with my company. He didn't want anyone to think that HandMade hadn't made the film, while all they'd done was provide the money. Denis's main involvement was to sign cheques and to cause problems at the final cut and that was it. We, Boyd's Co, made that film and we lost money out of it and we were not involved in the distribution and so weren't even allowed to participate in any of its success, limited as that was. And I have enormous resentment about that.'

Amazingly, when *Scrubbers* finally opened in America in February 1984, Boyd wasn't even informed by O'Brien. In New York at the time, it was left to a colleague to ring him up with the news. 'Do you realise your movie's opening?' Boyd rushed out to buy a copy of the *New York Times* to read for himself its flattering review. He couldn't believe it.

In spite of what happened, *Scrubbers* remains a film Boyd looks back on with unreserved pride. 'It's a really good film. Mai did a brilliant job. I don't think it's better than *Scum*, but I think it's a very different film that works on its own level. Mai's big thing was that people had this independent spirit that could shine despite the hellishness of a repressed system. That was her message and it was a very warm message. If you look at the film you'll see that that pervades everything. These repressed environments people talk about in concentration camps and prisons, our individual personalities would rather kick against the pricks and demonstrate our desire to be as free as possible within that repressed set-up. She felt that very passionately about women, that women's dignity should survive. That's what she was on about, dignity, and I think she succeeded.'

If *Scrubbers* was hardly Denis O'Brien's cup of Darjeeling – and there is probably much truth in Boyd's accusation that he left it to wither on the vine – it was very much to the taste of Ray Cooper. And it amply demonstrated where, artistically, these two very different men were coming from. Cooper remembers 'one of my first philosophical run-ins with Denis. We got into an interesting heated discussion. I said, "Well, Denis, if, say, *The Long Good Friday* had come to your desk as a script, would you have made it?" And he said, "No." And I said, "Well, I would have." We defined at that early stage some areas of differences.'

O'Brien, it seemed, was still keen to exploit the worldwide brand name that was Monty Python, even though after *Meaning of Life* it was unlikely the team would ever make any more films together. Steve Abbott's view was 'it was absolutely clear that they now wanted to do their own movies. Gilliam was going to do *Brazil*, and already from 1981 Charles Crichton was on the books of John Cleese's company and was being paid to develop the script that later became *A Fish Called Wanda*. So just the logistics of setting aside a year where they'd all commit to doing a joint project made it unlikely.' But Denis still saw to it that the comedy group continued to influence and colour HandMade's production portfolio for the foreseeable future. 'Denis's basic reference point to side-splitting humour was Monty Python,' Cooper says, 'he was a huge fanatic, which is wonderful. Unfortunately, he tried to imbue other material with that sensibility, which is very difficult, but that was always what he was trying to look for.'

If was as if O'Brien couldn't let go of the Pythons both spiritually and, more importantly, financially. Abbott believes, 'Denis was forever courting them individually to make films for him, but as a group, anyone who knew them at all knew that a group film wasn't going to be forthcoming, certainly in the four or five years after *Meaning of Life*. And, of course, it never happened, and once Graham died that was it anyway.'

Python meant bums on seats and no one knew that better than Denis O'Brien. Gilliam says, 'When Python left, and it was our stupidity, we never made an announcement, we just said, "Goodbye, Denis," and walked away from it. We never put a press statement out – you know, "Python leaves HandMade", "Python rejects Denis O'Brien and everything he stands for". We didn't do that and Denis for another ten years played off that, he was still selling it as the same thing. That's why a lot of people were attracted to it, people didn't know that Python was no longer involved with HandMade Films, especially in Hollywood. And he just kept using us and George.'

One couldn't really help but continue identifying HandMade with Python, though, when members of the group (John Cleese, Michael Palin and, much later, Eric Idle) were only too happy to return and make films for O'Brien. Gilliam asserts, 'But I thought it was wrong. I could never get the others to get angry enough about it to do something.'

Several pseudo-Python projects did almost come to fruition under the HandMade banner. During one Christmas party, Terry Jones approached O'Brien with an idea to do a Viking musical. Brian Shingles says, 'But Denis always maintained that films that had boats in them were very expensive.' So he passed and the film was eventually made under the title Erik the Viking. Jones openly admits, 'But I very much valued Denis's involvement in some of my other projects. He was keen to do this film of mine about the peasants' revolt. But I wasn't quite sure whether Denis really got the idea. I think he thought it was a comedy, and it really wasn't.'

Graham Chapman also interested HandMade in his pirate romp Yellowbeard. 'More bloody boats,' O'Brien must have feared. While Cleese had Fawlty Towers, Idle had The Rutles and Palin and Jones had Ripping Yarns, Chapman was enjoying no high-profile success and was desperate to get Yellowbeard off the ground. After much preparatory work, HandMade let the project go and it was picked up later by Orion. The film ended up a box-office disaster despite one of the all-time great comedy casts – John Cleese, Eric Idle, Peter Cook, Marty Feldman (who died during the last week of filming), Madeline Kahn, Cheech and Chong, Spike Milligan and Chapman himself whose unbelievably eccentric performance makes the film almost worth watching.

O'Brien appeared to favour one particular Python above all the others – Michael Palin. Busy working with the rest of the gang on The Meaning of Life, but frustrated that progress was slow, Palin began ruminating over the possibilities of a solo project: 'People were doing lots of different things at the time and were absent from discussions, whereas they weren't in Life of

Brian, people were always around. There was a feeling then of everyone spreading their wings and doing their own things. So that's why I thought I'd have a go at *The Missionary*. And I remember when I had the idea. I was actually running over Hampstead Heath and it suddenly came to me, this idea of a missionary as a central figure.'

In spirit, *The Missionary* is closer to Palin and Terry Jones's *Ripping Yarns*, those affectionate parodies of *Boy's Own* adventures, than it was to Python. It was also a paean to Palin's schooldays when he'd sit fascinated listening to visiting missionaries whose lectures barely touched upon religion but were instead full of heroic tales about paddling up the Limpopo and avoiding being eaten by tigers. Palin's own fictional hero, Reverend Charles Fortescue, is returning after a lengthy and liberating spell in Africa to an Edwardian England steeped in hypocrisy and social prejudice. He is given a new responsibility of establishing a refuge for prostitutes in London's impoverished East End with orders to 'find out why they do what they do, and stop them doing it!'

Michael Palin explains, 'I wanted to go back to the whole area of *Life of Brian*, sort of hypocrisy and double standards. The idea of a missionary who has a lustful sex life when he's out in Africa and then he gets into trouble when he comes back home because of the attitudes towards sex and prostitutes. I thought this had comic possibilities with a serious theme underneath it.' Palin even went to the meticulous lengths of researching prostitution at the British Library, just to see if during that period there had been any serious attempts at reform. Alas, his suspicions were proven right; the Edwardians treated prostitutes as wicked women, considering it their duty to clean them up with carbolic soap and prayers.

Funding the £2 million project, which at one time was playfully entitled *The Missionary Position*, was simplicity personified. Palin says, 'I went to see Denis and we were all on quite good terms then because *Time Bandits* had been this unexpected success, so Denis was happy to work with people who'd worked on that. I'd also done *Life of Brian*, so I had an enormous track record. George was reasonably happy. I don't think it was actually a film that George particularly wanted to do. But what is important is that Denis supported me at a time when I wanted to make a film like *The Missionary*, and later helped finance something like *A Private Function*, because those films may well not have been made, certainly not made with the amount of control we had, with anybody else. That's definitely on Denis's credit side.'

The Missionary represented a considerable step forward in Palin's professional ambitions, his first project as star, writer and co-producer. And it was a real opportunity to find out what he could achieve on his own away from the slightly restrictive world of Python. He balked at the prospect of directing it himself, though. 'I've never been tempted to direct. I'm more interested in writing first, acting second, and I think to write, act and direct is extremely difficult, very few people do that successfully. I haven't got the sort of concentration, quite honestly, to do all three, it's a 24-hours-a-day, seven-days-a-week job. I've seen others do it – Terry Jones and Gilliam become almost different people, utterly and completely absorbed and weighed down by the responsibilities which are ultimately yours right through the film. So I'm quite happy for someone else to take that responsibility.'

Palin's ideal director turned out to be Richard Loncraine, with whom he'd wanted to work for some time. Having just finished shooting Dennis Potter's gothic *Brimstone and Treacle* with rock star Sting, the idea and challenge of doing a comedy was certainly appealing. 'So I literally came off *Brimstone* and went on to *The Missionary*, which was not a good idea for all sorts of reasons that my ex-wife will tell you about. It was a pretty exhausting time. But I've always liked comedy because I think it's so hard and so dangerous. The thing about comedy is that you can't get it half-right; if they laugh they laugh, if they don't laugh there's no excuses. You can have a horror film that's a little bit frightening, but if it's a comedy and nobody laughs you've got something wrong.'

Pretty much from the word go, Loncraine found himself at odds with Denis O'Brien, something Palin realised early on. 'Richard is a London boy with a very good line in patter, but fairly scatological and fairly fruity in his language. We all had a meal together to sort of meet up at a rather smart restaurant in Chelsea and Denis was sort of doing his bit and talking to Richard and saying I want to do this and I want to do that ... there was a bit of bargaining going on here and there. And at the end of it, Richard said, "Well, Denis, you know what you are, don't you?" And Denis looked rather pleased with himself. And Richard said, "You're a cunt!" It was just wonderful. Denis collapsed. It was just quite brilliant, not really what anyone normally says to a producer who's prepared to give you a lot of money. And it was said with a certain amount of affection to it, and I've never ever forgotten that. Denis was quite taken aback, but I think after that understood Richard much more.' Loncraine still fondly remembers the insult. 'I couldn't think of a more articulate word at the time.'

To appear opposite Palin in what was essentially his first real dramatic screen role, Loncraine cast arguably the greatest actress of her generation in Maggie Smith. She plays Lady Isabel Ames, the sexually frustrated wife of a bigoted peer of the realm, who offers to finance Fortescue's home for fallen women on the condition that he goes to bed with her. The acquisition of Maggie Smith was a real casting coup and a daunting prospect for any actor. Palin remembers, 'I'm just in awe of her really because she's so good, so easy to work with. It's a bit like working with John Cleese, doing comedy, you just know they know exactly what to do, they just don't make a false move. Some people find Maggie difficult to work with because she doesn't suffer fools at all, she can be quite tetchy sometimes, a very quick wit, but that's good, that keeps you on your toes. I absolutely adored working with her.'

The two stars make an appealing team and Palin more than holds his own against the future theatre Dame. He'd come a long way indeed from the parrot sketch.

On set, Maggie Smith was never less than a real trouper and enjoyed the experience immensely, but like most stars needed to know that she would be treated with the respect her status deserved. 'I learnt a few lessons with Maggie,' Loncraine observes. 'She's a hard taskmaster and was a bit of a handful, but I've always been very straightforward with actors. Maggie doesn't fall into this category but many of the big Hollywood stars surround themselves with sycophants, but they hate you being sycophantic to them. With actors, it's about them trusting you and the moment you start lying to an actor your game's up. Some actors have got great brains, some have got very little brains, but all of them have an instinct for when they're being bullshitted. Let's say, if you do a take and they're obviously bad and you go, "Wonderful, darling, marvellous, terrific ... Let's just do one more," They may not say it but you know inside they're going, "What a wanker, it was real rubbish." If you've really got the relationship right, as I did with Maggie, I could blow a raspberry and go, "Rubbish, Mags," and everyone would laugh and she would laugh and we'd do it again because she knew that I cared about her, respected her and it was no threat.'

A cherished memory of Maggie was during location work up in Scotland. She'd finished for the day and went to leave as another shot was being set up. Loncraine recalls, 'I'm on this very high cliff and I see Maggie walking about 300ft below on this little goat track and I shout, "Goodnight, Maggie." She looks up and just ignores me and I said to the guy next to me, "Silly bloody woman," and I kicked this little stone out of frustration and it rolled down the hill. But it hit another little stone, and another one, and it created an avalanche of really quite big stones, some of them a foot across, enough to break your legs, and they went round Maggie and she was running backwards and forwards in this great crinoline dress dodging these boulders. Eventually, it all rolled away and she stood there looking up at me and you could hear a pin drop in this valley. She looked up and she said, "You stupid, stupid child," and walked off back to the hotel. She worked with me again on *Richard III*, so she can't hate me that much. The timing of that insult though was absolutely perfect, she waited until the last boulder had dropped … it was like waiting for an audience to calm down before you do the next line. Oh, she knew how to play it.'

The film's supporting cast, too, featured thespians of the highest calibre. Working with actors of real distinction, as opposed to mere comedians who may hanker for dramatic recognition, was deliberate and began on *Ripping Yarns* when, instead of going for obvious comedy casting, Palin brought in actors he admired and whom he knew could do justice to the material. 'I remember getting Denholm Elliott to be in one of the first of the *Ripping Yarns – Across the Andes by Frog*. It was a great coup because we didn't see why there should be this barrier between serious actors and comedy actors. If you wrote material which had to be played seriously but the humour was in how well it was played, then you should go for those people.'

Elliott turns up again in *The Missionary* as a bombastic Bishop of London. Loncraine remembers, 'Denholm was a complicated man. I mean, it's complicated enough being a heterosexual, I find, so being a bisexual … But I liked him and he was such a good actor. He was a bit hard work, he'd have loads of tricks if he dried because he never bothered to learn his lines properly. If he dried, he'd turn and say, "Oh, darling, please don't move that when I'm trying, you're in my eye-line, lovey." He knew every trick in the book not to take the blame.'

Then there was Michael Hordern whose delightful cameo as a forgetful butler who can't find any of the rooms in his master's vast stately home almost steals the film. Loncraine's view was that 'the stuff with Michael getting lost at Longleat, I don't think there's funnier comedy. I saw previews of the film in America and people were falling off their seats. And I became very fond of Michael, a sweet man and a fine actor. He was a joy to work with. I'd say to him when we were filming, "I think we can get you off by about three this afternoon, Michael." "Jolly good," he'd say. "Thank you ever so much. I'll see if I can get you one," because he'd go off fishing, he was a great trout fisherman and he'd come back before we'd finished shooting with a trout for me and anyone else he could find one for. He was a really lovely man.'

Undoubtedly, the most difficult personality was Trevor Howard, perfectly cast as Lord Ames, imperial bigot and fascist by appointment to her majesty. According to Loncraine, 'It was very sad because *Brief Encounter* is one of my favourite films ever. Trevor played the pompous canon wonderfully, but he was just so drunk and didn't know where he was. The scene we did in Longleat when he's writing this letter – "How do you spell decapitate?" – he couldn't learn his lines. He wouldn't put on glasses so he couldn't read cue cards and he was very aggressive; actually, he behaved unspeakably badly in the end. Then he wouldn't come in and do post-sync, and really it was making him look better. But he was an alcoholic … what can you say? He woke up one night in the little hotel we were staying in when we were filming in Longleat and his dresser two doors down heard this screaming and went into his room and he'd got into the wardrobe and couldn't get out. He was completely gone and looked like shit. This was about a year I think before he died.'

Filming had got under way in March 1982 on locations ranging from the West Country and London's East End to Scotland. There was also a brief sojourn to Africa. Palin says, 'We had to battle to get that Kenyan sequence. Denis wasn't really very keen to go off to Africa and felt it could all be shot in England, but we won the battle to go. The shooting itself was extraordinary, everything I hoped it would be. We managed to get this little church built for the sequence where I'm playing the organ and a congregation of Africans is singing. I thought it was a nice comment on what we taught people during colonial times and the way they picked it up and went with it. It also makes a comment on the attitude of those who think colonialism was something inflicted brutally upon people. Not always; there were times when people rather liked singing these silly Victorian hymns.

'We had our problems ... I remember the Masai women would not go bare-breasted in any of the scenes, which, of course, they would have done in 1906. The Masai women said they'd been told that the American tourists wouldn't come by any longer unless they covered themselves up. That was a bit of a disadvantage, it was actually quite important because the whole film was about sexual embarrassment in England but not in Africa.'

Palin holds the opinion that going all the way out to Africa was important for the integrity of the production, making it stand out as something that everyone had taken the trouble to do properly. Loncraine agrees. 'One of my fondest memories of *The Missionary* was Michael and I on the recce; just he and I went out to Kenya. And I will never forget as long as I live sitting in the back of an open Toyota Land Cruiser with the sun going down. And those sunsets in Africa are amazing, literally driving through giraffe and buffalo and Michael doing the Python sketches for me and, of course, he could do all of the characters. And I just remember crying and asking him please to stop because I couldn't get my breath. That, I think, is one of the great moments that I will never forget.'

The African filming was largely done at a small and remote village called Lerata where the inhabitants were as helpful as they could be to the travelling English crew. Palin recalls, 'As a thank you, we asked is there anything you would like that we can leave behind and they said, "You could put a roof on our school." They were building a school at the time and couldn't afford even to put a roof on. So our carpenters put on a corrugated iron roof. That was 1982 and I went out there in 1991 when I was doing the BBC *Pole to Pole* series. We went down through Lerata and the roof was still on and I met the children and told them all about my connection with the village and gave them my blow-up globe because I'd carried it all the way from the North Pole. And really I gave it to them so they could learn geography and they ended up kicking it around like a football.'

Still smarting perhaps from the 'cunt' jibe, O'Brien's relationship with Loncraine never really reached even cordial status. Both were, in Palin's words, 'at loggerheads, though in a reasonably pleasant way. They gave as good as they got to each other.' Loncraine's view was that 'Denis would never come on the set and throw his weight around, he would stay in his office. I think he was looking after the next deal, he was always on the next picture. He might sometimes say, "I don't think we can do it that way," or have a mad idea about casting. He had like 50 bad ideas and maybe 10 good ones, but you had to navigate through the rubbish, so that got a bit frustrating, but no more frustrating than half the people I've worked for. You could drop Denis into Hollywood today and he wouldn't be out of place. Denis wasn't a stupid phenomenon, he was just a product of the industry, really. As for George Harrison, he came down once or twice, but again just to smile and say hello. He was always a figure in the background. Denis was difficult at times but charming. I don't find many people intimidating unless they've got a knife at my throat. I certainly didn't find Denis intimidating. I was very lucky and protected because Michael did the battles. I would shout at Denis and we'd have the odd screaming matches. But he was very fond of Michael so, when we needed something, Michael would say to Denis, "I think we need this," and we had it. So I was very cushioned.'

One particular battle involved the film's opening titles. Loncraine was determined to get it right and wanted large brass lettering that would spell out the words of *The Missionary* with a golden gleam. Palin remembers, 'Denis said, "Brass! Why can't it just be plastic or special effects?" And Richard said, "No, it's got to be this brass lettering." So Denis got the estimate and said, "You know how much this brass lettering costs? About £1,000 a letter." But, in the end, he did it. And about a year later, I was meeting Denis for lunch in this restaurant and in he comes with this huge great rectangular parcel under his arm, enormous great thing, and he's laughing even before he sees me, this high-pitched cackle. And then he comes up to the table and I'm looking – "What is this? Is he going to shoot me?" It's like someone coming in with a machine-gun in a case. I was a bit worried. And he rips the paper off and there is "The Missionary" in brass lettering, the original panel that we had done. And he gave it to me as a present.' Today, it resides in a garden shed at the bottom of Palin's London home.

As with all HandMade films, the final cut of *The Missionary* resided not with the director but with the company itself, a policy that was rigorously enforced by O'Brien. Not that it was actually much of a concern here. 'I've never had final cut and indeed wouldn't want it,' Loncraine states. 'My feeling about final cuts is it's not worth the paper it's printed on, the reason being if a studio spends $50 million on your movie and you have final cut and they don't like your cut, what are they going to do, spend another $30 million on promoting a film that they don't think's going to work or bury your movie? Many a director has found out that the way you maintain final cut is maintaining your position as the dominant force on the job. But having it contractually isn't worth it because they just dump you and they bury your film.'

The Missionary opened in London in March 1983 to largely positive notices. For the first time, critics drew parallels between HandMade's new brand of English film comedy and those golden greats from the Ealing studio. 'Not since the Ealing comedies have the quirks of English character and absurdities of English eccentricity received such an affectionate and entertaining ribbing,' gushed the *Sunday Express*. This sentiment was echoed by the *Sunday Times*: 'The film quickens towards a rowdy end that smacks of Ealing at the top of their ludicrous form. Jolly funny.' And the *Sunday Telegraph* purred, 'A gloriously eccentric comedy of Edwardian manners. Both a satire and a morality. It is that rare thing in the contemporary cinema, a picture you could wish to last longer.'

Unlike *Scrubbers*, *The Missionary* attracted good press attention and benefited from a more concerted ad campaign, undoubtedly due to Palin's popularity. Indeed, Brian Shingles recalls that Ray Cooper received a phone call from David Puttnam lamenting the fact that HandMade's film had got a higher profile than his own current release *Local Hero*. Puttnam's film, though, went on to take more money and is regarded now as a mini British gem, while *The Missionary*, alas, is rather forgotten. Loncraine says, 'When I say to people I made *The Missionary*, they go, "Oh, I love that film with the waterfall in South America." A lot of that happens and I have to go, "No, unfortunately that wasn't my movie."'

Opening in America in November 1982, *The Missionary* was greeted just as warmly by critics. The *Hollywood Reporter* declared it 'a sumptuous and dry-witted comedy reminiscent in tone and execution to many of those priceless old Alec Guinness and Peter Sellers rib-ticklers of yore'. Of course, the film did no business whatsoever Stateside. Loncraine believes that O'Brien made the mistake of opening it on far too many screens instead of letting it out slowly in order to build and find an audience. It also pissed him off that the publicity surrounding the release inevitably revolved around the Python connection. 'There was this chap called Marvin whom I used to call "the black hole" because every creative thought disappeared into his dark suits when you gave it to him. He was head of marketing at Columbia, who were distributing *The Missionary*, and I was over in America at the launch of the picture. It was a Monday morning meeting and we were all sitting around in this think tank with these young executives and Marvin is walking up and down and he's got the poster and he's saying, "We've got the one-sheet for the Monty Python *The Missionary*. This is a Monty Python presents *The Missionary* starring Michael Palin of Monty Python." And I said, "Sorry, Marvin to interrupt you ... this is Richard Loncraine, director. Marvin, this isn't actually a Monty Python film and if we bill it as a Monty Python film I think people, with respect to Michael, may be disappointed that they don't see the other Pythons and they won't recommend it to their friends. But what do I know ... I'm only the director." And he looked at me, put his arm on my shoulder and said, "No, no. Directing is a real contribution." And he wasn't taking the piss, he was genuine. So that was one of the problems in America, it was billed as a Python film and it simply wasn't.'

The American backers also tried to sell the film as a sex comedy, as opposed to Palin's view of it as more of an elegant look at Edwardian morals and manners. But he wasn't stupid and realised that it had to be packaged a certain way for mass consumption. He visualised this mythical but representational couple in the mid-West planning their evening's entertainment. 'Well, we can either go to a rodeo or go see "an elegant look at Edwardian morals and manners".' As Palin joked, 'It just wasn't on.'

The Missionary is a minor joy, not as funny as perhaps it ought to be but as pictorially stunning as any film of its era. This was intentional. According to Palin, why shouldn't a comedy be made with just as much care and attention to detail as the most elegantly realised drama of, say, the

Merchant/Ivory school? The *Voice* in America described the cinematography in *The Missionary* as 'virtually indistinguishable from *Tess*', but also made the point that 'comedies can't be too exquisitely mounted; beauty mitigates the joke'.

Looking back on the film today, both Palin and Loncraine are brutally honest about its shortcomings. Palin says, 'I think a lot of it was very funny in the first 40 minutes, I'm very happy with it. But I certainly could've done better with the story, tightened it up a little bit. But that's what you learn from everything that you do ... you can never get everything absolutely right.'

Loncraine admits, 'I think the problem with the movie commercially, seeing it from a distance now, is that we fucked up the ending, basically. I think the end in Scotland just didn't work. I'm still proud of the film, there's some wonderful stuff in it, but I think we weren't sure what we were making, a comedy or a drama. I think we were trying to do too much. The film doesn't know quite what it wants to be; if it wants to be a comedy then it's not funny enough after a certain point, it changes its tonality, and I think the audience felt let down by that. It should have been more of an outrageous, out-and-out comedy. But it's the happiest film I've ever made. Working with Mike was a joy from beginning to end. He's a tough old cookie, but he's very funny, charming, witty and a fine actor. I remember during the filming we'd say cut and no one would go home, we'd stay around. People would sit around the set drinking and chatting. It was a very sociable movie.'

CHAPTER 6

STIFF UPPER LIPS
ON PARADE

After the distinct Englishness of *The Missionary*, HandMade's next project had almost as much of a colonial feel to it. *Privates on Parade* began life as a play first performed by the Royal Shakespeare Company in 1977 to critical and commercial success. Written by Peter Nichols, it was based very much on the playwright's real-life experiences in an entertainment unit during his National Service in South-East Asia after the war, where he served alongside comedians-to-be Stanley Baxter and Kenneth Williams and future film director John Schlesinger.

In fact, it was Kenneth Williams whom Nichols saw as perfect casting for the leading role of Terri Dennis, the impossibly camp old queen in charge of a concert party entertaining British troops. Nichols was much put out when Denis Quilley got the role, exclaiming that the Shakespearean actor was 'much too straight'. It was the play's director Michael Blakemore who persuaded Nichols that Terri Dennis was a part not for a comedian but for a proper actor capable of going screamingly over the top but also with the subtlety to shade in the vulnerability, too, of portraying the agony behind the camp ecstasy. Denis Quilley recalls, 'Somebody wrote to me and said, "One so often sees these camp characters portrayed as cartoon characters or something to be laughed *at*. Thank God you played him as a human being that we could laugh *with*." And I thought, yes, that's true and that's because I'm an actor and not a comedian. A comedian would have got more laughs out of it probably, but it might not have been so believable. And there are moments of charm and pathos in it, too, which are very important. Danny La Rue was dying to do it. When it was announced that we were doing the play, I was standing in Soho and this fur-coated figure sidled up to me and said, "I say, you're muscling in on my territory." And I said, "Danny, it's not your territory at all." And it's not, but he was convinced that it was a great vehicle for him.'

Quilley did, though, have severe doubts about the part. 'Michael Blakemore wanted me to do it. He knew me well and had great faith in me. It wasn't that I was worried about playing a camp part, it was just that I didn't know whether I had the skills for it. I met Peter Nichols and the producer for lunch and I said, "I reckon I'm all right as an actor but impersonation is not my bag. I don't know whether I can do Noël Coward, Marlene Dietrich, all these people." '

The highlight of both the play and the film are the wonderfully performed comedy routines and songs, a superb mixture of pastiche and tat, that makes the production come over like *The Virgin Soldiers* meets *Cabaret*. Quilley continues, 'They plied me with drink and persuaded me that Terri Dennis was slightly over the hill and he'd probably never been a terribly good female impersonator in the first place. I mean, for Carmen Miranda all you have to do is put a bowl of fruit on your head and a pink dress with frills, come on and they say, "Oh, that's Carmen Miranda." So they persuaded me ... it wasn't that I was thinking of turning it down, not really, because it was such an ace part that I couldn't resist it.'

When Denis O'Brien saw the play he recognised its potential immediately and bought the film rights. At first, he intended casting all the Pythons in the various roles, an idea rejected outright by the group. Palin says, 'Denis was always very keen to gather all of us together to help each other out and be in each other's films. I've always resisted that only because I think to get all the Pythons back together without calling it a Python film would be a cheat and very often it would be something like *Yellowbeard* turned out to be, sadly. I felt Python had naturally run most of its course and what was better now was that people went off and did separate things and then came together to make films, or stuff like the Hollywood Bowl, rather than be all continually interlocked in each other's material.'

Unperturbed, O'Brien instead saw *Privates on Parade* as an ideal solo vehicle for John Cleese, whose current photograph in *Spotlight* (the actor's directory) had him dressed as Queen Elizabeth. Cleese saw the play and thought he might have a shot at the part performed by Nigel Hawthorne, that of Major Giles Flack, a jingoistic and bible-punching officer and supreme upper-class twit combating Commie uprisings and gun-running from his own officers. It would represent the first time he'd ever played a proper leading character in a film, as opposed to the multitude of characters he usually adopted in Python productions. He was then 42.

'I had absolutely adored *Privates on Parade* on stage with Nigel Hawthorne, who was absolutely wonderful and much better than I was in the film because, in a sense, the part came quite easily to me whereas I think Nigel had to work much harder at it and consequently came up with something better. My weakness as an actor is sometimes simply to try and see what the writer's done and to try and interpret that instead of perhaps bringing a bit more to it, and I think I might've brought a bit more to Flack. But it was an easy part for me to play.'

O'Brien next took the major gamble of hiring the play's original director Michael Blakemore to helm the film, despite him only having one professional assignment to his credit, a short documentary about surfing in Australia. This marked the beginning of HandMade's fruitful policy of giving new directors and writers their first major break in movies. Although, in this instance, it must be said that Cleese played a pivotal role in the choice of Blakemore. The two men had known each other for years ever since collaborating on a comedy home movie spoofing BBC canteen food. Blakemore was also familiar with Simon Relph, the producer O'Brien had brought in to oversee the production, having worked with him at the National Theatre. Since then, Relph had worked as line producer on films such as *Reds* and *Yanks* and arrived full of enthusiasm for the HandMade organisation and the way they conducted business. 'It was a very unique thing that HandMade were actually out there looking to fully finance movies. It's what we all dream of, a single source of financing and get left alone to make the movies the way you want to make them.'

Blakemore's overriding concern was whether or not the play he'd directed so well on stage could be turned into a film. 'I did have some misgivings because I think that plays are much more difficult to adapt to film than are novels. Peter Nichols adapted it himself. It was rather difficult because he was wedded very much to the play and it was quite difficult to try and get him to really commit to a film script simply because any playwright who's seen his work on stage will not forego dialogue. They remember how well it worked, what a big laugh it got or whatever, and I'm very sympathetic; why should they throw something out that's been proven to work? But you have to in film, you've got to be quite ruthless. We worked very closely on the script before we started to shoot, but we didn't have enough time, we were working up against deadlines. It really needed another couple of months of really considering this material very closely and being very tough. But one of the problems was that John Cleese, because he was very much in demand, he had this window in which we had to do the film, there was no other time it could be done. So I think we went into it without really quite enough time to turn the play into a film on the page.'

It is a point of view shared by Peter Nichols. 'It was a rush job to fit John Cleese's availability and no one's fault that we didn't ever quite agree about how it should be done.'

The biggest stumbling block was how to make a play that was almost music hall in origin work as solid film drama. Quilley remembers, 'Peter Nichols rewrote it, really, in order to give it a more natural and normal narrative structure because in the theatre it was deliberately done like a series of almost sketches. He had to knit it together into a more conventional narrative whole, putting in a lot of exterior scenes, opening it out, which he did with great skill.'

Ironically, it was Quilley's own character that was the main casualty of the rewrite. In the play, Terri Dennis often spoke directly to the audience and Quilley desperately wanted to preserve that aspect of his performance. 'I pleaded on bended knee to Peter Nichols to keep it in and he said, "No, direct address doesn't work in the cinema." And I said, "Well, you know Michael Caine did it in *Alfie*." But he wouldn't do it and I bitterly regret losing my asides to the audience because they are some of the best lines in the piece. But you can't have everything.' Still, Quilley delivers some blisteringly funny dialogue, like his casual comment to a wild-looking native, 'Love the blow-pipe. Very you. Who does your hair?'

To further 'acclimatise' the play for the screen, Blakemore insisted the actors rehearse prior to shooting. 'Michael was aware, as we all were,' says Quilley, 'of the need to bring down our stage performances to a different kind of reality, which we achieved by rehearsing beforehand which you don't often get for a film. We rehearsed for about ten days in a rehearsal room, I think at the Old Vic. Michael had it all worked out and that's when we got familiar with the new script, but most importantly brought our performances down to a film level without losing the energy that it had on stage which is quite hard to do.

'For my own performance, what I tried to do was to keep the same amount of flamboyance but just project it less. And I relied a lot on Michael there, who has a very good instinct for the essential truth of a scene ... even at its most outrageous and camp it's essential to keep the emotional truth of a scene. And Michael's very good at that, it's one of his greatest strengths. Michael can say, "Oh, Denis, I didn't quite believe it when you ..." He has this unobtrusive way of saying, "I think you've got it all wrong." And he did that with everybody on the film and in the play, always going for the reality. Also, when you run through a scene, Michael will say, "Yes, very good, very good, not a lot to say about that, really. Very good. Well ... one or two things," and then you get about half-an-hour of detailed notes, all from memory, no little note books, and all pertinent and to the point.'

The final hurdle was finance. The budget was tight, just under £2 million. Simon Relph remembers, 'One of the big decisions we had to make was whether we were actually going to go and shoot on location in Malaysia. Peter Nichols and I went out there, we did a recce, but we all felt that wasn't a good use of money, to spend it all on locations, because we thought that actually is in the end not the point ... the point is it's about this little community of people. So we went round Malaysia, looked at places and thought about how we could copy that back in England. But it was fun, going back with Peter, staying at places like the Raffles Hotel.'

In the end, the whole South-East Asian theatre of war was replicated at the Duke of Edinburgh barracks in Fleet. Blakemore's impression was 'it was absolutely perfect because it was built in the 1930s, very much the way a British army base would be built in Asia with little wooden huts with little verandas, it was extraordinarily apt. And it had a big parade ground. It served us very well. There were Gurkhas on the camp but it was rather curious because, as we were making this film, which really mocks a lot of army thinking and army routines, it was during the Falklands War and these Gurkhas who were playing small parts for us in the film were preparing to go off to fight that war. So during the filming there were operations of huge troop helicopters flying in and people scrambling aboard up long ladders to go off and fight, which made our endeavours seem even more flippant.'

Unfortunately, though the production enjoyed one of the better English summers, the fake tropic setting did look as if, in Quilley's own words, 'we'd stuck a few palm trees on the slip road of the M3'. It was duly noted by the critics, too. 'I never thought, in 1982, that I'd see a movie set in the tropics but filmed in England with some potted palms stuck in a field,' derided *Films and Filming*.

There was also consternation at the decision not to film abroad back at the HandMade office. Shingles says, 'I remember saying to Denis, "Why didn't you go to Malaysia and shoot just a few scenes?" and he said, "It doesn't look so terribly different." But it does, somehow, shooting around Bucks or wherever, you don't feel like you're in a steamy jungle. It just looks like the *Carry Ons* go to Black Park around Pinewood.'

The budget really was something of a handicap and it shows all too evidently on screen, leaving Peter Nichols particularly unhappy. Blakemore observes, 'When Peter saw the film, he didn't really like it, but he had no idea of the budgetary constraints we were under. He wanted something far more spectacular with many more big army sequences with hundreds of people on the parade ground and we simply couldn't afford that.'

In spite of such problems, filming itself went smoothly, a view with which Quilley agrees. 'The whole thing was a completely enjoyable experience. Everyone got on very well. John Cleese and I used to do the *Times* crossword in the morning and compare notes after about half-an-hour. John's manic energy was extraordinarily effective in the film. And it was quite extraordinary seeing him driving around these streets in Hampshire in a tank with a bit of a palm leaf in his hat, a token bit of camouflage.'

Cleese certainly endeared himself to the crew. Relph thinks, 'John is a very interesting guy, very serious. I've a lot of experience of working with very funny people and they're often very serious people, rather tortured, and John at that time was still a bit of a handful. But lovely, we had a nice time and I think he was very good in the part. But we had a problem with O'Brien who was always trying to impose in the film things that came out of what was his enjoyment of John Cleese and the Pythons, which actually had nothing to do with the piece itself, silly walks and things like that. The silly walk, for instance, that was something which Denis forced on us.'

Following unenthusiastic test audience reaction to *Privates on Parade*, O'Brien orchestrated some additional, more typically wacky Cleese material for inclusion, hence the star's Ministry of Silly Walks-style routine at the end. Relph remembers Cleese being unhappy about doing it but finally agreeing, supportive of the film and the difficult position Blakemore had been placed in. Cleese says, 'There was this idea of a little song and dance at the end and it was suggested that I should do a little bit of eccentric dancing. But I actually had an argument with Denis because he put a little bit of that in the trailer and I thought that that was a mistake because it gave people the wrong impression of what the movie was like. The style of that little song and dance at the end is completely different from the rest of the film, so using a bit of that in the trailer I thought was misleading. But I think he'd realised that it was not going to do well at the box office and people get a bit desperate when that's the case.'

For some, Cleese's 'silly walk' in *Privates* was a classic example of how O'Brien tried to integrate Python elements into projects that didn't suit them. This was certainly Cooper's view. 'John Cleese, that was huge, painful miscasting. Denis was right to love the play, it was a wonderful play, but then to try and squeeze again those Python selling points – the silly walks at the end, which John did, to be fair to him, under some level of protest, I think. But he did them.'

During the bulk of shooting, O'Brien was happy to stay pretty much in the background, leaving Blakemore alone to come to terms with making his first feature film, the prospect of which was suitably terrifying. 'I was very, very nervous. It's difficult on a first film because nobody tells you much and I didn't quite know enough about what I should demand and ask for. You have on a day-to-day basis the advice of the assistants, like your cameraman and your sound man, but it's very hard to get a lesson beforehand. I was just sort of pitched in. It was very scary. I don't think there's anything as scary as the first day of a big movie. It was frustrating because as I began to work through the film, I began to get far more of a feeling of what I should be doing, how it should be done. I could sense it in the attitude of the crew who began to nod approvingly at rushes.'

During editing, O'Brien's opinions and views were welcomed by the film-makers and, where appropriate, acted upon until the final cut was one everyone could agree on. Relph recalls, 'The day after it was delivered, the editor of the film, Jim Clark, a top editor, rang Michael and I up and said, "The most extraordinary thing's happened this morning. I've been called by Denis O'Brien ... he wants me to go back and re-cut the film. What do you want me to do?" So we said, "Hold on a minute, we'll both talk to Denis." I rang Denis and said, "Denis, I don't understand this. We showed you the film, listened to everything you said and I thought we had agreed on the version of the film." And I remember he said to me, an extraordinary thing, he said, "Look, you've had your go and now I'm going to have mine. It's my film. I paid for it. It's my right to do this."

'What he tried to do was effectively remove the most obvious sort of homosexual cross-dressing elements. It was the most bizarre thing. It was like he hadn't really completely grasped what the whole point of the thing was.'

It seemed very strange indeed. Gilliam observes, 'Denis had made this film and, at the end of the day, he decides, wait, it's about poofs, and he's trying to cut it out, he's trying to cut the whole homosexual side out. Denis Quilley is the main character in the piece and he's side-lined by John Cleese's character who suddenly is inflated, is wrong for the film and John does a silly walk which is really obscene. And I thought, This is awful, because the play is clear what it is. John went back and did reshoots on it, added bits and the part was inflated. John, I think, deserves some criticism for letting that character get blown out of shape and to do funny walks. I mean, John, what are you doing? John just seemed to be a collaborator, in the World War II sense, with Denis on that film.'

The film-makers were left bedraggled, dazed and betrayed. Blakemore felt 'manipulated by Denis. We didn't see very much of Harrison, he was a very benign presence, as indeed Ray Cooper was. But Denis was the controller and he took it upon himself to make a lot of, I thought, very ill-judged artistic decisions. He took the film away from me and re-cut it, not seriously, some songs went, that wasn't so bad, but it was just the way he did it. HandMade said we are going to do this now, whipped it away and did it all themselves without reference to anybody and it was quite unnecessary and quite brutally done in a way, very high-handed like the worst of the American film industry, and one thinks of HandMade as being a very admirable English institution. John Cleese was very supportive of me and was outraged by what they did. But, at the end of the day, I didn't care because I didn't feel that I'd perhaps quite done the film we should have done. But then I did the best I could under the limitations of time and budget.'

Privates on Parade opened in Britain in January 1983, but this bitter, sardonic look at army life during the butt end of the British Empire sunk virtually out of sight after a couple of weeks, despite a gallant promotional tour undertaken by John Cleese. Audiences flocked instead to that other and palpably more appealing military movie *An Officer and a Gentleman*, preferring to wait longingly for Richard Gere famously to flash his tackle than see Denis Quilley in a dress.

Critics, on the whole, liked it. '*Privates* transfers radiantly to the screen as a comedy of wit, style and compassion,' beamed the *Sunday Express*, and the *Sunday Times* called it 'A flight of bravura that brings theatre into the movie house with operatic aplomb'.*What's on in London* wrote, 'This is what the British film revival should be all about. *Privates* is exhilarating, witty and intelligent entertainment. It has the same kind of delirious delight that the best of the Ealing comedies displayed.'

Others, like the *Guardian*, disagreed. '*Privates* simply does not work as a screen entity. But Nichols's play is simply too good to be beaten and the performances are a lasting pleasure even within a botched framework.'

The failure of *Privates* was a personal disappointment for O'Brien. Shingles says, 'I've always been very fond of *Privates on Parade*, it deserved to do better. Denis had real high hopes for that film. He thought initially it would do a *Life of Brian*.'

Poor old John Cleese also did promotion when *Privates* finally opened in America in April 1984, where it bombed even more disastrously. 'But we got a rapturous press in New York,' Blakemore adds. 'Indeed, it was on the *New York Times* ten best of the year list. So it went over very well in New

York, where they weren't aware of the stage production and also where the subject was very exotic. But it didn't do any business outside New York. It was a bit too shocking. There was a lot of language in it.'

Not all New York's critics were bowled over by it, though. 'What made anyone want to film this stage play in the first place, let alone distribute it outside of England, is unfathomable. Some private matters aren't worth bothering the public about,' whined the *Voice*.

As for the version of *Privates on Parade* shown in America, it was slightly different to the UK print. Shingles explains, 'The film was cut in America. Denis trimmed it by a good ten minutes and it did lose a lot of its oomph. Denis was often worried about the American market. *Privates* hadn't worked in the UK and Denis thought maybe they could do something to salvage the film when it opened in the States.' It's a common dilemma, the creatively sensitive artist versus the cold, unblinkingly practical businessman. The artist understandably wants to keep his original vision intact at all costs, even if, monetarily at least, it has failed, while the businessman is more flexible when it comes to changing or adapting the product to suit other markets. 'And neither party understands the other,' Shingles says. 'An artist will say, "It's my movie, it's my vision, why should it be tampered with?" And the argument is, if you want your film to be successful and seen around the world and for us to sell it, then you have to compromise. But sometimes compromise is almost impossibly difficult.'

Some who worked on *Privates on Parade* didn't quite see it that way. Today, they share conflicting views about the merits or otherwise of how the film turned out.

Relph believes, 'Denis O'Brien was a very clever operator and I think he had quite good taste in what he liked. He chose both interesting talent and interesting projects. It's just that his attitude towards talent was, in our view, quite appalling, really, in the sense that he felt that the fact that he and George were making the money available entitled him to do all kinds of things to the work. Although I think George liked the film very much. I remember years later we were all going to organise this dinner, all the producers who'd worked with Denis, and we were going to have this empty chair so that we could all share in our memories of how we'd been abused. We were all like abused children.'

Cleese rationalises the partial failure of the film by saying, 'I think the problem was that it was never quite substantial enough to make a real film story out of it. The stage show was brilliant but it was a little bit of a confection; it was quite impressionistic, and in the film we tried to strengthen the storyline and I'm not so sure that was the right approach. So although there was some very nice stuff in it, I don't think it was much liked outside Surrey.

'I was very fond of Michael Blakemore, he is a friend of some long standing now, and I love working with stage directors because they know how to direct actors. A lot of film directors don't have much idea. So I liked working with Michael enormously, but it wasn't much of a hit, in fact it wasn't a hit at all and it sort of faded away, which is rather a shame.'

Nichols says, 'Quite a few people enjoyed the film because of Denis Quilley's wonderful performance. Michael and I were wrong to give the "plot" too much prominence. It lacked a cohesive style but had its moments. Still, it would have done far better if the producers hadn't smothered the poor thing at birth.'

Quilley is complimentary of the finished product. 'I had my fingers crossed as to whether the play would work on screen but, to my amazement, it did. When I saw it at the press show, it was getting lots of laughs from hardened old hacks. I think it's a jolly good record of a super play quite well translated into cinematic terms.'

'On the stage, it worked absolutely wonderfully,' Blakemore continues, 'there was a terrific audience response, but somehow people who had seen it on the stage didn't like it nearly as much on film. But it had a lot in it that I was quite proud of, innovative stuff, like mixing black-and-white with colour, fake newsreels. I think in the time between the stage play and the film, the material had got tarnished rather by things like *It Ain't Half Hot Mum*; it just didn't seem as fresh.'

Indeed, Peter Nichols was halfway through writing *Privates* when he saw the BBC sitcom *It Ain't Half Hot Mum* and stopped then and there and threw his play into the bottom drawer thinking, Well, that's it, they've beaten me to it. It was only much later that he was persuaded to resurrect the project.

Like *Privates on Parade*, HandMade's next venture also began life in the theatre, and could also have shared the same director. Dick Clement (who with Ian La Frenais, was part of the comedy writing team responsible for

The Likely Lads and *Porridge*) recalls, 'There was talk of me directing *Privates on Parade* and I very much wanted it, actually, because I had some more radical ideas for doing it. Michael Blakemore had done it on the stage and I think a fresh eye might have been different for it. I found it a little overlong. But, in the end, it was a very maddening situation because I was also up to direct a movie in America called *War is Heck*, which, in the end, never got made. I met John Cleese and we talked about directing *Privates* and I was looking forward to doing it, but HandMade were trying to get the deal together and were umming and aahing. Then suddenly the producers of *War is Heck* made what they call a "pay or play" offer, literally about 24 hours before Denis O'Brien was going to make me a firm offer on *Privates* and, of course, I'd taken the other one. And then the studio that was going to make *War is Heck* collapsed, so I ended up making neither. Very frustrating. But certainly that flirtation about *Privates* had opened up a dialogue between myself and Denis.'

At an audition for the aborted *War is Heck* in Los Angeles, Clement met and got chatting to Chicago-born actor/comedian Ron House, swapping anecdotes about, of all things, Bulldog Drummond, of whose literary adventures Clement had been a boyhood fan. By a wonderful stroke of luck, House was at the time performing in a popular stage show entitled *Bullshot*, an affectionate parody of the Drummond character and all those British '30s *Boy's Own* thrillers, complete with cliff-hanging moments. Would Clement and his writing partner Ian La Frenais be interested in the possibility of turning the revue into a feature film?

The road to *Bullshot*'s American stage success was long and fraught. The Low Moan Spectacular was a fringe comedy group formed in the early '70s by House, along with Britons Diz White and Alan Shearman. Its base was the Oval House in South London, an Arts Council-subsidised theatre-cum-workshop that accommodated a variety of other groups that boasted among their number future artistic luminaries as actor Stephen Rea, director Mike Figgis and Pierce Brosnan, who often practised street theatre with Shearman.

The group began working on *Bullshot* after Diz White came across an old Bulldog Drummond book at Portobello street market and, finding its chauvinistic views so hilariously outdated, thought it ripe for send-up. After a successful provincial tour, the show ended up at the 1972

Edinburgh Festival playing back-to-back with another Low Moan comedy revue *El Grande de Coca Cola*. It was a sell-out. Alan Shearman remembers, 'There was this American guy in the audience who came up to us and said, "Hey, I love that *Coca Cola* show, would you be interested in doing it in New York?" And we said, "Yeah, of course, we'd love to do it." We didn't believe him at all, we thought it was a load of hogwash. But the following February we went to New York, thinking we were going to be there for about six weeks. We were pretty naïve, it doesn't work like that in New York, if you get a rave review in the *New York Times* you run for ever. If you get a bad review in the *New York Times* you close that night and you're back on the plane home. We were lucky, we got fantastic reviews.'

After six months, Low Moan handed the reins of *Coca Cola* over to a second cast (replacing Shearman was the then unknown Jeff Goldblum) in order to take the show on tour to San Francisco, where it met with equal success. 'Then in October 1974,' Shearman continues, 'we opened *Bullshot* in New York and this time we saw the other side of the coin. We didn't get a good review in the *New York Times* and that was it, we're closing, and we didn't even have the money to get back to England. Meanwhile, our *Coca Cola* show is still running off-Broadway but we can't get in it, so we were sort of trapped in New York.'

Bemused by the critical reaction to *Bullshot* but not dispirited, the group decided to put the show on themselves in San Francisco where *Coca Cola* had gone down so well. Shearman says, 'It was a very good move, we raised the money ourselves and *Bullshot* ultimately ran for over four years in San Francisco. It was a huge hit there and became almost part of the community. We were in a nightclub and strip-joint area of San Francisco and when all these strip-club owners saw the lines around the block for our show, they started saying, "What's going on there?" Believe it or not, two or three strip clubs became legitimate theatres as a result of all this. It was a very interesting time.'

Finally, in 1978 *Bullshot* opened in Los Angeles and was an instant smash, much to Shearman's delight. 'What was so exciting was because so many celebrities live in LA they were all popping up in the audience, every night there'd be some legendary face like Charlton Heston, Steve Martin, Mel Brooks, Hugh Hefner. We were the toast of the town, meeting all these famous people, setting up deals to write screenplays, we'd finally made it. But what was ironic was we had to leave after six weeks because we'd committed to do the show at the Ford's Theatre in Washington DC. Now the Ford's Theatre is where Lincoln was assassinated and it's essentially a museum, it's like a live museum. It was so bizarre because people would wander in and they'd say, "Oh, look, there's a show on stage, how quaint," and just sit and talk all the way through it. I don't know what they thought they were watching. It was a disaster is all I can tell you.'

Upon returning to LA, a local cable TV company filmed a concert performance of *Bullshot*. Now the group possessed an excellent broadcast-quality copy of the show that they could tout around town. One of the first to see the tape was Dick Clement who grasped its potential and took it with him on a trip to London to show Denis O'Brien. Within weeks, O'Brien had confirmed his interest. Everything passed off without a hitch. As Clement liked to joke afterwards, it was like driving down Melrose Avenue in Los Angeles with all the traffic lights green.

Clement and Ian La Frenais were very deliberate in choosing HandMade; to them, here was a very British company for a very British film. Indeed, it's difficult to imagine any company making a film like *Bullshot* other than HandMade. 'Everyone is talking about a renaissance in the film industry in Britain today but HandMade were making good pictures like *Time Bandits* even during the so-called depression,' La Frenais said at the time. 'HandMade is just that. Their films are, well, hand-made. They're hand-crafted, very careful, very meticulous.' Both writers were also pally with Ray Cooper, an association going back to when their company, Witzend, made a film of Elton John and Cooper touring Russia, which later went out on a double bill with Clement and La Frenais's big-screen version of *Porridge*.

In direct contrast to *Privates on Parade*, *Bullshot*'s transition from stage to screen was relatively straightforward. The whole gimmick of the play was that they were doing a movie on stage with all sorts of special effects – car chases and the like – but crappily executed with cardboard cut-outs and hopeless models. Clement explains, 'They were deliberately on the stage making a virtue out of their inadequacies. We obviously said that if it was going to be a movie, we would want it to have different production values, open it out more. So Ian and I developed the script with them very closely but we were always at pains to say that this was their baby and not ours.'

On the other hand, Clement and La Frenais's experience was instrumental in what was ultimately a successful adaptation, a point acknowledged by Shearman. 'They really did give us a crash course in screenplay writing. We needed to turn it into the typical detective B movie, but very tongue in cheek and just show how silly those films were, and Dick and Ian were very helpful in steering us in that direction, particularly in the internal logic of the plot, making sure there were no loose ends and so on.'

The original stage plot, in which Bullshot Crummond comes to the aid of a dotty English rose-type whose scientist father has been kidnapped by beastly foreigners out to steal his secret formula, was pretty much left intact. Clement says, 'The basic character of Bullshot was already there, the essential speeches where he's doing his deductions and the fact that beneath his bravado and his lantern jaw there was this terrible fascist who mistrusted foreigners of any shape or kind. There was a lot of humour in that. And the running gag that actually all the people he'd met who still remembered him faithfully he'd maimed in one way or another.'

Bullshot Crummond is a wonderful and much under-rated creation. In its own way just as well realised and performed as that other great British send-up, Austin Powers. Over the years, numerous actors had played the dashing Drummond, notably Ralph Richardson and Ronald Colman, but the eventual choice for Bullshot was the little-known John Lodge. 'I just loved his slicked-back hair,' Shearman says, 'he was very much the image I had in my head of what Bulldog would be like because I had actually read all the Bulldog Drummond books as a kid, I loved them, I thought they were terribly grown up. Oh boy, people really do get killed in these things, this is serious, this is a step up from Biggles.

'As for my original stage performance, funnily enough, I was already performing it before I realised what was the correct way to play him. What happened was we did a try-out of just Act I and we took some photographs and I saw one of these pictures and I said, that's it, that's what he is, he's always got this sort of glint in his eye of suspicion, he's always terribly alert. And so whilst I should say as an actor I should have done all kinds of sense memory preparation, it was actually a photograph of me doing it all that gave me the hook, and once I'd found it it was easy, everything else fell into place. It was a kind of arse-about-face way of approaching the character.'

Filming on *Bullshot* began in April 1983 around London and the Home Counties. Pictorially, like so many of HandMade's early output, the film is stunning to look at, belying its limited budget. Clement reveals, 'We made it for under $3 million. Considering that we've got vintage cars, aeroplanes and an octopus – it's only got five tentacles but you can't tell that, we couldn't run to eight – we put a lot on the screen for the money.' Particularly impressive are the scenes at Henley Regatta and the derring-do stunt work involved which, at times, bordered on the nerve-shredding. 'My recollection is that there was only one stunt I didn't do,' Shearman admits, 'but I was so into it I wanted to do all my own stunts. There was one hairy moment when Diz White's stuntwoman during a train sequence slipped and nearly went under the rails, but all my stunts went fine. Though I can't say I wasn't nervous, when you're hanging on to a plane that's roaring along the ground and you've got a huge propeller a few inches from your face, it's a little unnerving.'

Besides the tight schedule (just 35 days) which meant shooting was always a race, the crew running flat out the whole time just to make sure they got everything done, the biggest headache was in getting the tone of the film right. For Clement, '*Bullshot* was the sort of film where every scene had to be funny. Because it was a spoof, each day you had to say, "How can this scene be funny?" Whereas other films you've got the odd day when you're shooting something which is either dramatic or romantic, or something else. This was the film equivalent of farce, really, and therefore you've got nothing else to fall back on so you feel very exposed. If it's falling flat, it's just failing, so you had to keep that energy up the whole time. It was tough because the sort of stuff that Ian and I write is more naturalistic comedy which is based on character, when you can occasionally be sad, dramatic or whatever, so in a way *Bullshot* was an aberration from what we usually write. But we liked it so much we just said, "Let's go for it." '

On the whole, the mood was good during filming and, unlike some of their predecessors, the film-makers enjoyed a fruitful and collaborative relationship with Denis O'Brien, who Shearman says 'was totally available all the time. I can't say he was hands on, it never felt like that. It was very useful having just the one man at the helm so that you weren't going through panels of committees and all the rest, he could just say yay or nay. It was also fabulous that Denis was happy to let us play our original stage roles and didn't say, "Oh, it's a great play but let's have big stars doing it." We didn't meet George until we were filming down in Henley. He came to the set to meet us and invited us up to his house. Actually, I got to know him much better after we finished filming because he got involved with the music soundtrack. George, Dick and myself wrote together the end title song. It always makes me chuckle that I actually wrote a song with George Harrison. And we get royalties every now and again. I get a couple of dollars because the movie aired in Sweden or somewhere. To make a friend with George was wonderful. I just think he was the most extraordinary human being.'

Bullshot emerged as one of Harrison's favourite HandMade films. Alas, it was a view not shared by others, for when the picture opened in Britain in October 1983, it was to an unfair barrage of abuse. In a headline that read WHAT A LOAD OF BULLSHOT!, the *Daily Mirror* tore into the film: 'A more depressing load of old rubbish it would be hard to find.' Other critics were even less kind. *Monthly Film Bulletin* said, 'Unrelievedly ghastly. Even canned laughter would be hard-pressed to raise a titter.' And the *Daily Express* declaimed, 'It could have been fun but the cast signal every joke with a wink and a nudge in the ribs and grimace to such an extent that it looks as if they are suffering from nervous diseases.' Hardly surprising then that *Bullshot* stiffed at the box office.

Bullshot's home reception was both hurtful and unexpected, especially as it was, in both taste and style, a very English comedy. Clement says he was 'very disappointed by the critical reaction because we thought we'd made a film that, whatever else it was, was an enormous amount of fun. So I was really surprised by the British reaction because obviously it's the British you'd expect to get the joke. Sometimes, you sense it coming and sometimes you don't and I didn't because all the early response and people working on the film had enjoyed it. That can be misleading. I don't like to get over-carried away by how the crew reacts to a joke on the set, but there was a very good feeling about the film when it was put together and people saw it, but then somehow it just didn't connect with the public.'

In America, where the film belatedly opened in August 1985, the story was a little different. Yes, the public stayed away, but some American critics did warm to it more than their British counterparts. 'HandMade carries on its delightfully barmy tradition with *Bullshot*, a daft and often delightfully nutty send-up. Those who have acquired the taste for English humour will find it a timely respite and welcome tonic from summer aliens,' glowed the *Hollywood Reporter*.

It's indeed odd, given the subject matter, how both the stage show and film of *Bullshot* played better in the States than they did in the UK. Shearman thinks, 'It was because many Americans have a stereotypical view of English people anyway, they're either cockneys or they're upper-class and that's all we had in *Bullshot* anyway, stuck-up Brits or cockneys, and it very much typified an American's ideal of British stiff-upper-lip and all that stuff. And it amazes me that in America it's become a bit of a cult thing. I look back on it today very fondly. It was just a dream, an absolutely wonderful, positive, exciting experience. It was such a trip.'

CHAPTER 7

SWINE FEVER

Bullshot was the fourth HandMade release in a row to disappoint at the box office. The company now hadn't enjoyed a proper hit since *Time Bandits* and, to a certain extent, were still living off the success of those early movies. Looking back, Denis O'Brien probably had the wrong start in the movie business. On *Life of Brian* and *Time Bandits*, he'd made all these killer deals, and because the films were so good they brought tons of money into the coffers at Cadogan Square. The distributors also made a packet from their distribution fees because there was so much money to go round. The problem was, when O'Brien went back to the same companies for the next wave of HandMade releases, he always insisted on tightening the deal; in negotiations, he always wanted to turn the screw one final notch. If he'd made a deal with a distribution fee at say 25 per cent, he'd go back and want it down to something like 22 per cent.

Take Australia, for example. *Life of Brian* was one of the most successful ever releases there, but when O'Brien went back with the likes of *Privates on Parade* and *The Missionary*, those same distributors took huge losses when they underperformed at the box office. Steve Abbott says, 'This is where Denis's ego was his own worst enemy. There was no give and take, he should have made it fair, he was crippling these companies who'd got rich with him on *Life of Brian*. Sadly for HandMade as an entity, Denis's pride would not let him make fair deals, he always had to have the last word with people, he always wanted to get the better of the other side, whoever it was, which is great when you're making hits, not when you stop. HandMade just had the wrong start to the business; you've got to recognise that most films at best aren't going to make money.'

For the majority of HandMade's existence, the job of funding movies was an overriding concern. The growth of the company had so far been entirely self-financed, there was no outside funding, unlike Goldcrest who had successfully cultivated merchant banking interests, enabling them to draw on millions of pounds to finance projects on the scale of *Revolution*. HandMade was able to protect itself by keeping very tight controls on its budgets. 'We don't put money into overheads. We don't hire actors who ask for $1m. And we make films for a quarter of the cost of any major,' Harrison boasted to *Screen International* in 1984.

O'Brien was always on the look-out for new ways to back his film endeavours and one such avenue was a possible tie-up with Thorn EMI video. One of the first companies to take advantage of the video boom of the early Eighties, principally by exploiting their own film library, Thorn EMI was a market leader until titles dried up and it became obvious that outside product was rapidly needed. Principally because of the success of *Brian* and *Bandits*, HandMade were the obvious people to try and latch on to. EMI's head of acquisition at the time, John Kelleher, approached O'Brien with the idea. Certainly, it made sound commercial sense to get into bed with a major video distributor and, during the deal-making, O'Brien was impressed with Kelleher's talents and offered him a job. Kelleher remembers, 'At the time, EMI was in a lot of turmoil and so it seemed to me like a good time to leave and HandMade seemed an interesting place, so I thought from the outside.'

Kelleher's appointment did not best please Wendy Palmer, now back at Cadogan Square after her sojourn in Guernsey. 'I came back because I just couldn't stand living on Guernsey any longer. I just hated it. So I told them, "Look, I'm going to come back to London. I'd like to work for HandMade, but if I can't, so be it." Denis was quite angry with me because it was going to upset their tax structure, but eventually they reorganised things so that I could do the same job, but in London.' Palmer found herself reporting to lawyer Marc Vere Nicol, until his sudden and unceremonious dismissal. 'That was pretty miserable. Denis would just get rid of people, basically. Not many left of their own volition because we did have a "cruisey" life. He didn't pay brilliantly, but he didn't pay badly. He always gave decent bonuses. There was a wonderful family spirit there, so there wasn't any good reason to leave. Also, it was the only thing that was happening in films at the time in Britain, so what else are you going to do?'

After working in the cramped and soulless Guernsey office, Wendy found Cadogan Square an invigorating breath of fresh air. 'The office atmosphere was always fabulous. Denis was hardly ever there which was great. He was always such the focus of everybody's anger that all the rest of us got on terribly well. It was so easy to be nice in comparison to Denis. The rest of us really had fine relationships with the film-makers. It was always us against him, really.' Promoted to Acting Head of Sales and Marketing, Wendy found herself quickly sidelined by the arrival of John Kelleher.

Coming as he did from a vastly bigger corporation like EMI, Kelleher was surprised to find that everything within the HandMade structure operated on such a secretive level. 'I think I very quickly realised that there was very much an "us" and "them" thing. Denis was very secretive, he gave people information on a need-to-know basis, so you felt that you never really knew what was going on. Denis ruled with a rod of iron. He decided what films were going to be done. I don't think George Harrison was really involved in that decision-making at all. He seemed to me very other-worldly in any conversations I had with him about the movies. George wasn't involved in the film business, he really was just interested in making music, his garden and having an easy time.

'George was very close to Ray who was very protective of him. Ray's a very interesting guy, I like him on the whole, but he's very complex, very mixed up, he certainly was in those days. He regarded anyone new coming in as a kind of threat to his position in the world.'

Following Goldcrest's lead, since the winter of 1983 intense and painstaking negotiations had been taking place between O'Brien and City financial institution Prudential. If a deal were to be ratified, HandMade would go public and become one of the biggest independent film companies in the UK. Palmer thought at the time that 'This was going to make us all rich. We were going to get X amount of shares.' For some, such a development was perhaps too ambitious, too big. Cooper recalls, 'I think Denis went to Wall Street as well, as an American. We were all on a promise, we were shareholders, life was looking extremely rosy. It would have been an interesting process, but by that time George wasn't quite sure what was happening with his money and what was happening with what he was being a front of, what the banks were expecting from him, because he was always the front man in that sense. I think he suddenly thought, This is getting big, that's not what I thought it was going to be. I came in it to help my mates. And he never really moved away from that core generosity. So it was Denis who had the big picture.'

O'Brien was confident that the deal would go through, enabling HandMade to increase film production significantly, freeing them from the frustration of having to wait sometimes a year or more to recoup the money spent on one project to invest it in another. 'We want to take what the City has to offer but retain the management we've always had,' O'Brien told the press during the height of the negotiations. 'We're the ones developing the films and screenplays. Nothing in life is worth doing if you have to give up your independence for it.'

It was on this issue that the deal ultimately foundered. City investors wanted the final say on what films to develop and this was not acceptable to either Harrison or O'Brien, whose bitter comment afterwards was that he wished the negotiations hadn't taken up so much of his time. The failure also put into sharp focus the unwillingness of the business fraternity to invest in the British film industry. 'The City has been anti-film business for years,' O'Brien lamented.

O'Brien tried hard to disguise his obvious disappointment over the Prudential deal falling at the last hurdle. So serious had he been about it that he'd even shaved off his beard, much to the surprise of friends and colleagues, to assume a more businesslike persona. At the same time, he was gearing up his staff for the possible merger. Cooper says, 'Suddenly for the first time ever in my life, I had to do a CV, which was farcical for me. There were all sorts of things going on at that time, we were becoming very "Americanised", which was freaking me out. O'Brien also wanted each of the directors, myself included, to do a handwriting test which would then be submitted to this handwriting expert to see if we were all compatible. And I said, "Denis, I can tell you right now I'm barking mad and I'm not compatible to anybody. I'm unique. I'm alien to all of this. So hands up now, I'm out of the building, there's no fucking way I'm gonna do a handwriting test, sorry." He laughed, "Ray, you're so funny." But he was deadly serious, and so was I. And I never did it. The whole thing about creativity is you're not compatible but you find ways of becoming compatible for that project. That's the whole thing of creativity.'

Despite the City flop, HandMade announced their busiest filming schedule yet with three films slated for 1984 and plans to tackle as much as five films per year in the future. It was a very loud return to production duties for a company whose sole release in the previous 12 months had been *Bullshot*. The industry pondered whether O'Brien and co had taken a break to reassess and reorganise after a string of box-office duds. It was time enough for their detractors to label them as just a bunch of rock stars (Harrison and Cooper) and nothing more than one-hit wonders and cinematic flash-in-the-pans. Too often in the past, HandMade attracted publicity relating to their Python/Beatle connection. With this new production slate, it hoped to be judged in its own right as a substantial player in British films. For a joke back at Cadogan Square, the staff had begun referring to themselves as a 'mini-major'.

The three new projects couldn't have been more different, and yet all were quintessentially English. *A Private Function* hailed from the pen of Alan Bennett and starred Michael Palin. *Water* was another comedy from the long-standing writing duo Dick Clement and Ian La Frenais and boasted the heavyweight participation of Michael Caine. Finally, there was *Travelling Men*, a comedy thriller helmed by *The Long Good Friday*'s John MacKenzie which aimed to reunite Caine with Sean Connery for the first time since 1975's classic *The Man Who Would Be King*. It was a mouth-watering package, reflecting both O'Brien and Harrison's fondness for off-beat comedy and original British scripts. It also bolstered HandMade's commitment to providing first-time opportunities to writers and directors and imaginative support and careful handling for projects that did not immediately present themselves as smash hits. 'HandMade did have a philosophy,' Cooper explains. 'Fairly broadly, it was the best that we could endeavour to do of every part of drama and comedy. Comedy was the leading player, it started with comedy with Python and moved into drama because I love drama. I loved dealing much more with the *Mona Lisa*s. But it never mattered as long as it was of the best quality work, its morals were in the right place and it had a good quality of entertainment about it. That was our broad philosophy.'

The aim was also to strike a balance between art and commercialism. Yes, to take risks with unfamiliar and controversial material, to make films that would stimulate as well as entertain, but at the same time to make sure they made enough money for the company to stay in production. It was also being seen by the industry to be brave in what it chose to make. Cooper adds, 'It was a signal, like beacons being sent out or jungle drums saying, "That's a good home." And you got these wonderfully eccentric and strange people coming in and wanting to make films for us.'

Although *A Private Function* and *Water* began shooting within days of each other in May 1984, both films enjoyed very different fortunes. *A Private Function* was the brainchild of BBC director Malcolm Mowbray, who'd long been fascinated by the black-market boom of the late 1940s, a by-product of severe post-war rationing. Pork was particularly scarce and the illegal keeping of pigs was rife. Mowbray was convinced here was fertile ground for a comedy drama. 'The black market in England just seemed a really interesting area, the way it showed up the social strata via food. You were deemed what class you were by what food you could get hold of. It exposed English society in a rather interesting way.'

Mowbray had just written and directed a television film, *Days at the Beach*, that so impressed Alan Bennett, the acclaimed playwright wrote personally to Mowbray congratulating him. The two subsequently met and Bennett was invited to collaborate on the black-market film. Apart from an abortive project for John Schlesinger, Bennett had never written a screenplay for the cinema before. Mowbray recalls, 'It took about from 1982 to 1984 to get the script together. I think Alan rarely writes stuff that doesn't come from himself, so it took quite a time.'

The story that emerged was set in Yorkshire (not surprising, given Bennett's heritage) and concerned a genteel chiropodist caught up in the shenanigans of local town big-wigs rearing an illicit pig to be the centrepiece of a banquet celebrating the wedding of Princess Elizabeth.

Bennett explains, 'Malcolm wanted to do a film about a pig and I wanted to do a film about a chiropodist, so that's how the two elements came to be combined. And, of course, the period he was talking about, the Forties, was, as it were, a historical period for him, but it wasn't for me, that was part of my childhood. I wrote a first draft and we both went through it. I rewrote it, and then we did it in a way like doing homework, doing section by section and cutting it down and throwing stuff out and so on. But I didn't think of it as anything other than a long television script, really. Television plays in those days were an hour-and-a-half ... well, they still are, I suppose, but they don't get made, so that wasn't any different from what I was used to doing.'

Water had also been a joint collaboration. Clement and La Frenais had made a television pilot in America with a man called Bill Persky who came up with this idea of a mythical island, a sort of Caribbean Ruritania, seeking independence from Britain, and together the three of them hammered out an initial screenplay. 'We finished it and nothing much happened to it for a while,' says Clement, 'well, nothing much happened at all, actually. Bill wanted to direct it originally; he'd directed one movie called *Serial* which didn't do a lot, so his bankability was a little low on the totem pole. And then we took it out of the bottom drawer after *Bullshot* when Denis was saying, "What else have you got?" And again it was Denis who absolutely loved the script and really responded to it, and said, "Let's do it." So we then wrote another draft and, as a result of that, Michael Caine came on board. He read the script and fell in love with it overnight and called me up and said, "It's the funniest thing I've read in ages. I'd love to do it." And we were thrilled because we knew that meant we would get the film made, and suddenly it was a go project.'

Caine, in fact, hadn't been first choice for the role of the island's colonial governor. Alan Shearman admits, 'Right after we finished *Bullshot*, Dick and Ian started writing *Water* and I had always hoped that I would play Baxter. But when you have a chance to get Caine, well, obviously, they went with him.' Shearman was instead rewarded with a small role in the film.

Consistent with O'Brien's desire to hire a Python wherever possible, John Cleese was also offered a part. 'I liked Clement and La Frenais a lot, but I wasn't crazy about that particular script,' Cleese remembers. 'The part was for some English colonial-type who I think had a couple of bed scenes with a dusky maiden.' Despite such an inducement, Cleese turned it down flat.

Obtaining a suitable backer for *A Private Function* was a more convoluted affair. For Mowbray, two obvious candidates stood out – Goldcrest and HandMade. Because *Function* was a comedy and HandMade had made its reputation with comedies, Mowbray was naturally drawn to them. Gilliam's wonderfully innovative and charming logo also heavily appealed to the director. With producer Mark Shivas, whom Mowbray knew from his BBC days, now attached to the project, everyone agreed the best strategy would be to approach HandMade with a star name already signed up. Shivas had previously worked with Michael Palin on a long-forgotten TV comedy and personally approached the actor, aware that out of all the Pythons it was Palin who'd retained the closest links with HandMade, and particularly O'Brien. Bennett concurs. 'I think that Michael Palin once said that he was the only one of the Python people who would still work with Denis O'Brien. None of the others would.'

Among his Python colleagues there was consternation and bewilderment that Palin was still in contact – indeed, on friendly terms – with O'Brien after all the management bust-ups and financial irregularities. Palin confesses, 'I felt so long as you say to Denis where your limits are and what you will do and what you won't do, he was quite useful. He was consistently interested in the sort of films that I was interested in, not big Hollywood epics but smaller films with interesting characters. All right, there were times when he could be persistent, manipulative and just downright wrong in the way he dealt with us all, but then this tends to happen in lots of relationships. I felt that one just had to play him along a bit and he probably played us along, too, whereas with Eric and John, Eric particularly, there was a great resentment of Denis after a certain point. But I'm very loath just to sever relationships just because you have a disagreement over money or whatever. Perhaps I didn't know enough, being naïve about these things, but I always felt that Denis put more work our way rather than take it away. And the deals seemed to me to be reasonable enough, although we're still not being paid any of the money back for *The Missionary* or *A Private Function*. But I still don't see any need to end a friendship, and it was a friendship for quite a considerable

Above: George Harrison and Denis O'Brien. The Beatle and the banker.

Inset: The famous logo Terry Gilliam designed for HandMade.

Above: Saved by a Beatle. The *Monty Python* team on location in Tunisia for *Life of Brian. From left*: Michael Palin, John Cleese, Graham Chapman, Eric Idle, Terry Gilliam and Terry Jones.

Below: Bob Hoskins and Helen Mirren in *The Long Good Friday.*

Above: The Time Bandits. *From left*: Og (Mike Edmonds), Fidgit (Kenny Baker), Strutter (Malcolm Dixon), Randall (David Rappaport), Vermin (Tiny Ross) and Wally (Jack Purvis).

Below: Monty Python in *Live at the Hollywood Bowl*. The cheeky barber shop quartet who open the show.

Above: Dennis Quilley and John Cleese head to head in *Privates on Parade*. There was conflict in the cutting room and the film was the first of HandMade's flops.

Below: Going down the plug hole. Michael Caine and Valeri Perrine get tied up in *Water*, another box office stiff.

Above: Seven distinguished feet. Alan Bennett, Maggie Smith and Michael Palin talk chiropody on set in *A Private Function*.

Below: Michael Palin, in his dressing gown, regards a pig. Note the infamous bucket.

Above: Michael Caine as the chilling Mortwell with Cathy Tyson in *Mona Lisa*.

Below: Bob Hoskins and Cathy Tyson together in *Mona Lisa*. The performance earned Hoskins a BAFTA and an Oscar nomination.

Top left: Sean Penn sports an all too prophetic tie in the box office disaster *Shanghai Surprise*.

Top right: Madonna and George Harrison on set. He intervened personally to ensure that things ran smoother between Mr and Mrs Penn and the rest of the production team.

Below: Richard E Grant and Paul McGann as *Withnail and I*.

Top: Eric Idle and Robbie Coltrane in *Nuns on the Run*.

Bottom left: Terry Gilliam and Ray Cooper. Gilliam and Cooper formed a life-long working partnership after he helped Gilliam with the soundtrack to *Time Bandits*.

Bottom right: 26 Cadogan Square. The former HandMade offices as they are today.

time. We spent a lot of time together and that gives you time to detect how much someone really cares for the work that you do, what they value, what you value.'

When Palin heard about *A Private Function* and Alan Bennett's involvement, he was almost already won over. A meeting was set up at Bennett's north London home, with Shivas and Mowbray also in attendance, clutching a copy of the script which at that time was quaintly entitled *Pork Royale* (another scrapped title was *Saturday Night Swine Fever*). Palin remembers, 'The three of them were sat on the sofa against the wall, like a Spanish inquisition, but in a very gentle way. I couldn't quite see them very well, I just remember a row of knees and lower legs and they were very quiet, they're all very quiet people, none of them are at all extrovert or ebullient in any way. I like them all tremendously, but they were just terribly quiet and I wondered what was going on here. And out of the darkness came, "Well, we've got this script." And I thought they were going to say, "You're the only man to do it," and they said, "Do you think that HandMade would be interested in making it?"

'So what I was there for, really, was as the HandMade Films man, to be a messenger, because they'd obviously got nowhere with it. So I said, "Well, I'll go and talk to them." '

Shivas meanwhile had met with O'Brien, an encounter the producer today recalls with incredulity. 'The first reaction we got from Denis O'Brien was that he didn't believe we had Michael interested, because Palin generally said that he would never appear in anything that he hadn't written himself. So being told that you're a liar, this is not a very good start to a relationship. Denis then said, basically, this is the kind of film that would never work in America, to which you could only say, "Well, we'll see, won't we?" It was quite off-putting, first telling me I was a liar because he thought I hadn't got Michael and then when they found out that we *had* got him, then the film would never work in America!'

For the duration of the project, a strange kind of mistrust built up between O'Brien and the film-makers. 'We were always very genuine in our dealings,' says Mowbray, 'but I always got the sense that Denis thought we were trying to rip him off in some way. The HandMade people were wonderfully supportive, Ray Cooper and the company secretary who was in a small office the size of a broom cupboard that wouldn't hold a broom.

We'd go to Cadogan Square for innumerable meetings. I remember reading on some wall, just noticing a letter from Denis to the staff saying he'd been round checking the litter bins on a Friday night and discovered that people weren't using both sides of the paper.'

Indeed, O'Brien could be pretty mean around the office. Kelleher observes, 'He didn't like money being spent on things if it could be avoided. There is a particular kind of person who likes to spend money on himself but doesn't like to see other people spending money. I mean, he had this yacht which must have cost a fortune.'

Palin had since read the *Function* script, fallen in love with it and agreed to play the lead role of Gilbert Chilvers, a meek and mild-mannered chiropodist driven to extreme acts by an overbearing and socially ambitious wife. Palin, it seems, is naturally drawn to such characters and, during filming, Mowbray was keen for Chilvers to exude an atmosphere of dullness. Palin qualifies this by saying, 'But it was very important to keep the centre realistic and not to fall into being a caricature, to be dull but interestingly dull. If you played it dull, then it wouldn't work, there has to be a certain sort of spirit and involvement there, but it is basically someone who is fairly quiet and unostentatious. I kept thinking of Alan Bennett when I was doing it, that's the way it was written, it wasn't for overacting at all. Malcolm and Alan were very keen on keeping it down, not giving an over-the-top comic performance. But there was a danger that, at certain times, I'd become rather too animated and lively and probably Malcolm had noticed this, but after about 10 days he hadn't said very much about my performance and so I said, "Are you sure it's all right?" And he said, "Yeah, just keep it dull." So I was doing it all right.'

Palin is essentially playing the straight man to the rest of the cast's more colourful and eccentric characters. 'So they got the laughs ... I didn't need to overdo it to try and get laughs, they would come from the way I reacted. I think a lot of comic acting is reacting, how somebody takes in what's going on around them and how they work with the people they're working with. Chilvers was a bit of a reacting role.'

Still, O'Brien was desperately unsure about the project. Palin says, 'I showed it to Denis and George. Denis said, "Michael, do you think this is funny?" And I said, "I think it's very funny." Denis asked, "But will it knock 'em dead in Dayton, Ohio?" And I had to say, "Well, I'm not sure about

that, but if you get the right cast together it could be very good indeed."
And Denis was swayed. George was OK about it, very nice. I know it
wasn't his kind of thing, but they trusted me and that's rather touching. I
do remember Denis asking me why I wanted to play a chiropodist.'

For Palin, one of the joys of the film was working with Alan Bennett. 'I
think it made it easier because I was also a writer. And because we're both
writers we realise that you've actually thought about the lines. I don't
particularly like actors who come along and change everything just
because they can say it better. I mean, they've accepted the role, the
writing's been done, you say it how it's written. Alan was on set a lot. He
was quite interested in how we actually staged a scene, how we played
something. Alan is so discreet in a way, you would see him behind the
cameras trying to find some quiet little spot where he wouldn't be noticed
while we were doing a take.'

It's unusual for a writer to be so visible on a film set, although Bennett
retorts, 'It's not unusual for me. I used to like doing it, I like it less now
as I've got older. If it's a Yorkshire piece, which *A Private Function* was, you
often have to be there to say how the dialogue should be spoken, a kind
of unofficial dialogue coach. And also it was shot in Ilkley and I live not
far away.'

Bennett's unobtrusive presence on set was taken for granted by many
of the cast and crew, including actor Richard Griffiths. 'I remember Alan
as always constantly schlepping around the place with carrier bags. People
would say, "What have you got in the carrier bags? You're not going
shopping for sausage rolls and porridge down at Marks and Sparks?" He'd
say, "No. I've got awards in them. They keep giving me these awards and I
don't know what to do with them, so I'll have to go to my Auntie Eileen's.
She likes polishing them." '

Bennett's penchant for visiting the location gave rise to one memorable
occasion, recalled affectionately by Michael Palin. 'We were doing the
scene where I get the pig into the car which is one of the most crazy and
surreal moments I've done filming Python or otherwise, trying to get this
bloody pig into the car, it was a huge thing. They'd smeared the car with
fish oil and it just wasn't having any of it so you had people out of sight
pushing the backside of this pig into the car. Eventually, it got inside. Then
it leapt for the door and got its trotter right into my crotch. I was having

to let the brake off while holding this trotter away from my privates. And, of course, it got very excited and the car was covered in shit, an awful nightmare. The man who'd lent us his vintage car was a Yorkshireman and he said, "Who's that up there?" pointing to someone chewing his tie. Alan used to chew his tie when he got nervous. And I said, "That's Alan Bennett. He's the writer." The man sort of nodded his head a bit and then looked at the car and the pig being pushed in and said, "He's no Ibsen, is he?" '

After their wonderful partnership in *The Missionary*, it was decided to team Palin once again with Maggie Smith, playing his wife, a role Shivas guessed Bennett had written expressly with the actress in mind. 'Maggie and Michael loved each other, and although she's not the easiest person in the world – there's that reputation – she was great, there were no problems at all. We were staying in, I think, Ilkley's only fairly large hotel. I got there the day before shooting. Maggie was already there, she had arrived there first of all so that she could choose the room that she would have. We'd got her what we thought was one of the best rooms and she'd changed it before I got there. I asked, "Maggie, how's the room?" She said, "Well, I may have done worse, but by God I've done better." '

Prior to a scene, Maggie would invariably sit in the make-up room with Bennett in attendance and the two of them would laugh hysterically and keep each other amused, nothing like the difficult and temperamental star her reputation suggested. Griffiths recalls, 'Maggie was treated as Madame la Tempestuosa. "Here be dragons" ... you know. We'd be told, "She's not very good in the morning, so don't, whatever you do, get her going because she'll fuck the day up for everybody." And everybody walked on eggshells when she came in. Nobody could take her waspish tone, they were all whipped by it. But I must say, I never once saw Maggie behave out of order, she was an absolute lady, the soul of charm and grace. She never once gave any credence to this notion that she was a dragon.'

Another *Missionary* veteran was Denholm Elliott, replacing first choice Ian Richardson who'd been excused to do a television series in America, in the role of a town doctor who despises his patients. 'Denholm would sit there between takes and be devilish,' says Griffiths. 'I remember he had the tip of his thumb shot off in the war and they managed to cobble it together again, but the top had grown out like a spike. He sort of hinted in a naughty, silly way that it came in very useful for sex. He was so salacious, and it didn't matter what age, height, size or sex it was, he could have sex with anyone and anything. And he was always, as it were, on the look-out. I think that's why women just fell down in droves for him, and not a few men.'

A feature of the early HandMade films are the wonderful casts, made up predominantly of English character actors and comedians, and completing the strong line-up in *A Private Function* are Liz Smith, Alison Steadman and, in an early film role, Pete Postlethwaite. Griffiths observes, 'Pete's got this incredible, insouciant sort of cheeky face. Those bright red cheeks, slightly too prominent, and his eyes, glinting and shining out at you with this half-laugh in them. He has a line where he's got his mistress's dress off and she has to reveal her backside, which the poor actress really suffered from, she felt really odious and embarrassed about, and why not, but it was a rather shapely bum. And Pete revealed her bottom to the mirror and then he caressingly puts his cheek against it and says, "Look at this darling, cheek to cheek." And then he strokes the bum and says, "Oh, if I had this on my bacon slicer." And that made her squirm. The actress was desperately unsettled.'

Needless to say, all of these fine thesps were effortlessly upstaged by the pig. Shivas says, 'We went to a company called Intellectual Animals some months before the film was shot to choose the pigs … they had to be trained from birth. Pigs are supposed to be clever; my theory is that they are so intelligent they never want to do take two. The pig trainer's advice was to get three female pigs because male pigs are too aggressive to be well trained. I remember Maggie Smith encountering the pig for the first time for a publicity shot on the first day of shooting and it wouldn't come and have its picture taken, it would wander off, and she said, "I see this is going to be a breeze." '

Mowbray was determined to integrate the pig properly into the film, not relying on stagy cutaways, and as this was in the days before animatronics that meant the live pig had to be on set with the actors for everything from long shots to close-ups. To prepare his cast and crew, Mowbray organised a week's rehearsal beforehand using a stuffed pig as a stand-in. But no one was quite prepared for the real thing. 'Before a scene,' Palin remembers, 'the cast would sit and wait and, at the last moment, when everything was absolutely ready, the pig was brought in – Betty.

There were three pigs in all, but only one that could act, so Betty was brought in. It was a bit like the arrival of some mega Hollywood star; you all had to be quiet and then she'd come on to the set and immediately the clapper boy went "Whack!" for action the pig would panic, the way a lot of actors probably do as well but they're better at controlling it. So we'd have to clear the set while the carpet was cleaned and shampooed rather rapidly and then we'd start again.'

Not unreasonably, the pigs didn't take to what the crew wanted them to do and devious tricks were often employed to get the animal to perform. Mowbray explains, 'For example, there was one scene where a girl is having a piano lesson and the pig wanders into the room and they have to get rid of the pig without the girl seeing. To get the pig to follow a circuit, that was incredibly difficult. Although it's trained and the trainer has mock-up sets built and everything, the reality is when you try to do it, he'll say, "It's the wrong carpet. I thought it was Axminster and it's Wilton. Pig can't do it on Wilton." In the end, sardine oil proved very, very useful. There was a fishing rod with sardine oil in a piece of cotton wool above the camera to lure it.'

There was the smell, too, remembered vividly by Alan Bennett. 'I remember being in this upstairs room in this suburban house in Ilkley while we were waiting for the shot and this lingering smell everywhere of this terrible pig. We used to go back to the hotel at night and you'd have a bath and a change but you still somehow smelt of those terrible pigs, and you'd see people looking at you askance. There was no getting rid of it.'

While watching the creature in action one day, Bennett got into a bizarre conversation with Richard Griffiths. 'You know,' he announced suddenly, 'when she's running away from you it puts me in mind of one of those secretaries in the old days. Know what I mean?'

Griffiths nodded. 'Yes I do. Very tight little bum and just mincing along in her high heels.'

Bennett agreed. 'Yes, yes. She's got little slingbacks on and she scuttles along with those very tempting buttocks.'

Griffiths paused. 'Tempting in what way?'

Bennett quickly replied, 'Oh, to eat, my dear.'

'Yeah. Fine. Remember the Coward song, "he took to pig sticking in quite the wrong way"?'

Bennett shook his head. 'Oh no, we have none of that round here. This is Yorkshire.'

Griffiths said, 'I bet it goes on.'

Bennett was adamant. 'Oh, not in this film.'

In the end, the defecating animals proved not just a hindrance but a near health hazard and something had to be done. Shivas says, 'Some of the crew had such a bad time with the pigs, because they would shit all over the place, some of them were asking for special clothing allowance because they had to change their clothes so often. They were eating more bacon butties in revenge.' Finally, a solution was found. Palin explains, 'There was a boy who used to hang around the set at Ilkley, just wanted to do anything to get into film. We said, "Anything?" And he said, "Yeah." So we said, "We'll give you this plastic bucket and whenever the pig comes on set and you see anything happening at the back of the pig, you just whack that bucket under there." And it worked, it speeded up the filming, it avoided having to clean the carpet every time. I think it was the only credit ever in films for "Bucket Boy".'

After shooting wrapped, the pigs escaped the abattoir to enjoy contented retirement on a farm, oblivious to their fame, not even invited to the film's royal West End opening. Shivas admits, 'We couldn't take the risk of them shitting on the carpet of the Odeon Haymarket.' The audience's warm response to the pig was something the makers hadn't reckoned on and they were forced to delete a scene in which the culled animal is seen dead in a bath. 'We showed a rough cut of the film to the public,' Mowbray says, 'and by that time in the film the audience had become so attached to the pig that when they saw it dead in the bath they were shocked and drew back from the film, and so anything that followed that scene they weren't engaged with. So, in the end, we thought it was more beneficial to the film to lose that scene.'

As shooting progressed on both *Water* and *A Private Function*, there developed some resentment at how differently both films were perceived by the HandMade hierarchy. Those toiling away on *Function* saw themselves very much as the poorer cousin. Palin's view was '*Water* was over in the West Indies, a lot of big stars, and there was us with an incontinent pig in a rather draughty part of north Yorkshire.'

Function's budget was extremely small and O'Brien had also beaten them down to a tight shooting schedule of just six weeks, meaning scenes involving the pig that were too complicated and time-consuming to stage had to be excised. Bennett feels that 'the problem was they were making *Water* in tandem, the budget of that was much higher and any spare money was channelled into that. They'd obviously thought either we were a loss-maker or were not something to be banked on. You didn't get the impression that they had much confidence in it, really, and so any money they had went into *Water* and we were absolutely cut to the bone.'

Richard Griffiths clearly remembers the day representatives from HandMade arrived on location and took over the catering bus for a showdown meeting with the production team: 'As this secret meeting drew on, a bad feeling began to emerge. Then the suits came off the bus and smugly walked to their car and got whizzed off and we never saw them again. A disconsolate Alan came out, along with Malcolm and Mark, all with faces that were crestfallen, thunderous with rage. They'd been asked not to talk about it so they were wanting to wail and gnash their teeth but they tried to be honourable about it. Eventually, it turned out that what had happened was *Water* was all over the place and needed more money and HandMade said, "Look, there's a budget sitting there in Yorkshire, we can nip a bit off that. It's only a little tiny movie." So they came over to Ilkley and said, "We want a quarter of a million pounds out of your budget." '

According to Griffiths, these executives already had a strategy worked out. On the way up to Ilkley, they'd gone through the script deciding what scenes could be cut. 'It was just butchered by these money people. And if it was O'Brien, then we can spit on that and say, "Well, he's the same bastard that fucked up the company. And, of course, when *Function* came out, it was successful and *Water* went straight down the sewage plug hole. It's just a crap, self-indulgent, fuck-all-going-on type of movie.'

Astonishingly, when *A Private Function* was forced to go over schedule by just one day in order to complete the shooting of two pivotal scenes, there wasn't a penny left in the budget to cover it. Shivas reveals, 'Denis said, "Well, you can have an extra day's shooting but it will come out of your salary and Malcolm's salary – £5,000 each. If the film makes money you'll get it back." Needless to say, although the film made money we never saw a bean. Then he had the gall to say when he saw the film, "I think that's the funniest scene in the film." Not remembering if he'd had his way, that scene would never have been shot.'

To be fair to O'Brien, he did have a very firm notion of budgets. Kelleher agrees. 'It was one thing he was good at. Denis was very clear that the budget was the budget and if you didn't keep to it then you had to cut shooting.' As Harrison also said, 'It's nice to let people have as much artistic freedom as possible, but I'm the one who has to pay back the bank. If they want total freedom, they have to get their own money and make their own films. It has to be give and take. But I think we're quite reasonable.'

For *Water*, though, the cheque book always seemed open. Where *Privates on Parade*'s jungle setting had been poorly replicated in Aldershot, this time HandMade allocated huge resources into filming in a far-flung location. Clement and La Frenais's story called for a Caribbean island so, after a painful selection process, St Lucia was selected, despite the logistical nightmares involved. The biggest problem was having to ship everything out there by sea because of the absence of any film-making mechanism on the island. Clement says, 'We shot most of the film on St Lucia. The studio stuff was done at Shepperton and we did the oil rig scenes in Devon during a pretty good summer. We had quite a lot of sunshine, though I remember one morning when we were sitting waiting for the fog to lift, which you don't get very much of in the Caribbean.'

For St Lucia, the filming meant prosperity. Local extras were earning $35 a day. 'It's better than a ganja, man,' one smiling Rastafarian informed a travelling British reporter. But despite the sun, a major cloud was looming. Clement reveals, 'We were rewriting the ending as we went along and that's never good. Ian and myself suddenly looked at each other and thought, The ending isn't working. And then we wrote another ending while we were still shooting it and, in hindsight, I always think you need to get those decisions out of the way before you get on to the set. But, on the whole, it was a good shoot. Michael Caine was a fantastic trouper on the film, he was really a joy to work with, enormously supportive. I can't be more appreciative of his work on it and how professional he was. In a way, Michael had the straightest part in the film, he was almost the straight man. He kept saying to me, "You realise I'm having to carry all the plot here?" '

Caine's unlikely co-star was Billy Connolly, a cult comic star in Britain, though largely unknown anywhere else, who misguidedly viewed *Water* as both his big break in movies and the chance to crack America. 'Billy had a special relationship with HandMade,' Clement recalls. 'They were always trying to put him into a movie because Denis was convinced that Billy Connolly was the funniest man in Britain … he was way ahead of the pack there. He said, "You've got to find a part for Billy in *Bullshot*." And we said, "Fine." So that part of an accident-prone blind man, was written with him in mind. Again, Billy was in *Water* because of Denis. He was actually cast before anybody else.'

Back in the far less exotic Ilkley, someone had come up with a brainwave. Because most of the action in *A Private Function* takes place inside the household of Palin's character, it was decided to buy a local town villa, get the art department to do it up in a Forties style and shoot inside. Other rooms housed the make-up and wardrobe departments. When the film was over, according to Richard Griffiths, the art department moved back in to redecorate the property and then flogged it for something like £20,000 profit. It was probably the first time a crew has ever used a location and walked away with 20 grand more than they started with. Bennett says wistfully, 'I often go past the road where that house is and think about it. I look back on the film now and have very happy memories. There was a good atmosphere. We had such a wonderful time. If you watch the film, particularly Richard Griffiths, you can see that the cuts always come just when he's about to break up. Every time they had to put the fart noises in for the pig, he could keep his face straight for the next half-minute but then he'd suddenly start laughing out loud. So you can see when the cut comes just as he's breaking down. The whole cast were a lovely lot to work with. It was very happy in that way.'

Griffiths' corpsing got so bad that Shivas one day took the actor quietly to one side. 'You're having a good time doing this movie, aren't you?' he said.

'Yes I am. I love it,' Griffiths replied.

Shivas grew more serious. 'Only I've noticed watching the rushes that you crack up a lot.'

A broad smile came over Griffiths. 'Yes. It's so funny, isn't it? And I can't help it, everyone just makes me roar out laughing. I mean, normally I'm good at keeping a straight face, but it's so ridiculously funny.'

Shivas continued. 'Yes. You realise, of course, that this movie is roughly costing about £100 a minute between the morning call and the evening wrap. Do you see what I'm saying?'

Griffiths nodded.

Shivas went on. 'And so far, your cracking up has cost me about £17,000. So I'll be grateful if you could take it a little more seriously.'

The congenial atmosphere on the set of *Function* was probably a result of the fact that Denis O'Brien rarely ever paid them a visit. Shivas says, 'I think Denis came on set once in Yorkshire with his Doris Day-lookalike girlfriend, had his picture taken, smiled, then mercifully went away and let us get on with it.' As for Harrison, he seemed to shun the picture altogether. Bennett admits, 'I never met George Harrison. He was no help over the money, he was totally a united front with Denis O'Brien. I mean, there was no sense of fellow artists about it.'

Despite the crew shooting for a few days in Henley, just down the road from his mansion, Harrison chose not to go anywhere near them. This didn't deter a pair of girls, though, who followed the filming everywhere in the hope of catching sight of the former Beatle. According to Shivas, 'The reason that George didn't come anywhere near the film when it was being made was because of *Water*, which was always held up to me as being the perfect production – it was going terribly well, it was bigger, it was more professional, etc, etc. Every time I had a problem, Denis or somebody would say, "Well, *Water*'s going well." But George, I believe, doesn't terribly like confrontations, and why should he bother with confrontations when he doesn't have to? He didn't come near us because he thought it was difficult ... he knew my relationship with Denis wasn't particularly good and stayed away because he thought he'd get an earful when he came to the set.'

Harrison did, however, throw his considerable weight behind *Water*, not least in a stunning rock concert sequence set in the United Nations building where he was responsible for roping in a few pals like Eric Clapton and Ringo Starr to play especially for the film. 'Although George was very leery of appearing in his own company's movies,' says Clement, 'that was a big help to the film. We called in a few favours and, obviously, the Harrison connection didn't hurt. We hoped that scene would be a big selling tool for the movie ... didn't work out that way, but it was a good idea.'

The whole thing was shot in a single day at Shepperton Studios. Producer David Wimbury remembers it well. 'We paid these stars the musician's minimum rate for a playback session on set. At lunchtime, I gave them the little brown envelope of cash, not much, I think about 40 quid, and they had to sign for it. They were well pleased ... it was the first real wages they'd seen in a brown envelope for many years, I guess. They got a big kick out of it.'

When *Water* and *A Private Function* were complete, Harrison sat alone in a Wardour Street screening room to watch them. 'He thought *Water* was very funny and didn't think *Function* was at all funny,' Shivas remembers. 'It wasn't until he saw both of them with an audience that he realised that *Water* was not a success and that *Function* was.'

As *A Private Function* entered post-production, tensions mounted. First, there was a problem with the rushes. From Shivas's viewpoint, 'Denis was a mysterious character. He would say things which boggled our minds like, "The rushes are too dark." But that's how they're printed! He'd made films before, so we were amazed he made that kind of comment. He would make very unprofessional remarks.'

Next came concerns over the film's length. O'Brien feared it was going to run far too long. Mowbray confirms, 'We always said it was going to be 90 minutes and he'd seen a rough cut that was longer than 90 minutes and became alarmed. That was a bit weird. When you make a film, say you're making a two-hour film, the rough cut is likely to be two-and-a-half hours long, but when somebody says, "Oh, that means you're wasting a fifth," it's kind of odd. So there was a bit of a fight about that, with Denis gnashing his teeth. But, in the end, the film came in at 90 minutes, just like we said.' Mowbray was also shocked when O'Brien arrived at one screening with his two daughters aged ten and eight. 'We were a bit embarrassed because the film was rated a 15.'

One creative stroke of brilliance O'Brien was responsible for was to have the film open with some period newsreel footage. After all, American audiences had no knowledge of rationing, neither, one supposes, did many back in Britain who were too young to remember the era depicted. 'So give him his due,' admits Mowbray.

The main battle, though, was still to come and that was over the music. O'Brien insisted that, because the film was a comedy, the musical soundtrack had to tell the audience that it was a comedy. The makers, meanwhile, wanted the music track darker in tone, indicating that this was no run-of-the-mill comedy but something a bit more subversive. It appeared that O'Brien was deliberately dumbing down the picture in order to get the biggest audience. 'They insisted on putting jokey music on it,' Alan Bennett observes. 'Obviously, as it's a comedy, you couldn't have Wagner, you wanted something reasonably light, but it was jokey in an old-fashioned way with the pig signalled by the double bassoon. Well, it's all right if it's *Doctor in the House* or whatever, but it wasn't and Malcolm and I were really upset about that. But they seemed to take this as a matter of course, almost, that it was their right to do this, they weren't at all shame-faced about it. And Ray Cooper, who one would have thought, since he was a practitioner himself, would have been more supportive, but he was entirely on the, as it were, management side.'

Ray Cooper's role as, essentially, a middle-man between Denis O'Brien and the creative community was one he saw as utterly necessary. Gilliam's view is that 'Ray was always the man trying to mediate, trying to find a middle ground, to smooth it out. Ray's got a wonderful ability to deal with creative people.' But, increasingly, this role had been causing him problems. Because of his artistic background, Cooper was always trying to be this metaphorical bridge-builder between the front office and the film-makers, who invariably saw O'Brien as a suit. Cooper had to break that down and was, at first, successful in doing so. 'But then we entered an era of physical interference with the film-making process,' Cooper states. 'We became very much bullish, hands-on editors and cutters and we alienated, I think, a lot of the creative society. We would do things that are very common practice now, unfortunately. We would have our own cuts made, our own visions. It was very painful to be involved in the process, especially as people I was dealing with were, in most cases, friends, and they knew me on a creative level, and I think it led to a lot of my own downfall because people would say to me, "What are you doing? Why are you doing this, Ray? Why are you on the side of Denis suddenly?" I'd say, "You don't understand, I'm not." It was sometimes a very difficult situation, sometimes a thankless task. Denis was paying my wages, even though I was a director of the company for ten years, it was still a wages situation. That's not an excuse, because it shouldn't be.'

For the most part, Ray was genuinely loved and fondly thought of by the film-makers. Many remember and acknowledge the support he provided. Some also wonder why he willingly placed himself in such a difficult position, often a no-win situation of trying to please sometimes two diametrically opposed camps. Denis on the one hand, and the artists on the other. Shivas comments, 'I could never understand why Ray put up with it for so long. He was forever, I'm sure, running between the producer and Denis O'Brien and getting the worst of both ends, no doubt. Very nice man.'

Clement today admits he was utterly unaware of the problems that were faced on *A Private Function*, although acutely aware of O'Brien's reputation within the industry. 'I know that other directors didn't always have a good time working for HandMade, but I had a great time, they were very supportive. I used to play tennis with Denis a lot, so we had a very friendly relationship. We had creative … I wouldn't even say disagreements … where we argued things through but we always arrived at a consensus. So it was nothing that, from my own experiences, was out of the normal creative process.'

When it came to distribution, *A Private Function* was again shunted into the corner to make way for *Water*. Shingles recalls, 'Everyone was saying, "Oh, *A Private Function*, you're never going to shift that." I remember we had screenings for distributors and Rank were there and we screened *Water* and *A Private Function* and they said, "We'll have *Water* but *A Private Function*, we're not interested." So we were forced, in effect, to do it ourselves and I think we did a bloody good job. If we could all be proud of one film, releasing it ourselves, because we were forced to, it would be *A Private Function*.'

By this time, HandMade were increasingly less inclined to distribute their own product, preferring to farm out films to other distributors. 'HandMade distributors didn't actually close,' Shingles says, 'I think it just fizzled out. I think we were seen as a fair-weather distributor; sometimes we'd do them, sometimes we didn't. People were never sure whether HandMade were going to release it or they weren't. And I felt that our relationships with some of the distributors were a little fraught. You have to be consistent, you can't keep messing people around. I can't say there was a day when they said, "Right, we're not going to do distribution any more." HandMade distributors existed right to the very end.'

A Private Function did win unexpected publicity when it was chosen in November to have a royal charity première in the presence of Princess Anne. Shivas remembers, 'Something I didn't know about royal premières is that somebody from the Palace comes to see the film to make sure it's suitable. They came to see an unfinished version of it and, of course, we put a large number of pig farts on the soundtrack between the time they saw the film and when Princess Anne came to see it. But she seemed to enjoy it.'

The film opened proper in December and was a surprise success, staying in the London top ten for over three months. It was also invited to be screened at the Cannes and London Film Festivals. HandMade were not only looking at their biggest hit since *Time Bandits*, but their most critically acclaimed film thus far. The British critics fell over themselves to heap praise upon it. The *Daily Telegraph* called it 'a comedy as ripe, rude and robust as any I can remember'; the *New Statesman* wrote, 'Blissfully funny. An all-round triumph. This deserves to become a classic.' The *Sunday Mirror* raved, 'A fine example of small-scale British film-making at its best.' And the *Evening Standard* even went as far as 'A morality play that will shake the rafters with laughter. I'd have hated to die before I saw it.'

Undoubtedly, *A Private Function* ranks alongside *Life of Brian*, *Time Bandits* and *Withnail & I* as one of HandMade's finest achievements. Maggie Smith's biographer Michael Coveney even described it as 'one of the funniest and most nearly perfect British films of the century'.

Function was later nominated for five British Academy Awards, including Best Picture and Best Screenplay. Palin's performance was also highly praised but, as usual, the actor is too modest to admit it: 'Chilvers was quite a reasonably easy part to play. I don't think it was as demanding, for instance, as some of the things in Python when you're playing lots of different characters, having to invent something new each time. In a sense, that's where acting skill is really important because you have a very short time to build up the character. I think people do tend to underestimate the sort of acting that goes into comedy films, especially group comedy films, because they go, "Oh, they're just larking about and having a good time," but it's a little bit more than that. And I did try with those Python roles, making sure each one was absolutely different from the other. That was about as demanding as almost anything I've done.'

Very little of the film's success trickled back to the actual people who put the effort in to make the bloody thing in the first place. Bennett says ruefully, 'They claimed it didn't make any money. Of course, film finances are famous, but I'd get statements of profit and loss and the cost of it mounted each time the balance sheet came round so it seemed to have cost £15 million by the time we'd finished and I couldn't see how this could be since I knew the budget was so small. But that's creative accounting. In the end, I wrote to them to tell them to stop sending me these absurd financial statements, saying if they sent me any more I would submit them as candidates for the Booker Prize for Fiction. But they'd no sense of humour. I think they wrote back and obviously hadn't seen the joke at all. But that was fairly typical.'

All Mark Shivas ever got from O'Brien (who, along with Mowbray, was supposed to have a percentage of the net) was a copy of the poster. 'It was mounted on a board, albeit in black-and-white when the poster was in colour, and it said something like "Fond memories", which I didn't particularly have.'

It had also been a cinematic baptism of fire for the mild-mannered Bennett. 'I never actually came to dislike Denis O'Brien, but I disliked what he did in the end. My experience of film producers is quite small, but he's the worst one. I imagine the problems we had weren't as different from the rows everybody always has with producers, but then I never had them on my two subsequent films with Sam Goldwyn Jnr, who's a model of good behaviour by comparison with Denis O'Brien. Maybe with Malcolm Mowbray being new to directing features, that might have had something to do with it.'

Is Bennett suggesting that O'Brien felt he could more easily push Mowbray around because of his début status? If so, then this brings a whole new slant to HandMade's overall willingness to hire first-time directors.

Bolstered perhaps by its home-grown success, *A Private Function* was given a big send-off in America, opening the British Film Week at the Los Angeles Film Festival on 13 March 1985. It turned out to be a disastrous evening. The venue was the famous Grauman's Chinese Theater on Hollywood Boulevard. All the principals were there, including Alan Bennett who'd never been to LA before and confided to Shivas, 'that it was too far to go for anything'. It was all very Hollywood, searchlights lit up the skyline and a troop of horse guards stood on duty outside. Somewhere along the line, though, the money had obviously run out as both Mowbray and Shivas had to pay for themselves to fly over for the opening of their own movie! Mowbray admits, 'I really wanted to be there and, as they weren't going to pay for me, I went off on my own. I was staying at the same hotel as Alan Bennett. We were meant to go to the theatre at about seven but nothing seemed to be happening so Alan and I went down to the lobby and sort of sat around when suddenly this film company girl comes up and says, "What are you doing here? You should have gone in the limo." "What limo?" we say. We actually ended up going there in the back of what seemed to be a fish van, roaring along to be dumped outside Grauman's Chinese Theater.'

Once inside, a troop of 'Highlanders' filed on to the stage, rather confusingly with trumpets, not bagpipes, and weakly blasted a fanfare heralding the arrival of the British Ambassador, the evening's host. Alas, his microphone didn't work and sections of the audience started barracking him. Next, Shivas, Mowbray and Bennett were introduced to the audience. A spotlight located them individually and they stood up, but the scattered applause hardly made it worthwhile. When it was Bennett's turn, he dutifully rose but was seated too far back in the auditorium for the spotlight to reach him. 'What's this guy playing at?' said someone behind. 'Sit down, you jerk.' Britain's greatest living comedy playwright obliged.

And the film didn't go down particularly well with the audience, either. When everyone poured out, Michael Caine, one of the few celebrities in attendance, sidled over to Shivas. The producer was hoping to hear some positive words, but all he got was Caine's prediction that his film wouldn't make a dime in America. Bennett says, 'Grauman's Chinese Theater was very dispiriting. The audience didn't really understand what was going on and nothing worked, the sound system didn't work, just everything was wrong. It was a parody of Hollywood glamour. And then Michael Caine saying what he did. I thought, Well, that's a bit rich seeing that they took all our money for their thing which really bombed, and ours didn't bomb.'

Caine was right, of course, but then *A Private Function* was never going to be another *Star Wars* in box-office terms. Perhaps the subject was too English; then again, it was the film's sheer Englishness, as opposed to *Water*'s tragic mid-Atlantic vapidness, with its imported American stars, that bowled over the American critics. The *New York Times* gushed, 'Not since the end of the golden age of Ealing studios has there been a stylish English comedy of such high-hearted, self-interested knavery as *A Private Function*.' The *Chicago Tribune* applauded 'a classic comedy of class struggle, expertly performed. Here's hoping that *A Private Function* scores at the box office and triggers a renaissance of British film comedy.' The *New Yorker* claimed that '*A Private Function* is like an Ealing Studios comedy of the late '40s, early '50s period as it might have been skewed by Joe Orton.'

Ironically, *Water* was something of a lame duck compared with how *A Private Function* turned out. In the words of Dick Clement, 'It didn't, to make an awful pun, make a splash.' Opening in London in January 1985, *Water* was in the top ten list concurrently with *Function*, but quickly dropped out after poor word of mouth and some risible notices. 'How on earth do films like this make the leap from drawing board to movie camera?' asked the *Financial Times*, while the *Guardian* suggested it 'might be called neo-Ealing in conception but comes out merely puerile in execution, with glossy production values only emphasising the TV-sketch thinness of the writing'. The most telling review came from *The Times*: 'Produced by HandMade who recently found great success with the modest, indigenous *A Private Function*. There is a lesson to be learnt here.'

It wasn't just the critics who found *Water* unpalatable; some HandMade staff couldn't help but show their disappointment with it. Shingles claims, 'You have to have a flair for directing comedy and I don't know that the director was exactly the right one for that. It was like a watered-down Ealing without any of the charm, basically. It had a great cast, but it just didn't gel.' To be fair, Clement himself openly admits the film to be flawed. 'I'm happier with *Bullshot* than I am with *Water*. I think *Water* just misses. I feel it's not quite connecting in the right way. I look back on it and I'm fairly uncomfortable. For me, I always did have a problem with fictional countries or places, I always like things rooted a little bit more in reality. I have a feeling that kind of thing works perhaps in fiction, but I always find that film is a very literal medium, you've got to sell stuff on the screen and I think it was slightly larger than life in a way that isn't quite comfortable on the screen and I don't think I pulled it off.'

Perhaps the film's approach was too old-fashioned, a throw-back to past glories like *Carlton Browne of the FO* and *Passport to Pimlico*, a comedy world of yesteryear out of place in Thatcher's post-Falklands Britain. 'I guess it was like an Ealing film,' says Clement, 'but it was not a conscious effort to recreate that style. I can see the analogies with something like *Passport to Pimlico*. And, again, in hindsight, as much as I love Billy Connolly, I think a black guy in that part would have been better. I think that would have helped the credibility of making it a Caribbean island and I think having to explain that Billy's character was half-Scottish, half-something else was a reach.'

Water fared even worse in America. Test screenings went so badly that a distributor was so difficult to track down the picture wasn't released there until April 1986, where it died a death at the box office and was critically mauled by those who bothered to review it. *Variety*'s comments can be added to the generally negative reaction: 'The film is totally devoid of a narrative centre and without sustained imagination it quickly becomes an overproduced cliché.'

In an attempt to recuperate some of the losses incurred on *Water*, O'Brien took the unusual, if rather novel step of flogging props from the film to any of his staff who wanted them. Kelleher remembers 'someone coming into my office and saying, "This is the suit that Leonard Rossiter wore in *Water*. Do you want it?" And I said, "How much?" And they said, "£150." It was anything he could get money back on. HandMade was a sort of cottage industry in that sense.'

The shoddy fate of *Water* was more than an embarrassment for HandMade. Some saw it as, excuse the pun, a watermark in the company's fortunes. Palin feels 'that it was a bit of a turning point in HandMade Films, that *Water* was such a disaster and yet so much money was put into it. Somehow the luck ran out, because judgement up to that time had been pretty good. Even *The Missionary*, which had not made a lot of money, had covered its costs.'

Palin still remained a favourite with O'Brien. A steady stream of scripts would usually find their way to the Palin household care of Cadogan Square. 'But I didn't think the quality was very high, to be honest. Denis also wanted me to direct. Denis's view of HandMade over the years we worked together was that it should be like a family where everybody sort of helped each other out and commented on each other's films and appeared in each other's films. It was a case of Denis getting names associated to projects that people knew and trusted. I think he asked me if I'd be interested in directing something like *Bullshot*. He wanted me to come along and give my name to it, but I didn't feel it was what I wanted to do. So Denis did want me to direct and couldn't quite believe why I wouldn't direct. But I always wanted to try and keep my own individuality within any set-up.'

Next O'Brien took to ringing Palin incessantly at home about projects, phone calls that became much more than just a nuisance. Steve Abbott believes, 'Years and years after the Python split, Denis behaved in a way that would have prompted law suits if someone had done it to him. Even though Anne James was representing Michael, he'd think nothing of bypassing our office and phoning Michael at home and trying to sell him something, as a producer putting a film together. It was an outrageously unprofessional way to behave. If we'd done that, if we wanted George for something, just picking up the phone to Henley, because we had the number, he'd have put writs out on us. Strange man.'

Still the phone calls kept coming. 'And to such an extent,' says Palin, 'that I got a bit twitchy after a while and was getting a bit of a thing about the name "Denis". So I thought I'd transfer it to something warm and furry and rather loveable, so we called our cat Denis. It was wonderful because it took on a different kind of significance, the name Denis. And I remember when Denis came round and we were saying, "Denis!" and Denis said, "Yes." And we said, "Sorry, we're talking to the cat." And Denis was ever so touched that we'd called our cat Denis.' Palin, though, was not to make another film for HandMade.

The third project slated for production during 1984, arguably the most anticipated of all, sadly never saw daylight. *Travelling Men* was a collaboration between director John Mackenzie and writer Peter McDougall and was to be a gritty and humorous thriller, a sort of road movie featuring two granite-strong leading characters. A script was produced along with the belief that, if the right actors were cast, this might turn out to be something very special. Mackenzie recalls, 'O'Brien heard about it and said, "It sounds great … I think it should be Sean Connery and Michael Caine." We'd already thought about Sean, because there's a Scotsman in it, but not of that combination, it sounded good. It was *The*

Man Who Would Be King, the two of them at it again. It would be great if we could get them both.'

Connery liked the project and visited O'Brien numerous times at Cadogan Square. But problems soon developed over the script. 'We had a wonderful script,' says Shingles. 'I remember thinking this could be really good, but it got watered down. For example, there's one scene where there's this yappy dog on a ferry and one of the characters just kicks it overboard. I loved it but Denis took exception to it and took it out, and that was the sign that the script was being emasculated in a way.'

Worse was to come, much worse. It was now not just a matter of dropping certain scenes but the entire shape to the story was gradually being altered, something Mackenzie knew absolutely nothing about. He'd been away working on something else, thinking the project was happily ticking away, when on his return he was invited by O'Brien for lunch at a plush restaurant. 'O'Brien said, "Well, look, we've just changed the whole concept." I said, "Oh, really. The whole film?" He said, "Yeah. And we'll set it in the highlands of Scotland." I said, "In the rain, I suppose." Having done a film in Scotland I didn't want to go back. I said, "Well, that's quite a big change." He said, "Yeah." I said, "Well, I wish you luck with it." He said, "What do you mean? We want you to direct it." I said, "No. I'm not directing anything that's taken out of my hands and done like this." "What do you mean?" he said. And it went on 'til he was shrieking at me, because he's a madman. Mad. "WE MADE YOU," he said. "You made me! What do you mean you made me?" I asked. "You made a lot of money out of *The Long Good Friday*, that's all you did." And he's crashing the table in this empty restaurant. I've never seen such rage. He was mad, his eyes went and you could see this man was out of control. And it was to do with his ego because I said, "You know nothing." And he was ready to kill me. So I just got up and left.'

Mackenzie not only left the restaurant but, true to his word, walked away from the entire project: 'I could see that there was going to be a lot of problems here so I thought, Is my life worth it? Then Sean Connery asked if I would go and see him one evening. I went to see him and I said, "I don't want this, it's changed the concept. I just don't want to do it, and I don't trust O'Brien and I'm well out of it." And then Sean said he was a bit worried, because he was thinking about his money.'

With Connery out, Bob Hoskins was drafted in and the project was touted around town, passing from one director to another. At one point, Alan Parker was attached to it. Meanwhile, poor Peter McDougall, ably assisted by Ray Cooper, who'd been involved in the earliest days of its inception, was slowly, and not unsurprisingly, growing disenchanted about the way he and his script were being treated. His anger finally boiled over with dramatic consequences. 'This was one of the best writers HandMade ever had,' Cooper fumes, 'a man whose project he'd seen going into all sorts of extraordinary circumstances. At the end of the day, Denis had the insensitivity to write to Peter to say that he would be considered for dialogue retouches, on his own script, which as you can imagine as a true writer, and Glaswegian especially, didn't go down well, and rightly so.

'He wrote a letter to Denis. I was on a week's holiday and I read the letter and rang Peter immediately and said, "Do you really want him to read that? If you do, I'll stand by you, but if it was one of those heat-of-the-moment things maybe we can find another way of doing it." And he said, "Well, it's up to you." I think he'd sort of slightly pulled back. Denis was away and he had a temporary secretary who was really stupid. I rang her up and said, "OK, this is Ray Cooper, you know me, Head of Production. Destroy that letter from Peter McDougall. OK?" And she didn't. And when Denis got back, he wanted to see me and he was white-faced and so angry and unforgiving. And that was the end of the project as far as I was concerned.'

Again, the crunch came in the elegant confines of an up-market restaurant. O'Brien could be very generous when it came to dinners, there were many of them, but this particular one carried with it an atmosphere chillier than the Chardonnay. Cooper recalls, 'Over this dinner, he said, "I'm going to say something to you." And I said, "What?" And he said, "You haven't performed well on this project." And that word "performed", for me, has a significant meaning. And I said, "What are you fucking talking about? I've given you the best script you've had, virtually, and you've taken it to pieces." So that was a very painful project for me. I had developed it with Peter, whom I adored. And that project sits on a shelf somewhere, unmade.'

Mackenzie still owns a copy of the original script, but he's never read it since and, when pressed, can't even remember the plot; the memory of it all has been purged from his mind. Only his bitterness over O'Brien remains. 'So it never happened and it's a pity because it could've been quite fun. With Connery and Caine it could've been great. But I'd rather not talk about it because I don't want to revive all that time. It was a very unhappy time. And O'Brien was crazed. He thought he knew about films … he knew nothing. He was a financier; he grew into this mogul-god that he thought he was, fucking useless … let him get the fucking money and shut his trap. I don't want to listen to all that stuff from someone I had no respect for.

'He was very odd, too. He'd by then left his wife and met some other bird but he didn't want to get caught for alimony and he disappeared out of the office and went abroad. Apparently, he was on a boat and we'd get these odd phone calls from I don't know where … Canada, he's up in some port like Quebec. Then he was down the coast in Maryland. All this because he didn't want to land and get handed a subpoena. The lengths he went to avoid it. Crazed!'

CHAPTER 8

'COLD AND LONELY, LOVELY WORK OF ART'

HandMade's promise to have sometimes as many as five films on the boil at any one time was looking good in 1985. Projects under consideration incorporated a gamut of diverse talent old and new, including veteran director Jack Clayton, acclaimed screenwriter Donald Westlake and the multi-talented Steven Berkoff. Cooper says, 'We didn't actually end up doing a Berkoff film, tragically. I wanted to do his first film *Decadence*, which he later made elsewhere. I adore his work and adore him as a creative, incredible force, a tornado. He's extraordinary. A magnificent creature.'

It wasn't just the Berkoff project that bit the dust. Suddenly, there was a general air of not much going on, of few if any projects being completely committed to. Or so it seemed to John Kelleher. And it was this strange hiatus, coupled with the fact that O'Brien was getting more and more secretive in his dealings, that forced Kelleher out of HandMade after barely two years in his post. 'It got much more difficult to talk about what films we were going to do and I felt that, since I was the one responsible for generating money from them, that it just was very unsatisfactory. You never knew what was going on with Denis, you just didn't know. He

171

didn't feel like making the effort, he didn't inspire any feeling of confidence or wellbeing in anyone. HandMade was also becoming for me a hard place to work, there was a lot of personal politics going on between the people around Denis and the people around George.'

For a brief period, O'Brien did start arranging board meetings in an attempt to have a more open management policy, but it really didn't last very long. 'We even had this one weekend retreat out of the office to a fancy hotel in Sussex,' Kelleher remembers, 'to say what we are doing, where we are going, with all the senior people. But I always felt that Denis was just paying lip service. I don't think he really paid any attention to us. He may have listened to see whether he could pick up anything valuable. He himself never gave anything in those situations, it was all coming from everyone else, about what kind of movies we should be doing, etc.'

When Kelleher was offered another job, he personally met O'Brien to inform him of his reasons for going. 'Denis wasn't particularly pleasant about it. I remember he made me give my company car back straight away. He accepted my resignation because we weren't getting on well by then, we'd had our arguments. He was fairly difficult about the terms of my leaving. It was basically "Never darken my door again".'

Looking back, Kelleher saw Denis as an astute businessman who wanted to be part of the creative mix but wasn't quite able to bridge those two very different worlds. 'When it came down to it, he had no taste himself. He didn't seem to value the creative people. He didn't understand that, in people like Terry Gilliam, he was dealing with genius. He was the example of what's been seen many times of people basically going "Hollywood" and thinking they know how to do it when they don't know anything, really, and they don't really understand creative people and the creative process. He also didn't understand the humour of the films. He was a very humourless man in many ways. He was always laughing but God knows what he was laughing at. It was more nervous laughter than anything else. It wasn't genuinely getting the joke.'

This, of course, left things conveniently open for Wendy Palmer, who, after all, had been handling the sales side of the company prior to Kelleher's arrival. 'When John went, Denis finally said, "Oh, you can have the job now." It was like, "Thanks, Denis." So now I was responsible for all the marketing of the films, the on-set publicity, getting interviews arranged. We were pretty hands-on. We did the launches of the films, selling the films, negotiating the deals, royalties and stuff.'

Wendy and Hilary Davis were also regulars at Cannes, as was Denis and his yacht. And there were other trips, too, but O'Brien didn't like his team to be on the road, he preferred wherever possible for business to be conducted from Cadogan Square. Palmer saw that as 'always a bit irritating, because if you're selling, my theory is you should be meeting your clients, doing sales trips to certain territories. I did manage to talk Denis into doing more of that, of actually going off to individual countries and meeting our clients. But he wasn't ultimately that interested in the foreign sales to be perfectly honest.'

His preoccupation was always the USA. All deals conducted in that territory were done under his personal supervision. O'Brien was also keenly involved in the UK market, but all other territories were the domain of Wendy Palmer. 'I'd go off and do all the donkey work, get the offers and Denis would say, "Oh no, that's not enough." He'd ratchet it up every time and I'd have to go back again and say, "Denis won't close the deal unless you do this." '

One of the few projects from this period that did eventually see the light of day actually turned out to be one of the best ever to pass through HandMade, and a bona fide modern British classic to boot – *Mona Lisa*.

In 1984, Stephen Woolley of Palace Pictures teamed up with maverick Irish film director Neil Jordan to make the haunting fantasy *The Company of Wolves*. A deep and lasting friendship grew from it – they even, for a time, shared a house – and conversation often turned to what they might do next. *Mona Lisa* was conceived from two disparate sources. A tabloid report about a criminal charged with assault, who pleaded that he was protecting young prostitutes from their pimps, first caught their imagination. Neil Jordan says, 'I had this conception of a romantic criminal story, a person imagining himself as a knight in shining armour trying to save these girls from perdition, this terribly naïve point of view, mixed in with a London underworld story.'

Then, one evening, Woolley was watching a television documentary about some Soho sex entrepreneur. 'He came across as being this very wealthy bloke, like a businessman, not at all like a criminal or a rogue. So the idea for *Mona Lisa* came out of this thing about how criminals have changed. How in the Sixties they were like the Michael Caines of *The Italian Job*, and then in the Eighties they were the well-dressed, well-heeled respectable guys, people who would exude the Thatcherite values.'

After thrashing out a rough story treatment, Jordan invited television and film writer David Leland to write a screenplay, having admired his work on the uncompromising *Made in Britain* quartet of TV plays. Leland says, 'I was given a very short synopsis, no more than a third of a page, which outlined the basic story of the film. After some conversations with Steve and Neil, I then wrote a first draft.' But Leland's script did not meet with overall approval. 'Like a lot of David's work,' asserts Jordan, 'it was very, very hard, very realistic, very tough and quite violent, and it kind of missed the romanticism of what I had in mind. I wanted to make a film about the inarticulacy and confusion of male emotions with regard to women, that area of total misunderstanding between both sexes. So I had a go at the script myself and it gradually changed.'

Jordan reworked *Mona Lisa* through six more drafts and Leland was invited back for meetings with both Jordan and Woolley to act as devil's advocate over Jordan's screenplay. 'It was a combination of David's work and my own at the end,' remembers Jordan, 'that's how it grew. The basic crime story was irrelevant, it was in the background. I felt this film was about character, it was about the way people look at themselves rather than what they do. So the movie was kind of a film noir but not a film noir, a love story but not a love story.'

Jordan's protagonist is George, an 'honest' villain who comes out of jail and finds himself in a London underworld where good old-fashioned crime has given way to drug trafficking and child prostitution. Finding a job as a chauffeur-cum-minder to Simone, a black West End hooker, he overcomes personal prejudices about her profession and skin colour and slowly falls in love with her. As originally conceived, George was a much older figure and Jordan and Woolley's first choice was Sean Connery.

Woolley recalls, 'I met Connery by accident in a lift between meetings at Orion raising money for *Absolute Beginners*. We chased him from golf course to golf course, basically, on the phone. He was very accessible and very easy to talk to; I'd literally call him directly on golf courses and he would answer the phone and say he really wanted to do it. He loved the idea of working with Neil. I think John Boorman had told him Neil was extremely talented and John had worked with Sean on *Zardoz*. And I think Sean has got this Celtic thing about Scotland and Ireland and he was really attracted to Neil. But I don't think he was attracted to the part that much.'

Everything changed when Bob Hoskins' name was put forward. 'He seemed to me to be the character,' Jordan concludes. 'I had several conversations with him about it and I rewrote the character with Bob in mind, incorporating his innocence and energy. I would write something and see how he responded to it and then write more dialogue. It was a very fluid experience. He's a brilliant actor and he inhabited that role with the kind of depth that you rarely see in movies.'

Watching the film today, it's almost impossible to see anyone else inhabiting that role other than Bob Hoskins. Woolley believes that 'there's a sensitive side to Bob. Everyone thought of Bob as *The Long Good Friday* and not *Pennies from Heaven*. *Mona Lisa* was much more that gentle side. He's got that anger from *Friday* but he's confused, he's not like a hoodlum, he's someone who's a bit mixed up and doesn't know what's going on and the world has changed around him and he doesn't know how to cope with it. So Bob seemed to be a perfect idea and EMI, who were backing the film, were very keen on Bob. Then EMI pulled out. They suddenly stopped making films, it was a weird period, they just suddenly said, "Sorry, we can't do it." And it was like, "Oh shit, what are we going to do?" '

It was a problem Woolley could've done without, embroiled as he was at the time in the small matter of shooting the overblown musical *Absolute Beginners*, which had unhelpfully been labelled as the saviour of the British film industry. Woolley now faced major problems in raising the £2 million required for *Mona Lisa*. When it came to the funding of UK films, money was a scarce commodity, despite the existence of HandMade and Goldcrest and emerging companies such as Virgin, who were becoming more entrepreneurial in terms of the film business, and also Channel 4 who were forging a reputation for backing original and controversial film subjects … though not *Mona Lisa*.

'Channel 4 never gave us any money,' Woolley reveals. 'They hated Palace. It wasn't until much later that we got serious backing from Channel 4. They rejected *Mona Lisa*, and then later bought it for television from HandMade. That pissed me off. That's why there's a joke in *Mona Lisa* when Bob's watching a porno tape and Robbie Coltrane comes into the caravan and says, "Channel 4, is it?" That's deliberate because Channel 4 rejected it; they said our script was pornographic, they said you shouldn't make this kind of movie.'

Luckily, the line producer on *Absolute Beginners* was David Wimbury, not long back from his Caribbean sojourn on *Water*, who suggested to Ray Cooper that he contact Woolley. Cooper was only too happy to visit the *Beginners* set, fascinated with the eclectic people involved like Gil Evans, David Bowie and Ray Davies. Woolley remembers, 'We had a very entertaining lunch and I started going on about *Mona Lisa* and Bob Hoskins and, of course, HandMade had released *The Long Good Friday* so they were very pro-Bob. So Ray said, "I'll have a talk with Denis." It was a really off-the-cuff thing. EMI literally that week passed on *Mona Lisa*. So Ray took the script, read it, spoke to Denis and I think within two weeks we were sitting in Cadogan Square having a meeting with Denis and doing the deal. It was that fast.'

Neil Jordan had already previously dealt with O'Brien and Cooper; they'd asked him about the possibilities of doing some script rewrites, though nothing came of it, and he was looking forward to working with them proper. According to Jordan, 'HandMade were perceived as kind of a boutique production company. Very well funded, so they seemed to be able to choose their projects quite carefully. They liked *Mona Lisa* a lot, though Denis O'Brien was very concerned about the seedy and the dark nature of it. Ray Cooper was really the creative force that I worked with at HandMade. He was the supporter of the project. And George Harrison was the nicest man in the world; it just seemed that he paid the bills. He was one of the sweetest people I've ever met in my life.'

Although Harrison did not intend to involve himself in the production, he still had to OK the script. Woolley remembers, 'We had lunch and he was absolutely wonderful. He said, "Look, it's not the kind of movie that I really understand completely, but I really love Neil." We talked a lot about the Pope, actually. He didn't like the Pope very much. He didn't like Catholicism. But George was great.'

One thing Harrison was adamant about was nudity. He didn't want any nudity in the film whatsoever. A pretty tall order when your story revolves around Soho, pimps and whores. Jordan says, 'It so happened that the first scene we did in the film was where Bob is in this bath house looking for his boss and he dives into this pool and we had loads of these guys swimming in the pool and, of course, they were naked, as they would be. We couldn't afford proper underwater photography so our cameraman Roger Pratt had this splash camera that you just shove down and vaguely hope to follow what goes on. So, as Bob dived into the water, Roger splashed the camera down and, of course, when we saw the dailies all you see are these dangling penises, about 200 of them. And that was the first shot George saw. He was quite nice about it.'

Things were different with O'Brien. Both he and Stephen Woolley repeatedly clashed over creative matters. It was undoubtedly the worst professional relationship in HandMade's history, one that would continue to reverberate right up until the company's final breath. Wendy Palmer calls it 'a personality clash of the deepest order. Both desperately wanted to be top dog.'

Woolley was one of those who saw Denis purely as a suit. 'Denis was about money. Everybody thought he was this genius with money – give him a fiver and he'll give you 15 quid back. So people were giving him fivers and he was giving them 15 quid back. It was all offshore stuff. I had nothing to do with that. I'm not a money person. I just wanted to get the film made. In my view, Denis saw films as an accountant. It was like factories. There was one factory where people made things, the cameramen, the designers. Then outside of the factory you've got the talent, which was like the crazy professor area where you've got Terry Gilliam and Neil Jordan, you've got writers, the Pythons, they're all doing the crazy clown stuff in there, that's their place. Then you've got the management, you've got Denis and his team of accountants. And anyone like me who's a creative producer doesn't have a home there, you're sort of running from one place to the other, there's no box for you with Denis. He'd say, "What are you doing here?" Wherever you are at any given point, if you're in the factory with the workers, or you're in the playroom with the talent, or if you're in the management office, you're not welcome. After we did the deal, I think Denis must have imagined that would be the last he'd see of me.'

The first rumblings of disquiet were over who to cast in the crucial role of Simone. After extensive tests with numerous actresses, Woolley and Jordan selected Cathy Tyson. Jordan remembers, 'I'd just seen her in a play at the Barbican. The casting director, Sue Figgis, said to me, "Go and see this girl," so I went to see her and she was quite brilliant, quite beautiful. But HandMade didn't want Cathy. They wanted somebody known and Cathy was totally unknown.'

In what Woolley describes as 'one of the most surreal conversations I've ever had in my life', O'Brien told him that he'd been walking past the Odeon Leicester Square and had seen the poster for the latest James Bond film *A View to a Kill* with Roger Moore posing back to back with Grace Jones. There and then he'd had the brainwave of casting the black pop diva as Simone in *Mona Lisa*. 'Can't you imagine it? Bob Hoskins and Grace Jones standing back to back on the poster.' He pitched. Steve and Neil patently couldn't imagine it. Grace Jones was about a foot taller than Hoskins for a start, so it was going to look stupid. But Denis was convinced about Grace Jones and genuinely baffled as to why Palace were determined to have Cathy Tyson, who was not a star and thus had no market value.

'The whole project almost ground to a halt,' Woolley recalls, 'and I had to confront Denis over why we wanted Cathy. Denis said, "OK. I'm going to talk to Ray about it. You have to go away and come back." So we went out for a cup of tea. I had no doubt in my mind about Cathy, I was determined. And Neil was like, "Do you think we should do this? Should we confront him?" ... blah, blah ... "Maybe there's another way around this." Anyway, we went back and Denis spoke directly at Neil, didn't even look at me. He said to Neil, "If you really believe in this actress, then we'll go with it." Not for one moment did he look at me, he was so angry, he was incensed. And that's what the relationship was like all the time; it was lecturing, no eye contact, no sense of ever feeling you were in the room with him. It was a relationship that was so antagonistic and personal, a personal vendetta, and I never understood it.'

After winning the Cathy Tyson battle, the Palace boys were less inclined to go to war when difficulties arose over the music. This being a modern-day movie, it made sense to everyone to incorporate a contemporary pop song. Woolley says, 'So we're talking about it and Denis suggests Phil Collins, and we're sort of wanting to be nice because we'd just all had these battles about Cathy, so we're like, OK, we'll go with Phil Collins. Of course, it's not Phil Collins, it's fucking Genesis. And then Denis signed a deal that we've got to put it in the film, so Neil had to cut a whole little sequence of Bob wandering around to this Genesis track. It was just mortifying. It was so like *not* what we would've done. Denis didn't really have a flair for movies, as such. It was just like somebody told him that Phil Collins was Number 1 in America, so why would you argue with that? Let's do it.'

Besides Cathy Tyson's anonymity with the cinemagoing public, O'Brien also had genuine reason to be concerned about her inexperience. *Mona Lisa* was going to be her film début. But Jordan and Woolley were utterly confident in her natural ability as an actress to be able to cope with the stresses and strains of it all. There was the odd hiccup, though. Jordan remembers, 'Cathy didn't really know what films entailed. There was one scene in a hotel room where Bob runs in smacking around the punter who's tied Cathy to a bed or something and she dresses and runs downstairs and goes out to wait for a car. So we had the camera set up at the hotel room and I did one shot and I turned round to do the next take and look for Cathy and nobody could find her. We went through the entire hotel. Eventually, I walked outside and there she was waiting for the car. And I said, "Cathy, what are you doing out here?" And she said, "I thought we were continuing with the scene." I said, "But the camera's upstairs, Cathy." She said, "Oh, I just thought it followed you." '

The first few weeks of shooting were difficult for the young actress and it was Hoskins who took it upon himself to guide her through the pitfalls of her first movie. 'Bob was fantastic with Cathy,' Woolley recalls, 'he'd give her so much time. He really enjoys working with first-timers, Bob, he's such a genuinely honest nice bloke, he couldn't stop himself helping you. With Cathy, he recognised that for the film to work, and for him to work, she had to work, and therefore he would do anything to make her work. So he was very patient, instructing all the time, never pulled the big star act with her.'

But there was one scene in particular where no amount of soothing would pacify her. It was a sex scene between Simone and George. Jordan had written a scene 'where after she and Bob are attacked in a lift by this pimp they go into her room and they're forced to lie in bed together. They don't have sex but something different happens. But Cathy didn't like being naked. I shot the scene but it didn't quite work. It was a scene that

I couldn't quite get out of her so I cut it. And I suppose, in the end, I concluded it probably wasn't appropriate in the film anyway.'

By this time, Woolley's other production, *Absolute Beginners*, was deep in the editing stage, and deep in trouble, too, with its director Julian Temple barred from the cutting room and the film's main backer Goldcrest in a near state of collapse. Woolley knew that he'd be flitting between the two movies constantly and would need someone to be a rock for him on *Mona Lisa*. So Patrick Cassavetti was brought in to help with the producing chores and filming began in August 1985 on locations around London. Jordan says, 'The most difficult thing in the movie was actually turning London into something that was kind of imaginary. I wanted London to be a character, drawing on the memories of when I went there first as a 17-year-old kid from Ireland, and there was this big metropolis and everything seemed strange and dark and mysterious.'

The Soho area of the capital was used extensively and, prior to shooting, Jordan and Cassavetti busied themselves with research tours of the district, seeing things through the punters' eyes. 'A lot of the stuff in the porn shops we did in a documentary style,' says Jordan. 'At the time, Soho was nothing but porn – it's a much nicer place now. Back then, it was nothing but little clip joints and peep shows. We shot in quite a few of them. It was very sad, really, a lot of the girls were heroin addicts, serving warm champagne to fat men from the North of England. It was quite like the world the film depicted. The proprietors were fine about us shooting there. Like most vaguely criminal enterprises, they like to be glamorised. We got no trouble. Nobody tried to chop our fingers off.'

From this murk and gloom arises George's boss, a filthy flesh peddler called Mortwell, a Dickensian name for a darkly grotesque Dickensian-type villain ... and a radical departure for Michael Caine. Although only appearing in a few scenes, it was a courageous risk for Caine to take on so nasty a piece of work. And, over dinner at Langan's restaurant in Piccadilly, it was Ray Cooper who convinced the star to play Mortwell. 'Michael said, "Well, shall I do it? What's it about then? Come on tell me." I said, "It's a great part. It's a lovely cameo." And he did it which was very sweet of him.'

Palace had wanted Caine for Mortwell almost from the beginning, writing personally to the actor and talking to his agent Denis Selinger, but it was really only after HandMade got on board that Caine was delivered, so important was he to their foreign sales. Jordan recalls, 'At the time, Michael was doing an enormous amount of movies, acting in quite a lot of routine thrillers and, for me, it was interesting because he would come on the set, and we only had him for about a week, and he'd be quite impatient – "OK, we can get through this quickly." And I'd say, "Hang on, Michael, just try this, will you?" And you'd feel he'd want to get it in two or three takes. And then I'd get him to develop it and develop it and suddenly he wouldn't want to go, he'd be into this thing saying, "Let's do it this way, let's try this …" It was like a man who really wanted to act seriously and here was a part he could get his teeth into. It was wonderful working with him because he is such a good actor. It was wonderful actually getting him to express the dark-hearted stuff. Michael loved playing that part.'

Another small but significant piece of casting was Robbie Coltrane as George's equally sad and displaced friend Thomas. Primarily known then as a television comedian, *Mona Lisa* was Coltrane's first dramatic break in movies. 'I'd met Steve Woolley a few times and he thought I would be suitable for the part so arranged an audition. Originally, I was going to play it Cockney but it was Neil that decided on Glaswegian. I can't remember exactly how but I ended up with a spanner in my hand and a 51 Pontiac Fire Chief to drive, so there was no acting required on that account. Neil was always surprisingly unprecious on the dialogue, considering it was his script, and always open to suggestions.'

Coltrane's casting certainly lent extra spice to the general heady creative mix. Woolley recollects, 'It was something of a liability walking around the streets with Neil, Robbie Coltrane and Bob Hoskins. I'd be frightened if we'd pass a pub because Neil could drink for Ireland, Robbie could drink for Scotland and Bob could drink for England.'

Liquid lunches notwithstanding, the entire cast got on extremely well and developed into a tight-knit little group. Coltrane remembers, 'Neil and Bob and Cathy were such good company. I was in awe of Bob, he had done a lot of great work, even then, but he was very friendly, had this great "anti-lovey", let's-get-on-with-the-job attitude, and is very funny so we got on well. I think it shows in the film. It is important to the plot, of course, because my character is Bob's only friend in the film. I remember Bob getting into a major slanging match with someone in the street when we were filming the scene where he trashes his ex-wife's house exterior. They thought it was for real and told him to behave. Being out and about with Bob in London was exhilarating because he is such East End Aristocracy.'

George Harrison also made a brief location visit. He'd been much criticised lately for not making the effort to get involved physically in the movies he financed. One producer told the press that he never met Harrison once and that he would drive up to the location when everyone was at lunch, get out his director's chair, take a few pictures and leave. It was sometimes left to Ray Cooper to impress upon Harrison the importance of putting in the odd personal appearance, meeting the troops, as it were, in the field. 'It was always nice when George went on the location and he knew that. And he would always be very generous, without interfering, and it was always a big boost for actors and actresses who hadn't met him to see him. He was always extremely kind to them and interested in what they were doing.' As for O'Brien, he was practically invisible. Woolley says, 'I don't think I ever saw him on set once. He wouldn't be on set, that would be like the management being with the workers. He lived in Cadogan Square with the money. He was too busy making the money work.'

He did, however, occasionally make an appearance at the rushes. And, like Harrison, he did not take kindly to the underwater 'knobs' shot. 'Denis looked at the rushes and didn't like them,' Woolley remembers, 'was very obtuse in his comments, was not nice about anything in the film. And there was a shot of Bob's penis which caused a lot of laughter in the rushes because you start off with this crotch shot and somebody said, "I know whose dick that is ... that's Bob's," and the camera pans up to Bob and it was very funny. And Denis said, "What are you doing shooting that kind of thing? You won't get a rating in America." And I said, "Of course you will." And we had this huge argument.'

But the big confrontation was yet to come. O'Brien envisaged the film as ending in Brighton, where George has tracked down Simone, and there's a brutal bloodbath in which she shoots Mortwell. This was followed by a shot of Bob rushing down to the beach. O'Brien wanted the film to end at that dramatic moment. Woolley says, 'They were literally coming into the cutting room and telling the editor what to do with the film, which to my mind was fucking ridiculous. And people like Ray Cooper, who I really did have a good relationship with, I really loved Ray, were doing his bidding because Ray was being paid by Denis. You see, Denis had people cornered, very few people would go against Denis because of the fiver to 15 quid trick, that's how he got his power. He was a man who could do a lot for you and so when Denis asked you to do a small thing, like "Oh, can you cut the end of the film off?" people would try and do it. So there was a lot of argy-bargy going on.'

Contractually, HandMade had final cut, so technically O'Brien had every right to see his demands carried through. He had, after all, fully financed the picture. Palace only had the UK distribution rights, which they had insisted on during their first meeting with O'Brien, in return for which Woolley and his partner Nick Powell took very low producing fees. But on this point, Woolley was fighting on principle and confronted O'Brien. 'Look, if you cut the end of the film, it's just about this whore who's, like, evil.' O'Brien turned to Woolley and, with utmost seriousness, said, 'Well, what else is it about? It's about a whore who deserves her comeuppance.'

That take on the movie was about a million miles from Woolley and Jordan's; their preferred ending had Tyson returning to see Bob one last time to explain her motives. 'So it's not about all that anger that happened in Brighton,' Woolley explains, 'and you realise that George has come on a journey. At the beginning of the film, you see him as a racist, a person who hates women. At the end of the film, he's someone who understands a person who's both black and a woman. So this was about someone who was able to change through the events that he saw, that his view of the world was probably not the best view to have. That was a really important thing to me and I would have done anything to stop Denis destroying the film.'

By this time, O'Brien had acquired a reputation for 'meddling' in post-production. Certainly he enjoyed and, to some, exploited his position as executive producer. Perhaps such behaviour was merely an extension of his personality, in that he was a very impulsive and decisive man. Wendy Palmer believes, 'Denis was a man who never doubted himself for a second. He was autocratic and didn't brook any arguments. And what he used to do when he got into the cutting room was terrible. He'd get a video and he'd cut the films himself. He'd go into the video-editing suite with a video of the rough cut and play around for a weekend and come up with his own version. He did that a few times. He might even have done that to *Mona Lisa*. It was horrifying. Then he'd hand them the video cassette and say, "Here it is." That used to get people cross. And people wouldn't watch it. There'd be all sorts of rumpuses over that. That was one of his favourite things to do.'

Though, to be truthful, it's difficult when you hold the purse strings not to want to impose your own views on a production if you have a vision yourself of what it should be like. But in the opinion of many, O'Brien took this privilege to extremes. Gilliam's viewpoint is, 'Post-production, that's the time as a film-maker when you're most vulnerable. You've just spent a year working on this thing, you're actually shagged out, and now this guy is telling you stuff and you say, "Look at the films that have come before and they've been big successes, maybe he knows what he's talking about." And you're very vulnerable then and I think Denis abused that position.'

But with Palace, O'Brien had more than met his match. Unbeknown to him, Woolley had a major ace up his sleeve. He was close friends with both Chris Blackwell, head honcho of Island, and Carey Brocal, who ran Island's film distribution arm Island Alive which planned to release *Mona Lisa* in the States. Woolley knew how important the American distribution for *Mona Lisa* was to HandMade's financing and personally showed the film to Brocal and informed him of the problems it was facing. Brocal reached for the phone and made a personal call to O'Brien, stating that if the ending of the film was altered in any way, Island would refuse to distribute it in America.

'And, of course, Denis went bonkers,' Woolley grins, 'and I don't think we've ever spoken since then. I was in LA and I got Carey to make the call and Denis was dining at Balmoral. We're not sure who he was dining with but it's rumoured to have been the Queen Mother. And he said, "Don't call me on this number unless it's an emergency." And I said to Carey Brocal, "Call him, it's an emergency. Call him now." And we got him out of dinner with the Queen Mother. And we won. He never changed the ending. When it came down to it, Island Alive's advance was more important to HandMade than their opinion of what should or shouldn't be in the film.'

As the film geared up for release, word of mouth within the industry was of nothing else but Bob Hoskins. Like *The Long Good Friday*'s Harold Shand, Hoskins made George his own, vulnerable and poignant, yet in a flash capable of head-butting a thug or smashing a pimp's face in. It was a sensational performance, one of the best given by a British actor during the 1980s. And Hoskins was suitably rewarded for it. He was voted Best Actor by the Los Angeles Film Critics and the National Society of Film Critics in New York. He also received a coveted Golden Globe. Hoskins was his usual self-effacing and joking self about such triumphs. 'Usually, all an award means is that it puts you out of work for 18 months because no one thinks they can afford you.'

When *Mona Lisa* was entered into competition at Cannes, Hoskins became the first English actor for two decades to receive the Best Actor Award. He'd arrived at the French resort with his wife and Neil Jordan, but left again for London after the film's gala showing. Woolley recalls, 'I didn't leave Cannes. Denis and everybody else had pissed off and I said, "No, we're going to win this award." And then they all flooded back on the Monday when he won it. I said to Neil, "I'm not going back. I'm not getting on the flight. I'm staying because I think Bob's going to win it. How can he not win?" I loved the film so much, how could these people not give him the award? So we stayed and Bob did win it and they had to bring Bob back on a private plane.

'Cannes was also hilarious because we'd walk down the Croissette and Denis would come towards me and then he would cross the road just so he wouldn't have to acknowledge my existence. We just really, really upset him.'

Mona Lisa opened in the States in June 1986 to good business for a British movie. The critical reaction was extraordinary, and fully justified. 'Neil Jordan has chiselled a dark, sleazily glamorous gem,' oozed *Newsweek*; *USA Today* acclaimed 'The most affecting love story in recent memory'; *LA Weekly* thought Hoskins had given 'the performance of the year'; and *Village Voice* declared that 'if *Mona Lisa* doesn't grant Hoskins semi-stardom, nothing will'.

The film's modest but significant success in America did much to raise the profile of Neil Jordan, essentially putting his name on the international movie map. 'It did well all over the world. I never saw any money out of it, but it did very well. It was at a time when independent movies like that never got released in the States, really. Looking back on it today, I think it's quite lovely. Every time I see a movie that I've made, I can't disconnect it from the person I was at the time. So, to me, it's a perfect expression of all those emotions I was going through at the time.'

The success of *Mona Lisa* also did much for the profile of Palace Pictures who, certainly in media circles, seemed to be the ones getting all of the plaudits. Another case of HandMade not banging its drum loud enough. Brian Shingles recalls, 'The Palace boys had problems with Denis. It was HandMade's money that made *Mona Lisa* and they took the acclaim and glory for it and that really infuriated Denis and everybody else.'

Opening in London in September, where it broke the all-time house record at the Odeon Haymarket, *Mona Lisa* played successfully across Britain and garnered near universal press acclaim. 'A film of the first rank which sets a benchmark for British cinema,' said the *Daily Telegraph*. The *Mail on Sunday* regarded the film as 'the most extraordinary movie to come from Britain this year'. Not surprisingly, Hoskins received the lion's share of the plaudits. 'It is a performance of remarkable subtlety, observation and compassion and it puts him in the forefront of contemporary British actors,' said the *Sunday Express*.

Mona Lisa was indeed the making of Bob Hoskins. His new status was confirmed when that year's Oscar nominations were revealed and he found himself in the exalted company of Paul Newman, William Hurt and James Woods for the Best Actor Award. No one, least of all Hoskins himself, was really surprised when Newman won for *The Color of Money*. Six times nominated, surely the Academy weren't going to shaft him a seventh time. Consolation arrived at the British Academy Awards. The ceremony was held at some grand West End hotel and Bob won. He'd been the favourite. But, even in victory, the chasm between the two sets of film-makers responsible for *Mona Lisa* was plain to see. Woolley remembers, 'There was me, Nick and Neil on one table, and Denis O'Brien and all the HandMade people and Bob Hoskins on the other table. It was a real "us" and "them". And I think we even had to buy our own table for the BAFTAs.'

Mona Lisa remains the archetypal Bob Hoskins movie. It's a piece of work of which he is as proud as anything else he has accomplished in cinema. 'If I popped off tomorrow,' he once said, 'I would feel that I'd left something behind that was worth it.' It's a sentiment shared by others. Coltrane says, 'I loved doing *Mona Lisa*. It was the first time I had done a proper movie with people I really identified with. It established me in a cache of players, like Jim Broadbent, who ended up in a raft of interesting British films of the Eighties. I am eternally grateful. The only hard part for me was when they cut a Jaguar in two to make filming easier! We used to play Mona Lisa on the radio, the only thing that still worked, to help our concentration. It's tough on those low-loaders, there is a lot of noise and the crew are very close, plus people shout and peep their horns, and then the background doesn't match, so there are always lots of takes, so you go round the route again. So we'd rewind the tape, have a quick blast of old Nat and we'd be ready for take ten. Whenever I hear that song, I'm right there in the Jag. Happy memories.'

CHAPTER 9

SHANGHAI COCK-UP

In 1985, Sean Penn and Madonna were the biggest celebrity couple on earth, the Burton and Taylor of the MTV generation (minus the charm). You didn't have to be Einstein to comprehend the potential box-office bonanza that awaited anyone lucky enough or with sufficient balls to grab them both to star in a movie together. Prior to them tying the knot that August, Penn and Madonna had already rejected a number of film roles, notably *Blind Date*, later a massive hit for Bruce Willis and Kim Basinger. It wasn't until they were personally approached by George Harrison to star in *Shanghai Surprise* that the couple found a project to their mutual liking.

Based on the novel *Faraday's Flowers* by Tony Kenrick, the plot of *Shanghai Surprise* is a mixture of a 1930s screwball comedy and *The African Queen* as a missionary nurse gets tangled up with a fortune-hunter out to steal opium and jewels from Chinese warlord gangsters. Hollywood producer John Kohn owned the property and wanted a Briton to helm it, sending the script to Jim Goddard, a highly respected TV director whose work on *Reilley, Ace of Spies* had so impressed Kohn. Goddard had never directed a feature film before. As it happened, Denis O'Brien had recently offered Goddard a project with HandMade, but it hadn't been something he'd wanted to do. Instead, Goddard sent O'Brien the *Shanghai* script. The next thing Kohn knew, O'Brien was on the telephone offering to back the entire project to the tune of $17 million. It was the biggest gamble HandMade had ever undertaken, their first venture into the realm of big-budget features. Certainly, it showed their commitment to UK film production. But there were many insiders, Harrison included, who were dubious about the project from the start. So, too, were the money men. With no stars signed up by this stage, the project almost floundered. Shingles recalls, '*Shanghai* was within days of closing down, of the project being dumped. It was only when Penn and Madonna signed up at the last minute the film really swung into action.'

Kohn had worked with Sean Penn twice before, in an executive capacity on *Bad Boys* and then as producer on *Racing with the Moon*: 'So I knew Sean very well and so I used Sean to get his wife, to get Madonna. Finally, I think she said, "Well, if I do it, *you've* got to do it." I don't know whether Sean was ever really in love with that role but, once she wanted to do it, I guess she talked him into doing it. Madonna reminded me a lot of Judy Holliday, whom I knew very well. Unfortunately, she didn't turn out to be Judy Holliday, who was an angel. One thing I'll never forget after we'd signed Sean Penn and Madonna, I took them out to dinner to celebrate and suddenly into the restaurant comes George Harrison and sits in the booth with us. And Madonna was so astounded and open-mouthed. George was his usual charming self, welcoming them on the picture and saying how he was looking forward to working with them, and then he left. And I remember Madonna said, "There goes a legend." '

The casting of Penn and Madonna was a massive coup for HandMade. No other British film company then operating managed to pull off anything quite like it. Interestingly, neither were Kohn's first choices for the film. 'I wanted to go for Tom Hanks. He'd just made his first hit picture *Splash*. But Denis thought, and he was right, that it would be a bigger talking point having Sean and Madonna together.'

O'Brien's keen commercial mind realised the huge publicity benefits of a film package that combined Penn and Madonna. But there was a downside – being the most famous couple in the world meant that everywhere they went hordes of press and photographers followed. It was the plague of the paparazzi and the consequences for the film were to be disastrous.

In January 1986, Penn and Madonna touched down in Shanghai. It was early in the morning and, unable to sleep, both ended up taking a walking tour of the city. Dawn had yet to break through but already the parks were filled with people doing their slow motion tai chi exercises. It was almost dream-like. Such serenity was shattered when the couple flew on to Hong Kong where the bulk of location shooting was to be carried out. The Shanghai authorities had refused any filming in their city because of Madonna's raunchy image. It was really only a matter of time before the press caught up with them.

The *Hong Kong Standard*, an English language tabloid, offered a $500 reward for information on Madonna's whereabouts. Frustrated that nothing was forthcoming, the paper's proprietor, Leonel Borralho, took matters into his own hands and waited for the couple to return to their suite on the eighteenth floor of the luxurious Oriental Hotel in Macao. When the lift door opened, Barralho jumped out and started taking pictures. Penn went ballistic and, in the ensuing mêlèe, a camera strap got entangled around Barralho's neck.

Penn then had to be forcibly held back by his own bodyguard. Barralho was not allowed to leave until he handed over the film, which he eventually did in exchange for the promise of an exclusive interview with the couple. When it dawned on him that no such interview was ever going to take place, Barralho filed assault charges against Penn and sued for damages of $1 million.

Angry and bitter that they were once again in the spotlight, thinking the paparazzi wouldn't pursue them to mainland China ('We thought we'd be safe here,' said Madonna), the film's veteran publicist, Chris Nixon, came up with his solution to pacify the growing sense of ill-will the production was generating. Penn was already being pilloried in the local press as 'the ugly American'. Nixon's idea was to get the couple to pose briefly for photographers in the hope that once they'd got what they wanted they might leave them alone. Penn wasn't playing ball. 'This film doesn't need publicity,' he insisted. 'People will go and see it because we are in it.' Penn demanded that Nixon be fired. He was.

The first real hint that everyone was in for a very bumpy ride occurred on the opening day of shooting in Hong Kong. The unit had employed a 19-year-old called Rupert, fresh from public school, to be the runner or general dogsbody. At six o 'clock in the morning he knocked on the door of Penn and Madonna's massive trailer where they were inside getting made up. 'Come in,' said a voice. Rupert entered and there was Sean Penn scowling at his appearance in the mirror. 'Good morning,' starts Rupert, 'Mr Goddard has asked me to come and let you know that there's absolutely no rush at all this morning. It's very relaxed. As and when you feel that you're happy with the make-up, he's asked me to say would you let us know that you're ready to start and I can show you down to the set where Mr Goddard would like to show you the first set-up. But, like I said, there's absolutely no rush, all the time in the world, bags of time. I'll just be outside the trailer should you need me. Oh, is there anything I can get for you now? No? Fine. Well, if you need me for anything, I'll just be outside.'

Although Penn's and Madonna's eyes never strayed from Rupert the whole time he was speaking, neither deigned to utter a single syllable as the eager-to-please runner backed out of the trailer ... thrilled ... first day on the job, he'd been in a trailer with Sean Penn and Madonna, what other 19-year-old gets to do that and get paid for it? After about eight seconds, a voice from within said, '*Discuss.*'

A perplexed Rupert tapped on the door. 'I beg your pardon, did you say something?'

Still looking in the mirror, Penn locked eyes with Rupert and said again, '*Discuss.*'

Rupert said, 'I'm sorry, I'm not quite up to speed. I've missed something. May I ask, discuss what?'

Penn answered, 'Go down to the set. Go to Mr Goddard and you tell him that, when we are good and ready, we are happy to move. And we will come down to the set and we will *discuss* the first set-up.'

Day one. Shot one.

Having succeeded in firing the unit publicist, Sean Penn next turned his sights on Bernard Hill, the actor who had been cast personally by Jim Goddard to play the villain of the piece. Hill's first scenes were with Richard Griffiths and shot in Macao. It was an elaborate sequence, recreating the nightmarish exodus of Shanghai's inhabitants as the Japanese army invades, and involved some 4,000 extras, 200 horses and cattle, and huge pyrotechnics. Hill and Griffiths were seated in rickshaws loaded with dope trying to get through the enormous crowd, looking like tiny little boats bobbing up and down in a sea of humanity. After six nights of strenuous shooting, the scene was in the can.

As cast and crew caught the hydrofoil back to Hong Kong, it emerged that Hill had been sacked and replaced by another actor – Paul Freeman. Griffiths says, 'It was none of my business. The only reason my heart sank was that it was my door that was pounded at 3.00am with this howling Wookie, like Chewbacca, banging on my fucking door, out of his mind, saying, "They've sacked me. I'm fired." And I'm sitting there thinking, Fucking brilliant, because if Bernard's sacked, I can't work any longer so they'll have to sack me and I'll get a cheque and I can go home, which I've never had before, which is heaven. You see, by then I'd already kind of lost it with the picture. You can imagine how bad a state Bernard Hill was in. Very few English actors have ever been sacked off a movie for acting reasons, which he was, patently, clearly, by the influence of Sean Penn.'

Amazingly, Hill had been fired without even playing a scene opposite Sean Penn, or Madonna for that matter. Bernard Hill states, 'Penn just saw the rushes. As one artist to another, you don't do that kind of thing, unless there's something seriously wrong with you. I haven't met Sean Penn – and I'd really like to.' Neither did Hill get to meet Denis O'Brien until much later, despite attempts to track him down, as he'd begun to suspect that studio politics might have had some part to play in his dismissal, 'Eventually, though, I did get to have a long conversation with O'Brien and I said, "I'm not sure what the truth is. I suspect what it is, I've been told what it is, but I'd like to hear it officially from you." And he wouldn't come out with it because it was obviously too political, he couldn't do it.'

The whole tawdry experience left Hill disillusioned and angry: 'It kind of set me back for a long time. My instinctive reaction was to pack the whole business in because I thought I just don't want to come across this kind of crap again. I would have sued them in a breath. A couple of years afterwards I thought, Actually, that's what I should have done. I should have nailed them to the wall. Given the reasons for the dismissal, which were just paltry. At the time I said, "If you let me get sacked, your film's fucked, basically, because Penn and Madonna will just think they can do what they like – and they did.'

Paul Freeman had, in fact, screen-tested for the part of the villain at the same time as Hill. The actor was at home when the call came through that he was urgently needed in Hong Kong. When Richard Griffiths was told that Freeman was flying in to replace Hill, he went cold, he says, 'Because they'd sacked Bernard the night before and the day after his replacement was landing, which meant that the decision had had to have been taken the week before because Paul Freeman arrived with his wardrobe and make-up stuff. He'd had all that work done during the previous week in London. So we were doing all those night shoots which were all doomed because the guy in the middle of it, Bernard Hill, was already sacked and didn't know it. And that was Sean Penn's doing. So Bernard got the cheque and went off gnashing his teeth. Lucky bastard. And the rest of us had to carry on.'

Tensions were rising, too, among the largely British crew while they watched, sometimes disbelievingly, as Sean Penn began flexing his muscles on the set and calling the shots. Griffiths remembers, 'Sean had this ace of trumps. He'd play the ace of trumps, win the trick and then put it back up his sleeve and then when the next drama was played, he'd pull out the ace of trumps. And the ace of trumps was this – in Madonna's contract, and Penn was very sore about this because he saw himself as the star of the movie, there was a clause and it said Madonna shall have the casting approval of her leading man. In other words, if you don't do what I say, says Sean Penn, I quit and, if I quit, she won't agree with any other guy playing my part because, hey, she's my wife, and you don't have a movie, so go and fuck yourselves. Do as I say or I'm out of here. Boy, did he know how to manipulate that situation with Madonna.'

According to Bernard Hill, the crew codenamed the two stars Victor and Daisy. 'It was interesting because they had two trailers and they used to put their initials on the door of each trailer and when you put the trailers side by side it said "VD".'

Not unnaturally, Penn's brazen attitude brought him into direct conflict with Goddard and there was only ever going to be one winner. John Kohn's perspective was that 'Sean and Madonna were a little bit upset because they didn't think the picture was going the right way, which it wasn't, and they started giving the director a very hard time, they made his job very hard.

And I think the director was a bit in awe of them. The two actors sensed that he could be pushed around. Penn made life difficult. The director was wounded and he kept sticking a knife in as much as he could and I tried to keep them apart, reminding Sean that he's got to be professional in every respect. And sometimes I could and sometimes I couldn't.'

Penn knew this was Goddard's début movie and exploited that heartlessly, thinking he could do a better job than the man who had actually been hired. Griffiths remarks, 'And as you can see from *The Indian Runner*, Penn's début film as a director, he's got no fucking taste and he's an arsehole. At one point, John Kohn said, "I talked to Sean's dad one time and you know he said to me, 'The trouble with Sean is, he has never known adversity.'"And he just had this towering, mountainous confidence which was underpinned by not the greatest talent I've ever seen on the cinematic screen.'

Back in London, George Harrison was monitoring the situation with growing disdain and was finally left with no option but to fly out to the set to pacify matters. It was something of an embarrassment for HandMade, having recently been honoured by the *Evening Standard* newspaper with a special Outstanding Contribution to British Films Award, to be seen legging it halfway across the world to save one of its own films from going down the pan. 'First they'd brought Alan Ladd Jnr out from Hollywood,' Griffiths recalls, 'and Sean Penn told him to fuck off. And the only thing that kept it going was when George came up because the pair of them had the most infinite respect for George because he was a Beatle. And that was the only reason that the movie kept going ahead, because of their respect for George.'

Harrison felt incredibly awkward about the position he'd been forced into. It went against his nature and was something he could well have lived without. Ray Cooper says, 'George at that point had stopped smoking. And he started again, unfortunately, after that. Denis was using George not only as co-owner of HandMade Films, but also as clout with Madonna and Sean Penn. It's not the way you do it, I don't think. George didn't want to be a threat, he just wanted to see the film done. And it was a mess. It wasn't a particularly interesting film, unfortunately, but George was committed, because of the money, to getting this film finished.' Cooper is convinced that *Shanghai Surprise* was the turning point in HandMade's fortunes. It was never to be the same again.

As filming continued in Hong Kong, other unforeseen external problems threatened to undo the film. Local mobsters began seeking huge pay-offs in exchange for access to film in certain areas of the city. Kohn recalls, 'We'd been shooting all night with Sean and Madonna on this pier in a lagoon. At 5.30 in the morning we packed up and started to leave but there was this car blocking the exit and it wouldn't move. Now, I had a lot of electricians and crew guys and they said, "We'll just throw the car off the road." And our guide said, "Don't do that. Don't touch the car. Don't do anything like that, you'll get in trouble." So we finally bargained, I don't know how much money it was, but it cost us to get that car out of the road. Now, things like that started to happen, and what we found out was there isn't just one organised triad, each area of Hong Kong has their own triad. So if I knew I was gonna shoot in a certain area I'd find out who ran the triad in that area and try to make a deal with him, but that didn't guarantee that if you shot in another part of Hong Kong you weren't going to get some kind of harassment.'

This kind of procedure was unorthodox to say the least and burdened the production with a headache they just didn't need. At no time was anyone's life threatened, it was more along the lines of "Your film may get exposed", or at one point a generator was sabotaged forcing the set to close down. But this kind of thing carried on throughout the unit's time in Hong Kong. Paul Freeman remembers, 'One of the location manager's jobs was to sort out this problem, but in a sense it was impossible. Quite heavy-duty men would arrive and demand more money when they'd already been paid off.'

Some of the locals hired for the film also turned out to be less than helpful. One stunt, involving jumping into a river, badly backfired. 'That was scary,' Griffiths recalls. 'One of the stuntmen nearly died. There were these bastard Chinese frogmen who were supposed to jump in if there was a problem and rescue our boys, but they wouldn't go in so the stunt co-ordinator dived in and got this stuntman out. And when he got out he screamed, "Those bastard, fucking Chinese. I'm sacking the lot of them." I said, "Why didn't they go in?" He said, "They didn't tell us but this stretch of river is infamous for water snakes." And, of course, the water is the colour of mulligatawny soup; once you're in it, you can't see a fucking thing. And this stunt guy went down about 20 feet with weights on his body, he couldn't get the weighted belt off and the current was dragging him down. The stunt co-ordinator was screaming at the divers to go in and get him and that was when they said no. They thought it would be OK just to collect the money and piss off. So he dived in, into the murky depths, he had no idea where he was, he just followed the safety line the stuntman had on, followed it down and grabbed him, helped him slide off the belt and they shot to the surface. The stuntman had taken a lung full of water. They got it out but, of course, it's shit river water and he was never the same. I think he was hospitalised for months. It was desperate.'

Just as desperate was the fact that a family of large black rats had made a home underneath Madonna's trailer. Such adversities were sometimes too much to bear. 'I kept saying, "I can't wait 'til I can look back on all this," ' Madonna said later. 'It was a survival test.' This coupled with her insecurities about any acting talent she might possess sparked rumours about whether the marriage would survive the experience. But, if anything, it brought them closer, each taking it in turns to be strong. According to Kohn, 'As big a novice as Sean was to the music business, so Madonna was a big novice to the film business. This was Sean's area of expertise and he taught her the ropes about movie-making. He was breaking her in, so to speak, in the various routines of film-making.'

It was nice to see as a couple they were a mighty force and clearly very much in love. 'Madonna worshipped the ground Sean Penn trod on,' Griffiths adds. 'There was much shagging in the marsh. I often wondered if that was part of her fitness programme.'

When the picture moved to England in late February for interiors at Shepperton Studios, and also the disused sanatorium HandMade employed for *Scrubbers*, the problem with the press exploded into farce. It started the moment they touched down at Heathrow. Reporters who'd been waiting hours in the pouring rain swooped on the couple's motorcade and in the crush a *Sun* photographer fell beneath the wheels of Madonna's Mercedes limo, badly injuring his foot. Meanwhile, an untroubled Penn was keeping another aggressive photographer at bay in his own unique manner, by spitting at him.

From day one until shooting finished, there was a tense stand-off between the Penns and members of the British press. Occasionally, it would flare up into violence. Reporters were shoved, beaten and at one point had fire hoses turned on them by the star's minders when they encroached too near. The tabloids retaliated by dubbing the pair 'the Poison Penns'. Griffiths admits, 'I have to say the press were perfectly wicked in the usual paparazzic way of theirs. They treat you like shit and you react and boil over and there's the story. Or you ignore them and then they come and treat you like shit until you react and there's the story again. And they can keep doing that with someone who's got virtually no fuse like Sean Penn.'

The press knew this and exploited it, hounding the couple wherever they went. Freeman says, 'We were shooting in mid-winter with snow on the ground, but the press were there at six o clock in the morning when we arrived to start work, and jeering at them trying to get some reaction. Very unpleasant, actually, the whole thing. I had a lot of sympathy for them because they were really hounded. The producer wasn't very sensitive, I didn't think, to their problems with the press. For instance, he would come in during shooting and show them what the front page of the *Daily Mirror* had said, which seemed bad timing to say the least. I had a sense that perhaps the producers thought that they were usefully employing publicity and, in fact, rather the reverse was true. I think they got so much adverse publicity by the time the film came out everyone was sick and tired of it.'

At one location near London, some 80 press men with cameras crouched on a wall about 20 yards away from the action; it was as near as they could get. Griffiths observes, 'Literally, the unit vehicles had been put into a circle and the press were like Indians on the war path. And they were crying out things like, "Hey, Madonna, I suppose a fuck would be out of the question?" Sean and Madonna were sitting having a coffee in my trailer and these calls were coming in and I said, "Now, please don't react to them. These wicked things that they're saying are designed entirely to get you mad, for you then to do something rash. And all it is, is they get a fucking photo or a story and they don't care whether you live or die, so just ignore them." But it was so tough.'

One tabloid offered ridiculous money for anyone who could sneak a photograph from off the set. 'So every now and then,' Griffiths says, 'a little selection of polaroids would appear nicked from the continuity book by some pieces of shit on the crew. I say "pieces of shit", but it was a big temptation. But it was so evil.'

When Penn and Madonna found out, the predictable fireworks ensued and they refused to go to work until the thief was identified. Denis O'Brien rushed to the location and pleaded with the pair for several hours before they finally relented to resume shooting.

Harrison was by now losing patience with the expensive delays his film was incurring and all the negative press attention. Seizing the initiative, he announced a press conference at a West End hotel in the hope of smoothing things over. The trouble was, Madonna was an hour late and Penn didn't show up at all. Inside, 75 journalists were crammed in from newspapers spanning the globe. All TV and radio reporters had been barred. Despite some hostile questions (and answers), Harrison's gambit worked – the event made headlines around the world. *People* magazine even carried a picture of Harrison and Madonna on its cover. And for the remainder of the shoot, the Penns were more or less left in comparative peace. For a man who was known for his hermit-like stance to publicity and the press in general, this was a savvy piece of PR manipulation on Harrison's part.

Despite all this, it wasn't the press who was the film's greatest enemy. Penn continued to behave in a difficult way. From the very first day of shooting, he came on to the set with his own director's viewfinder. He'd also 'volunteer' his own opinion of how scenes should be done, telling Goddard, who was making episodes of *The Sweeney* when Penn was still in shorts, where to position the camera. Penn also enjoyed great sway over Madonna. The two stars shared the same make-up artist but it was Penn who always insisted on getting his make-up done before hers, regardless of whose scenes were to be shot first, meaning that Madonna was invariably late on set. And whenever Goddard gave Madonna a note, she'd turn to her husband and ask, 'What do you think?' and more likely he'd rubbish it. Now, if Penn is telling the director what he has to do, then who on earth's in a position to tell Penn what he's doing wrong? It was a recipe for disaster. Freeman recalls, 'I think Sean Penn wielded as much control on the set as he wanted to. I know he was talking about getting rid of Jim Goddard but was persuaded not to do it. But Goddard also didn't behave very sensibly. He was sort of making rather stupid jokes while Madonna was around which I thought was bizarre. I think he didn't know how to handle them at all, really.'

Penn's entire approach to *Shanghai Surprise* can be encapsulated in one incident. It was a scene where his character is confronted with a newspaper photograph that reveals one of the villains of the film. He was to look at the paper, then we see a close-up of the picture and then Penn's reaction to it. Because no actor had yet been cast in the villain's role, the art department didn't have any photograph to use in the bit of newspaper. Griffiths reveals, 'Sean took one look at this and said, "Where's the picture?" and they said, "We haven't got the picture yet because the guy hasn't been cast." Penn continued, "Well, if you haven't got the picture, how can I do the scene?" We said, "We don't see it. We see it's a piece of newspaper, that's all we see, and then we're going to do a close-up of the picture from your point of view and then the audience will know who it is. So it doesn't really matter what the picture is now because nobody can see it. I mean, sure, there's a picture there but no one can see that it's not the real one." And Penn said, "If I can't have the right props, how can I do the scene? I'm not doing the scene." And he walked off the set and we lost an entire day's shooting. So fuck Sean Penn.'

Perhaps for the first time HandMade's 'policy' of giving first-time directors a chance backfired. What was needed on so mammoth a production as *Shanghai Surprise*, that incorporated two equally sizeable egos, was a seasoned pro who wasn't going to take any bullshit and who commanded everyone's respect. Goddard, through no fault of his own, lacked both of those qualities and was put into an impossible position by HandMade. His career never fully recovered. Any thoughts he may have had of a career in feature films was more or less wiped out. To this day, even with close colleagues, he refuses to discuss the matter.

It is ironic indeed that a film which generated more press brouhaha than arguably any other film during the 1980s should engender such total apathy on the part of the paying public when it finally hit cinemas. MGM, who'd picked up *Shanghai* for the USA, knew they had a total brick on their hands and dumped the film quickly and unceremoniously rather than waste millions on advertising trying to buy an audience. After three weeks on release, *Shanghai Surprise* had barely scraped past the $1 million mark and was averaging less than $1,000 a week per theatre. 'That's awful,' claimed James Greenberg of *Variety*. 'I've rarely seen a worse opening.'

The American critics, not surprisingly, tore the film to shreds. *USA*

Today's verdict was 'Sean Penn packs more punches in real life than he does on the screen. It should head straight into the rent-a-turkey department of video stores.' The *New York Times* blasted, 'The nicest thing about *Shanghai Surprise* is that you can watch it in near total privacy. At one screening, there were barely enough bystanders to make up a baseball team.' One reviewer in Cleveland wrote that the film was 'awesome in its awfulness, momentous in its ineptness and shattering in its stupidity.' Critics also complained about the surprising lack of sparks or romantic chemistry between the stars.

To add to its woes, *Shanghai Surprise* also made a undignified strong showing at the annual Razzie awards, a sort of alternative Oscars devoted to crap movies. The film was nominated in the Worst Actor, Director, Song, Screenplay and Picture categories. Madonna claimed the prize for Worst Actress.

The writing, though, had already been on the wall. When your two stars start bad-mouthing your movie before it opens, you know you've got problems. Before its première, Penn and Madonna had virtually disowned *Shanghai Surprise*, infuriating HandMade and MGM. 'The director turned out not to know what he was doing,' Madonna bitched. 'We were on a ship without a captain, and we were so miserable while we were working that I'm sure it shows. It was a great learning experience, that's all I can say.'

Penn and Madonna also refused to promote the film in any way, shape or form. Harrison had personally asked Madonna to produce a video to tie-in with the film, hopefully to help sell the movie to her legion of fans through MTV, but she declined. Having defended them before a hostile British press, Harrison felt they were now both turning their backs on him. There was the definite smell of betrayal in the air and, after the film crashed, Harrison was uncharacteristically curt in summing up the two stars. 'Penn is a pain in the ass,' he complained to the *Hollywood Reporter*. Of Madonna, as quoted in *Cleo* magazine, he said, 'All this aloofness and star stuff … it's bullshit. I'm not trying to be nasty, she's probably got a lot in her that she hasn't even discovered yet, but she has to realise that you can be a fabulous person and be humble as well.'

In October, three months after bombing in the States, *Shanghai Surprise* finally made it over to Britain. It needn't have bothered, vanishing as it did without trace from the nation's screens, though not before being smugly slagged off by the papers. The *Evening Standard* branded the film 'Chinese junk', while the *Daily Telegraph* called it 'a milk pudding of a movie'. The *Sunday Express* thought the charisma Sean Penn displayed in his role 'was about as detectable as a distant pinhead viewed through the wrong end of a telescope'.

Bernard Hill, still smarting from his dismissal, took no comfort in seeing *Shanghai* flop so spectacularly: 'I felt it was just an absolute fucking shame that it had been ruined by a couple of people who you thought might have known better, but given the light of revelation, you realise they're never going to know better. It was a real shame because a lot of people put a lot of hard work into it.'

Despite all the problems, *Shanghai Surprise* didn't turn out to be HandMade's *Revolution,* the big-budget film that helped bring down Goldcrest. They were fortunate that the deal Denis set up for *Shanghai* made sure it couldn't cripple the company. Brilliantly, he managed to protect his investment by pre-selling the film in most territories so it was not HandMade but the distributors who suffered the losses. After the commercial failures of *Bullshot*, *Privates on Parade* and others, O'Brien had shrewdly learnt that, wherever possible, he should pre-sell his movies worldwide, something that was becoming more and more of a universal practice, especially among the independents. Pre-selling overcame the problem of having all your investment out there and then waiting for the profits to trickle back slowly. Palmer says, 'If we could, we'd always pre-sell our movies, although Denis, if he didn't get the right money, was perfectly happy gambling. He was a big gambler. But with *Shanghai*, that was like fighting them off. It was the hottest thing. When Madonna and Sean Penn joined it just became a total frenzy. You could have given distributors a telephone book and they would have bought it.'

In an interview for *Film Comment* in June 1988, Harrison was philosophical about what had been a very public humiliation. '*Shanghai* proved to be very painful for most of the people involved – the technicians as much as anyone – because of the attitude of the actors. It was like "Springtime for Hitler" in *The Producers*. We got the wrong actors, the wrong producer, the wrong director. Where did we go right? It wasn't easy, but I was determined not to let it get me depressed.'

O'Brien was equally scathing in an interview for the magazine *Producer*. 'It wasn't easy when you had a major actor sulking in the corner and trying to fire the entire production. George and I were out there in Hong Kong and at Shepperton just trying to stop this crazy guy from destroying us.' O'Brien confessed that his fingers had been well and truly burnt, but was equally determined not to repeat the mistake of working with a 'movie brat' star and subsequently pulled out of several projects, 'where we had the smallest sniff that a star was going to misbehave'. One such project, *The Catfish Tangle*, was in deep development and had Mickey Rourke attached who, according to O'Brien, wanted to 'rewrite the whole script'. It was shelved.

So HandMade had survived to die another day. But the post mortem over *Shanghai Surprise* was intense. What happened and why? Shingles believes, 'Basically, the script was crap. The whole project was awful and you get beguiled by the names. When you look at it now, it's just embarrassing. The acting is embarrassing. It's more notorious for its publicity than for anything it contained. I think if only Penn and Madonna had delayed, deliberated longer and decided to do something else, we would have avoided that fiasco. This guy from MGM said the film took on an odour they could never remove. And really that was about right.' Others saw the film as being much more than just a colossal mistake but evidence of a deeper malaise, the reverberations of which were to prove terminal. 'Those early HandMade films gave George Harrison a good name,' says Eric Idle, 'a reputation in England which was nice for him, to be seen to be this philanthropic supporter of British films. HandMade was a home for film-makers originally, for people who couldn't get their films made anywhere else. But I think *Shanghai Surprise* was the writing on the wall. Once you get big Hollywood stars, then you're doing what Hollywood does, and they do it a lot better because they've got a lot deeper pockets.'

John Kohn still contends that, on paper, the film looked good and had the makings of a success. He also claims his relationship with O'Brien, even after the film bombed, was a positive one. 'He was one of the most gracious, generous heads of companies I ever met. There was no end to the wining and dining. You were bowled over by it. He was charming as hell.' In the end, it was the casting that sank the film. Penn was just too young for the role of the grizzled fortune-hunter, someone a bit more world-weary, like Harrison Ford, might have brought more of a swashbuckling panache to it. Kohn adds, 'And I don't think Madonna was really up to it, either. She had to be a Jean Harlow-type figure, that kind of very loveable bad girl, and she just never really got it. She wasn't a good enough actress at that time.'

On the positive side, that a film of any kind emerged at all amid such an atmosphere of back-biting, brawling and out of control egos is a miracle in itself. But Richard Griffiths is under no illusions as to where the spotlight of blame should rest. 'George was so upset about *Shanghai Surprise*, because it was another good idea and it was shafted by this cunt Sean Penn. It was so awful because the artistic decisions kept falling between Goddard and Penn and, whenever push came to shove, Sean Penn had his wicked way. And he had absolutely no right or qualification to impose on the artistic appearance of the film. It was power without responsibility and he used it, it seemed to me, ruthlessly. That's what killed the picture. It was pulled between these two polarities, pulled apart. It was this thing of him vying for control and status all the time when clearly the control should have been in the hands of Goddard and the status should have belonged to Madonna, and he would have been well advised just to keep his head down a bit more. After all, he was going to bed with Madonna every night, never mind getting paid x amount of millions of dollars for wanking around.'

CHAPTER 10

WHISTLER AND ME

Paul McGann had only just completed the controversial BBC drama serial *The Monocled Mutineer* when his agent rang with another offer of work. 'Darling,' oozed the voice, 'there's a script about Whistler.'

'What?' McGann said.

'It's called *Whistler and Me* or something.'

'What, the painter?' asked McGann.

'Presumably. Anyway, it's winging its way to you now so give it a look.'

McGann put the phone down. A film about Whistler? Not inconceivable, there'd been a rash of period movies recently. 'So I thought, well, all right, because I look quite good in a frock. I look quite good in period things. And it was a movie and I hadn't done a movie. And it arrived. And the first time I read it was on the tube. I was in hysterics and that's never happened before or since. People were trying to look over my shoulder at what I was reading because I was almost crying reading this thing.' The script, of course, was for *Withnail and I*.

The audition for *Withnail and I* was at a house in Notting Hill Gate rented by an American producer called Paul Heller. Inside, the director, Bruce Robinson, sat scruffily dressed in leather jacket, jeans and with a cigarette dangling James Dean-like from his mouth, his hand never far from a can of lager. McGann tried to act cool as he sat down and the director asked, 'What part do you feel you could do?'

That was easy. 'Marwood,' said McGann, guessing Robinson was testing him out. 'I'd really fuck that Withnail part up. I couldn't do that.'

Robinson nodded. 'Well, I'm glad you said that, because I saw you as the other one, too.'

McGann recalls, 'I was so nervous, because you want to make an impression, you want to get it right. And I walked in and I can't remember getting my coat off. I can't even remember sitting down. And Bruce said to me, "You've got the job." And I was struck dumb. I wanted to just burst.'

Robinson had more or less cast McGann already as the 'I' character (referred to as Marwood in the script but unnamed in the film), having seen him perform previously. Now he was merely curious to observe him in the flesh. After all, McGann was effectively going to be playing Bruce Robinson himself. The role is semi-autobiographical, it's Bruce 20 years ago, and the director wanted to make sure he'd got the right guy.

Because first choice Daniel Day-Lewis had turned down an offer to play Withnail, preferring to make *The Unbearable Lightness of Being* instead, McGann was asked if he might come in and read scenes with prospective Withnails, a character Robinson has described as an 'awful, fucked-up, quasi-homo bounder; this vituperative, nasty, acid git'. He agreed and over the next two days sat in this swanky house as actors – some famous, some less so – paraded in to read extracts from the script, specifically two scenes, the one in the kitchen with the untouched washing-up and the pair's haunting goodbye on the park bench in Regent's Park.

One of the actors McGann instantly recognised, as both hailed from the same drama school – Kenneth Branagh. Robinson did actually toy with the idea of casting Branagh as Marwood but he insisted on trying out for Withnail, despite his obvious unsuitability. Robinson saw Withnail as Byronic and emaciated, whereas Branagh, 'looked like a partially cooked doughnut'. Not very Withnail. McGann remembers, 'But Branagh's so confident. He came in and he was confident. He barged in and he took over. But the guy I thought would get the job, who was completely out there, was Eddie Tenpole Tudor. Eddie *was* Withnail. He's even a fucking Tudor, for God's sake! He's a toff, the guy was twenty-eighth in line to the throne of England or something. This is Withnail. He was completely right, as far as I could see, and he did a fantastic reading.

'There were these two American guys, friends of Paul Heller, who'd come over. They looked like the Thompson Twins from the *Tin Tin* books, and they were sitting side by side on this sofa watching us. And me and Eddie are reading this scene on the park bench. And in the film, Withnail gobs on the floor. So we're doing this thing and Eddie gets some gob from the base of his spine somewhere and he actually really gobs and it goes "Thwack" and this thing lands on the turn-up on one of these guy's trousers. And I can see the veins in Bruce's neck and he's gone the colour of a Marlborough packet trying to contain this laughter.'

McGann was convinced Tudor would land the job, even after a certain Richard E Grant walked in. Grant had been sent the script by casting director Mary Selway and was desperate to play it, though didn't believe anyone would be stupid enough to actually give it to him. Robinson didn't even want to see him, looking aghast at his photograph in *Spotlight* when Mary Selway showed him it. 'I'm looking for Byron, not a fucking fat, young Dirk Bogarde,' he said. Grant had never been to a film audition before. 'I remember Richard coming in and I actually didn't think he was much good,' McGann recalls. 'He was very, very nervous. And I remember Bruce saying later over a cup of tea something like, "What did you think of the South African?" I said, "I dunno." Bruce said, "There's something about him. I'm going to get him back in." So Richard came back and he was ready for it this time. And it was Withnail, stood in front of you. He had it. It was spot on. And good for Bruce, he got him back in. But then the cunt sacked me.'

The first McGann heard about his dismissal was when his agent called. 'I'm really sorry, Paul, it's not going to work out, the *Withnail* thing.' He couldn't believe it, having already been offered the role, though no contract had been signed, Robinson was now letting him go. And, worse, he hadn't had the guts to do it face to face. McGann admits, 'I remember feeling justifiably really fucked off about it. I'd been sitting there with all these actors, some of whom didn't know what they were doing, and my function as I saw it was just to be there and try and give them as much as I could. God knows what I was doing. I must have been just hamming it like mad and Bruce had sat there having kittens about what I was doing, panicked and turned me down. I said to my agent, "I'm not going to take this. He's wrong. Get me an audition. Get me back in, I can't let this guy get away with this. He's nuts." So I had to go back in on the Monday to audition for the job I'd been given on the Thursday. Extraordinary.'

By this time, Richard E Grant was firmly ensconced in the Withnail role, with Robinson's words of 'Granty, we're gonna make a fucking masterpiece' ringing in his ears. But McGann still had to pass the test all over again. 'So I auditioned again and sat with Richard who'd got the job. The boot now was on the other foot. How about that? Bruce tries not to remember that now. I've talked to him about it since. He said, "Did I really do that?" I said, "Yeah, you bastard." So we had to go through this embarrassing rigmarole of sitting there again and I got to the end of the audition and I looked at Bruce and there was this silence and he said, "Oh, all right then. You've got the job." '

Like McGann, the first time Grant read the script of *Withnail and I* it had a profound impact on him, perhaps more so. 'Never before or since have I read something that conveys what goes on in my head so accurately,' he later wrote. One of the reasons why the film works so brilliantly and has endured for so long is that the script was ready. Robinson began it back in 1970 and it couldn't be bettered, it had been in his head fermenting and maturing for 15 years. McGann observes, 'That script went on to the screen unchanged. Not a single line was altered. It's completely unique. Our camera operator said, "I've never known this and you'll never see this again." '

At a special charity showing of the film in 2000, organised by Richard E Grant to raise funds for his old school in Swaziland, Robinson decided to auction his original manuscript dating from 1970. And there it was, typed on his old Remington, with handwritten notes in the margin, some of it absolutely verbatim, word for word scenes from the film. It was that ready. The script sold for £7,000. The buyer was *Four Weddings and a Funeral* writer Richard Curtis.

Everyone thought Robinson was mad to sell the script and, after the event, he grabbed hold of Ralph Brown, the actor he'd cast in *Withnail* as Danny, the drug king, to tell him, 'Richard Curtis has bought my screenplay.'

Brown replied, 'Has he?' Then, after a short pause, jokingly suggested, 'Why don't we go outside and meet him in the foyer and just do him and nick it back?'

A few days later, when Robinson got home to his farm in Herefordshire, there on his doormat was the script. Curtis had returned it. Bruce called McGann to tell him that Curtis's gesture had been one of the nicest things anyone had ever done for him.

The story of *Withnail and I* is loosely based on Robinson's own experiences as a perpetually skint drama student living with a bunch of mates in diseased digs in Camden Town during the Sixties. As the decade wore on, his friends either married or got jobs until there was only Robinson and this other guy, a self-destructively hard-drinking wannabe actor called Vivian MacKerrell, left in the house. Highly educated, MacKerrell became something of a cultural mentor to Robinson, spouting at length about Keats and Baudelaire in between the prodigious consumption of alcohol. Eventually, he went, too, leaving Robinson alone with practically no money, hardly any food, a solitary light bulb and a mattress on the floor. It was the winter of 1969 and Robinson was unemployed and in utter despair. Returning one day to the empty flat, he found himself weeping uncontrollably and praying to the God of Equity for a job, anything, even a coffee commercial. Tears soon turned to laughter at the absurdity of his situation and he decided to write about his predicament and the friend who'd left him behind.

It started life as a novel, mutating later into a screenplay collecting dust on the shelf until 1986 when Paul Heller, whom Robinson knew from his screenwriting jaunts in LA, read it, loved it and recruited David Wimbury, whose close association with HandMade was instrumental in getting them involved. 'You've got to make this movie,' Wimbury insisted to O'Brien. 'This is a film you can't afford not to make.'

Certainly, it's hard to imagine any other company other than HandMade taking on such a unique film as *Withnail*. McGann says, 'At the time, it was only HandMade, I guess, whose house style was funky enough to touch it. For both its punters and performers, HandMade was the funky alternative. I remember the associated kudos of working for them. It must have been like recording for Stiff Records in 1978. It had that cachet.'

But not everyone at HandMade was so like-minded. Before he resigned, John Kelleher saw a copy of the script and wasn't keen at all. 'I thought it was the most horrible thing I'd ever read. I remember it coming in. I think Ray Cooper must have given me the script. Bruce Robinson was hanging around HandMade a lot then because he was part of a group that included Ray and George. Ray said, "We're thinking of doing this. What do you think, commercially?" The trouble with the *Withnail* script was it was very hard to get past the beginning in this rat-infested kitchen in Camden Town that Bruce described in incredible detail. And you just couldn't help being completely turned off by that. It was very hard to get past it.'

Prior to filming, Robinson organised a week's rehearsal for the cast in a vast wood-panelled drawing room in an old house on the grounds of Shepperton Studios. McGann remembers, 'It was owned or used by The Who. It was a big open space. In the corner was a kitchen area and a fridge full of booze. And we'd work office hours. We'd arrive at nine and go home at five.'

While at Shepperton, the supporting roles were cast. As the poacher the lads meet on their disastrous holiday break in the Lake District, Michael Elphick, then a big TV star as *Boon*, agreed to appear as a favour to Bruce, as they'd been at drama school together. They couldn't afford his rates. 'But he did it for a few quid and a bottle of scotch,' Robinson noted. Richard Griffiths, a HandMade stalwart, agreed to play Uncle Monty, a character Robinson had conjured up as being representational of all the people who'd harassed him as a drama student, those 'artistic gents who were after my bum'.

One important audition was for the part of the drug-dealer Danny, and someone who found himself up for the part was a little-known actor called Ralph Brown. 'They'd been trying to cast this part for months without success. I hadn't done any films at that point, so I wasn't exactly on top of their list of contenders. I think Mary Selway had seen me on stage and got me an audition with Bruce. I remember I sat in a nearby park for about an hour going over my lines before I went in.'

Brown arrived for the audition totally in character, bare-foot with painted black fingernails, long wig, eye shadow and shades. 'I looked a bit strange.' It blew everyone away and Robinson all but gave him the part there and then. Modelled partly on someone who worked at a record shop near London's Central Drama School, who sidelined in selling dope, Brown was given near *carte blanche* to create his own Danny, basing him on people that he'd grown up with in Lewes in East Sussex. 'Lewes was the kind of place where punk kind of arrived in 1982 … it was still very much a hippie backwater ... cider drinking and smoking joints. There were various characters around the town, one used to be in and out of prison for various nefarious activities including drug-dealing, others were in bands. I was only 13 or 14 and these people were really larger than life for me and they were slightly glamorous. One guy called Noddy used to attempt to roll the longest joint ever known to mankind and he had this stoned, serious take on life where he'd tell you something in very serious tones that was absolute bollocks. So I definitely understood Danny in that sense.'

As rehearsals progressed, Grant and McGann grew more familiar with the script and Robinson's intentions. Earlier, they'd had trouble with some of the lines. Aware they were meant to be funny, both tried too hard to make them funny, telegraphing the jokes almost. Robinson was so opposed to that, repeatedly stressing that the comedy would come from the characters and situations. McGann recalls, 'Bruce said to us, "There are no punchlines. Boys, get it out of your head now, there are no gags. This film will work because we'll play it for real. You've got to play it for real." '

Then the bombshell dropped – Grant didn't drink, he was allergic to the stuff. This was news to Robinson; he hadn't thought to ask, 'Oh, by the way, Richard, you do drink, don't you?' Taking McGann to one side, a panic-stricken Robinson blurted out, 'He doesn't drink. He doesn't drink.' Then turning to Grant, 'There's nothing worse in films than a bad drunk act. We're dead.' And Grant was sitting there, forlorn, saying, 'I know ... I know ... I'm so sorry.'

Some quick thinking was called for. It was Robinson who came up with the idea that Grant should have a 'chemical memory' of what it was like to be completely poleaxed. He approached the fridge in the corner of the rehearsal room. 'There were beers and coolers and these airplane miniatures,' McGann says. 'I remember it was an airplane miniature of vodka. Bang in a glass. Doused. And he drank it. What a sport. And Bruce is saying, "Richard, we've got drivers, if you don't feel well we'll call it off and take you home." And I thought, Bollocks, I'm having a beer. And it was incredible, Richard went through every single stage of being pissed, literally from that lovely moment when you have that first drink and you get that first mellow feeling, and then incrementally the stakes get raised and you get a bit merry, and then you have another one and you start gibbering and flirting and then you start knocking into things. Grant did that, visibly. But it happened in minutes, maybe 20 minutes, to the point where if the police see you they have to have a word with you. I fucking swear this happened.'

Robinson was quick to exploit the situation and got them reading and rehearsing scenes, any scenes with drink in them or scenes under the influence. McGann remembers, 'We were sitting together and an arm went round my shoulder and Richard looked at me and said, "You're such a fantastic actor." It's like the pub drunk going, "I love you, man." And he said to Bruce, "Thank you so much." And Bruce is going to him, "Do the scene, just do the scene." And I have to say he was great, the things he was doing were great and he was laughing and enjoying himself. And then he started making these noises, involuntary sort of whoops. And then these, like, Navaho sounds. It was absolutely hysterical. Then he stopped whooping and went green and looked for a window and threw up. It was awful, really. They got him out into a car and took him home. His wife was on the phone. "What do you think you're doing? What have you done to my boy?" And Bruce is wiping tears from his eyes. It was so naughty. As Richard's leaving, I swear Robinson's going to him, "Remember. Remember!" '

And the amazing thing is, it did pay off, the chemical memory Robinson was after worked. McGann confirms, 'He did remember, look at the film, he remembered. It's the best drunk performance I've ever seen. There's a scene when we're in the car leaving London and he's leaning out of the window shouting "Scrubbers" to some schoolgirls. Look at his eyes, that's acting. How the fuck do you do that? I worked with this guy and, even to this day, I have to marvel at what he did. And he doesn't drink. He got on it, whatever it was, he got on it. At one point, he looks straight at me and you look at him and you go, "Fucking hell, you are out there, you are miles away." Remember this is 9.30 on a Sunday morning. Who won the Oscar that year? Nobody was that good. Absolutely magnificent.'

McGann also recalls during shooting how first thing in the morning he'd hear, through the adjoining doors of their hotel rooms, Grant physically psyching himself up to get into character, little wafts of smoke coming under the door from the herbal cigarettes he used instead of tobacco.

The morning after the drinking binge, Grant woke up with a demon of a hangover and foul-smelling dribble on his clothes. As he later wrote, 'My stomach is on fire. Tongue stapled to the roof of my mouth, throat scorched and head housing an orchestra of pneumatic drills playing Beethoven's Ninth. All for art?' When he finally managed to grope his way downstairs, Robinson had left a message on the answer phone. 'Granty. You did it. Breakthrough. Gonna make a fucking masterpiece, boy.'

On 1 August 1986, Grant and McGann met at Liverpool Street Station to catch the train up to the Lake District where much of the film was shot amid the picturesque countryside around Penrith. The first scene in the can was the boys' arrival at an abandoned cottage in the middle of a howling night. McGann recalls, 'Both Richard and I had never done a film and Bruce had never directed a picture, so we tended to spend a lot of time just staring at each other going, "What do we do now? And, can we do this? Can we get away with this?" ' Sensing that this was their big chance, Grant and McGann really got stuck in and made the most of it. 'They were both well up to speed,' Griffiths says. 'They were like baby sharks, the two of them, and I was just holding my end up, as it were. Richard had landed this part, God knows how because he had not a clue about how to present himself, and it's probably one of the greatest performances he'll ever give in his life. And it was all because Bruce was so generous about letting him express himself. And McGann was funny. He was constantly trailing shots. In other words, there'd be two of them in the shot doing the lines and then they'd exit and Grant would just crash out of the door and McGann would leave his face sort of vaguely looking over the top of the camera, and then go. He was getting himself a close-up. And the cameraman would look up at Bruce who knew what was wrong and kept telling McGann to stop trailing his face. "If you get out of the shot, just get out. Don't stand there looking beautiful and then get out, just get the fuck out." '

On that very first day of shooting, Bruce Robinson did something quite unique. He assembled the entire crew together inside the cottage, stood on a chair and was man enough to confess that he'd never directed a film before, but that he knew what he wanted, it was all in his head, it was just from a technical standpoint he'd not the first clue and asked everyone that if they saw him make a mistake on the floor not to be afraid to pipe up. It was one of those 'we're all in it together' type speeches, very Henry V at Agincourt, and the crew responded.

Griffiths' view was that 'Bruce was truly amazing. He would go into a set-up in a scene, he'd look at it and we'd all stand around and he'd say, "I haven't got a fucking clue about how to do this. Anybody any ideas?" And you'd stand there in shock. Somebody was not bullshitting you. Because directors always do, they always pretend they know what they're doing, especially when they don't. And out would come this fountain of ideas and at the speed of light he would just flicker through them and say, "No, no, no ... Ahh, that sounds good, let's have a look at that." And then we could rehearse it. And he said, "Yes, that's good. Let's shoot this way." It was so liberating.'

Everyone knew the film was being made on a pittance, a mere £1.5 million, and that in itself created a bond of loyalty and togetherness, coupled with a sense of how special the script was. Brown recalls, 'It was everyone's first film – mine, Bruce's, Paul's and Richard's. The crew were fairly experienced. Peter Hammond was certainly an experienced cameraman and he directed the shots pretty much because Bruce didn't really know where to put the camera and would just say, "Pete, what shall I do with this scene?" And they'd work it out together. It was a really nice atmosphere. There was no tension, everyone was helping each other out. I think we all felt that maybe that's the way movies were. And, of course, we've all made lots of films each since then and they're not all like that. It was a lovely honeymoon, really.'

Robinson later admitted that shooting *Withnail* was like playing poker when you don't know the rules but winning every hand. Pure beginner's luck. Nervous on the night before shooting, he later spoke of feeling 'naked, sheer, edible fear', and confided in David Wimbury who tried reassuring him, 'It doesn't matter how good your script is or how good your crew is, if you don't get luck, you're fucked.' And Robinson was blessed with luck, everything fitted, not least in the way Grant and McGann related to each other in exactly the way he hoped they would. Robinson knew so much depended on the actors; if they didn't play then he was in serious shit.

But the film wasn't without its problems. Indeed, the first week was almost its last. Denis O'Brien had arrived on the location. Grant described him as 'a Bilko identikit on a giant scale'. It wasn't a friendly visit. Soon, he and Robinson were arguing. O'Brien was of the opinion that the film was running behind schedule and suggested that a scene featuring a close encounter with a none-too-friendly bull be cut. Robinson was livid. 'How can we be behind schedule?' he exploded. 'It's only lunchtime on the first day? Right, fuck you.' Robinson resigned on the spot, mumbling something about 'over my dead carcass will we cut the bull'. McGann and Grant, previously so happy to be finally making a movie, were now witness to it crumbling about their ears. 'It's just a ploy,' Wimbury told them. 'The American is trying to frighten Robinson and Robinson is calling his bluff.' Sure enough, by four o'clock that afternoon Robinson was back directing and the bull scene had been reinstated. It was a case of Robinson telling HandMade to shut up and trust him, he knew what he was doing. Still, O'Brien and others at Cadogan Square were on edge about the whole project right up until it finished shooting. 'They were just being a gang of cunts for the first couple of weeks. Fucking nightmare,' Robinson later ranted. Henceforth the cast and crew referred to their benefactors as Hand-Job Films.

When the first dailies were sent over to HandMade, news of what they thought of them was eagerly awaited. Paul Heller loved what he saw, but O'Brien was horrified. Robinson broke the news. 'O'Brien says it's a fucking disaster. He thinks it's all too dark and funny as cancer.' Well, it would be dark, wouldn't it, seeing the first scenes were shot at night!

Robinson tried arguing with O'Brien that this wasn't Benny Hill, joke-a-minute stuff, that the desperation in the character's plight was where the comedy would come from. But O'Brien wanted almost drum-roll punchlines. It was humour of the blackest kind and he just couldn't see that. It was a bitter blow to everyone. McGann says, 'As a performer, you want the rushes to come in and you want them to go, "Fantastic, absolutely brilliant, no problems, everyone's chuffed, you look like Marlon Brando, it's all going to be sweet." And it didn't happen. Bruce said to me, "Denis wants the Ministry of Silly Walks. He wants Monty Python." There were messages coming back saying, "I thought you said these boys could act." Denis was going, "I thought you said it was going to be funny. It ain't funny. It didn't make me laugh. What are they doing? Where are the jokes?" And then you shit yourself.'

O'Brien wanted Grant, for example, to be more like Kenneth Williams, all arms swinging about and screaming at the top of his lungs. 'He said it should be nostril-pulling camping around,' Grant later complained. 'I said he should have stuck to financing.'

O'Brien's attitude really galvanised a whole 'us against them' scenario.

'After two weeks of filming,' Cooper remembers, 'Denis was quite willing to close the film down. He really didn't get the film at all or its humour, because it wasn't Pythonesque. Strangely, I didn't suspect this at the beginning, but Denis had a very limited view of humour and of drama.'

As usual, Ray Cooper found himself flitting like a mad thing between Cadogan Square and a film's location, trying to appease both camps. McGann observes, 'I wished that Ray Cooper had been around a bit more. Personality-wise, it would have calmed things down a little. Because Ray's such a gentleman, whenever he's around it ups the atmosphere. He's a calming influence. He's generous and he's got a good spirit. We all knew we were working in an atmosphere. Bruce said one day, 'If Denis doesn't let me do what I want to do, I'm walking.' And we knew that was no veiled threat. He would have done it. That was real.'

Robinson worked himself up into such a paranoid state that even when the crew began reacting favourably to what was going on and picking up favourite lines from the script, he took this as an omen that the film was doomed. 'Bruce was superstitious,' McGann believes. 'During filming, the crew would fall about laughing. I've never known this since and probably will never see it again, but we'd be in a hotel or bar after a day's work and you'd hear the crew going, "What about that bit with the chicken?" And I said to Bruce, "Listen to that, it's fantastic." And Bruce sometimes would go, "No it ain't." He'd say things like, "If the crew fall about laughing, we're dead in the water." And I'd say, "What! Did you get that out of a fucking cracker or something?" And he said, "No, no, they're laughing, we're going to die." And I said, "No we ain't. They're laughing because it's funny. It's going to be funny." '

As shooting continued, the temperature heated up in what had become something of a personal war between Robinson and O'Brien. 'Every day there was some battle going on,' Ralph Brown remembers. 'Denis was the sort of aggro guy at HandMade who was making it difficult for Bruce, in Bruce's eyes anyway. There would always be a lunchtime discussion in the pub, it wouldn't be on the set, so it never interrupted the shooting, but Bruce didn't keep things to himself, he'd always share with us whatever problem he was having that particular day. During my scenes, I remember he was fighting with Denis over the title – HandMade thought *Withnail and I* was the worst title they'd ever heard. There were also problems over the famous "coal man" speech which they'd made him cut from the script. And Bruce came up to me on the day and gave me this bit of paper and said, "Learn that, they've cut it but I'm gonna fucking shoot it anyway." And like every other aspect of the film, Bruce totally dug his heels in and said, "No, that's what it is." '

According to Brian Shingles, O'Brien performed a complete U-turn over the film once it was completed. 'I remember going to a screening, one of the rough cuts, and everyone thought how wonderful *Withnail* was. We thought, 'We've got a really unique film.' Denis did make changes and I don't know what Bruce felt about them, but Denis had a very soft spot for *Withnail* as I recall. He felt, out of all of them, it was probably the jewel in the crown.'

David Wimbury, the producer, also found O'Brien accommodating. 'I found Denis fine, actually. I know he upset some people and could be a little obstinate, but I had a really good relationship with him. Although he wouldn't pay for a last day's filming we wanted to do, so we had to pay for it ourselves.'

Another battle was over O'Brien's interpretation of the way Uncle Monty should be played. Robinson wanted the part performed very straight, but O'Brien had in mind something approaching a cartoon figure. McGann comments, 'He wanted the campest show on earth.' Ironically, Richard Griffiths himself saw Monty as more camp than Robinson intended. 'No, we'll have to go again,' Robinson would be heard to cry during a shot. 'Richard, you mustn't do any of that stuff with your wrist, don't flap about and don't pull faces. Just say the lines.' At other times, though, he'd want Griffiths to pull a camp face or two. Griffiths says, 'In one scene, we're in the cottage eating this huge leg of lamb and McGann says something that Monty finds completely out of order and I pull a face at him. And Bruce said, "Cut. This is rubbish. Richard, you've got to give him such a shitty look. He's said such a fatuous fucking thing so you've got to punish him with a look." I said, "All right, I'll give a punishing look." He said, "No, no. I want a particular kind of look." I said, "What kind of look do you want?" And he said, "I know … I want a look that's something like a goat's arse." And I flippantly said, "Oh, you mean like this …" And he said, "Perfect." '

Griffiths saw Monty as a wonderful creature, a character people could warm to, in spite of his amorous leanings towards Marwood. His botched 'seduction' of the young boy is a darkly tragic moment. Griffiths recalls, 'I spent an hour-and-a-half in make-up being made up to look like Hermann Goering at an orgy. And I had the famous dressing gown on. And, of course, the bastards made me sit around the whole day waiting for this scene. I had lunch, sat around chatting, drinking, having fags and completely forgot how bizarre I looked, so when I went in to do the scene I was very natural and cool, because the dialogue was difficult enough to get through without cracking up.'

The script called for Griffiths to slip off his dressing gown and to spread his obese nakedness in front of McGann. When the time came, Griffiths approached Robinson. 'I can't cope with that. I mean I wouldn't even do that in private. And I think I can suggest an alternative. Let me keep the fab dressing gown on 'til I back him into the corner and the camera's behind me, then you can see him over my shoulder, and what I'll do is I'll flash him and it'll be funny.'

Robinson liked the idea and the scene plays beautifully. 'I remember at the première of the film,' Griffiths says, 'as Monty enters the room about four rows behind me this woman went "Uurrghhh! Beyond yucky." But by the end of the scene, which must be all of two minutes, I could hear her weeping.'

Towards the end of August, filming moved from Penrith to London where a condemned house in Notting Hill was made to look even more decadent as the boy's Camden Town squat. It was here, during the filming of the notorious dirty kitchen sequence, that George Harrison and Ringo Starr paid the film a quick visit, Starr commenting that the attendant squalor of the place reminded him of how The Cavern used to look. It was a big buzz for the team and a thrill for the actors. Richard E Grant comments, 'Very low-key were they … very awestruck were we.'

For most of these scenes, drug guru Danny takes centre stage, spouting immortal lines like, 'If I medicined you, you'd think a brain tumour was a fucking birthday present.' The role is such a one-off stroke of genius that Ralph Brown simply can't help but steal every minute he's on screen, though that was never the actor's intention. 'I just played the character as it was written. If you look at the way the scenes are in the screenplay, Danny really dominates them, he drives them, the scenes are very much about them reacting to him. In the last scene, Paul's getting stoned,

Richard's giggling and I'm being Bruce, actually. Those lines about hippie wigs in Woolworth's and we have failed to paint it black, stuff like that, is really the voice of the writer there. And I'm the classic holy fool being given these words of wisdom to speak, because Danny is so clearly a pontificating idiot, therefore if he sort of speaks the truth it takes the curse off it a bit, it stops it being preachy.'

Brown only worked for three days on the picture. On his last day, they filmed the famous Camberwell carrot scene where he sits spaced out smoking an enormous joint. Brown was determined to behave exactly as he'd seen rastas smoking ganja in Jamaica, what he calls 'professional ganja smokers'. That was to try and inhale through his mouth and breathe out through his nose at the same time, thus creating a cloud of reef smoke. That whole sequence had to be completed in one day, such was the tight schedule Robinson was under. 'Bruce was great,' Brown says. 'He was an actor for years so understood the process very well. But at the same time, he didn't let us run with it, he wanted it a very particular way. He could hear it all in his head and he could've played all the parts himself. In fact, quite often he'd give out line readings from the set. He'd let you try it and if you didn't get it the first two or three times he'd come up and whisper in your ear, "No, it's supposed to be like this ..." He was conducting the film, really, like a mad, drunken conductor with his flask of vodka he'd had for breakfast. He never appeared drunk at all; one was aware that he must be drunk because of the amount of alcohol he was drinking, but he never appeared to be drunk, he was always very lucid.'

During that week, McGann's *Monocled Mutineer* débuted on television to much press attention. Strangely, the final stages of *Withnail* curiously mirrored the relationship between Grant and McGann themselves. The scene in the cottage where Marwood receives a telegram offering him a job was played from the heart by Grant who dreaded a return to unemployment when shooting ended and envied McGann his success with the *Monocled Mutineer*. McGann says, 'That scene is my favourite bit of Richard's whole performance. I hand the telegram to him and he looks at it and just says, "Well done." Next time you see the film, look at his face, everything is in this beautiful bit of acting, fantastically bittersweet. It's the whole film. It's over. Their relationship is over. It's about to end. That's wonderful acting, and it proved that his performance wasn't just all those shenanigans and camp shit, he did a lot of really brilliant, clever stuff, too.'

Other memorable scenes included the boys nocturnal visit to Monty's posh London abode where he strains to let them in while holding a cat. 'The cat we used was hopeless,' Griffiths complains, 'a useless fucking cat. It was this blue Persian kitten that was just shitting itself with fear. I said, "What am I supposed to do with this?" They said, "You open the door and you've got a glass teapot in one hand and this cat in the other." I said, "And I open the door with the end of my willy?" And they said, "No, no, you've just got to struggle a bit and open the door." Well, I opened the door and this fucking cat just hung there. It had died and gone to hell. It hung in my hand like a friggin' wet dishcloth and so I was having to hold it up, it wasn't clinging to any part of my arm. I had to hold this thing up like you'd hold up a squid because it was slipping. And, of course, being a Persian they're very tiny, skinny creatures with all this mass of fur. Talk about fur coat and no knickers, there's no substance to them at all.'

Monty ushers the boys inside to the lounge and, at some point in the dialogue, the cat was to suddenly materialise on top of the couch, startling Monty. 'Well, you wouldn't believe,' Griffiths adds, 'it couldn't jump, and eventually they were lobbing it. They would throw it in the air and hope it would land near my head on the couch. They said, "Oh, don't hurt it otherwise we'll all get into trouble." I said, "Fuck that. Why don't we just pull it inside out and get another one?" But, no, they wouldn't have that. The cat hardly figures at all in the film, but, God, it dominated the time we were in that room. Bastard thing.'

Then it was off to Kensal Rise to film Withnail and Marwood's Jimi Hendrix-fuelled drive out of London. It was a drizzly, quiet Sunday morning, very early as the crew hadn't really gained permission to shoot there. They'd secreted themselves in the doorway of a bleak tower block to capture this battered Jag roaring past. McGann was driving and had to take the Jag on a lap of the estate a few times until the perfect establishing shot was in the can. 'On the fourth take, I've come to a stop at these lights and we're looking like a pair of cunts at the wheel in costume. The Jag's got like one headlamp and Grant's got a bottle of scotch between his legs. And I saw a parked Panda car and thought, Jesus. And I said to Richard, "Look." And he said, "Oh no." I said, "Don't worry, they haven't even noticed us." Then one of them looked up and saw me and nudged his mate, mouthing, "What the fuck?" And I thought, Well, this is it. And I don't know what possessed me, the lights were still red, I just stood on the Jag and took off. And they didn't waste any time, these guys were right behind us pretty quick. Richard was already a ball of fucking claws next to me, he was going like, "You've got to stop, I'm gonna get fucking arrested." I think he imagined he was still an illegal alien or something. He'd only been in England a couple of years. I said, "All right, don't worry." And we get back round to where the crew are and I mount the pavement doing about 50 and, before I've even brought it to a stop, Richard had the door open and he did a stunt exit from this car and was off. He'd gone.'

The car was now stationary, and a policeman came tapping on the window. It was then that the first assistant came out of the high-rise to calm things down. McGann remembers, 'But we couldn't find Grant for five minutes. He'd completely disappeared. They found him hiding in someone's garden down the fucking road. And Bruce was going to him, "Fucking hell. If this had been Los Angeles you'd have been dead, they'd have shot ya." It was great. It was so exciting.'

Early in December, the cast saw the film for the first time in a small screening room in Wardour Street. Brown recalls, 'Richard E Grant was there and he's actually never seen any of his work since then because it freaked him out so much. I was appalled by how slowly I was speaking. I thought, Fuck me, this is terrible. And I was sitting next to Richard Griffiths and I said to him, "I'm talking too fucking slowly." And he went, "Don't worry, dear boy, it's marvelous." '

Then came the test previews. The first one was a disaster. Shown to a small, hand-picked audience in the West End, Robinson sat there mortified as his film raised not one titter or semblance of a laugh. Only later was it discovered that the audience had comprised of German tourists hijacked from a nearby hostel.

For a time, it looked like *Withnail and I* might be doomed to collect dust on a shelf somewhere as distributors shied away from releasing the film. David Wimbury recalls how he would be on the phone trying to flog it, saying stuff like, 'No, it's just two boys. Talking. No girls.' Just how do you pitch something like *Withnail and I*? Grant believed the film would never see daylight. Palmer confirms, '*Withnail* was so difficult to sell. We couldn't do anything with it. God knows, we tried. For me, that was probably my personal biggest disappointment that we couldn't find it a proper distributor.'

One achievement was getting it a showing at the Edinburgh Film Festival, which Robinson attended. Checking into his hotel and not liking the room, he declared, 'This room is so small I couldn't even get an erection.'

Eventually, Recording Releasing took the film on but, being a relatively small outfit, they couldn't give it the wide release it deserved. Stupidly, O'Brien, still smarting over his encounters with Stephen Woolley on *Mona Lisa*, refused to let Palace have the film when they put in an offer. 'Denis wouldn't let Woolley have it,' Palmer says, 'and Palace were the company to distribute it. If anybody could've made that a success, it was Palace.'

Woolley had already seen the film and loved it. 'HandMade were looking for a distributor and, again, they had no idea what to do with it, they were lost, and I saw it and after ten minutes I had literally collapsed to my knees, I was just laughing so hard I could feel the tears coming down my cheeks. And I really wanted us to distribute it, and we did everything we could to try and get it released under Palace, but they wouldn't let me have it. Denis was quite cruel, and I feel cruelly treated by him on a personal level.'

Withnail and I opened in London in February 1988 and was widely welcomed by critics. The *Observer* proclaimed, 'A funny, curious and oddly affecting slice of anti-nostalgia.' The *Guardian* said, 'One of the most original and certainly the most personal film of the current British revival.' The *Face*, however, found it 'ineffably patronising, tedious, unconvincing and irretrievably self-indulgent'. It was the *Daily Telegraph* that perhaps said it best: 'In many ways, *Withnail and I* is what the British film industry is all about. It is an eccentric, intimate and well-written independent production that would never have seen the light of day in Hollywood.' Strange, then, that HandMade chose to open *Withnail* first in America, during the summer of 1987, cannily at a time when other off-beat British films like *Personal Services* and *Prick Up Your Ears* were finding appreciative, if small, audiences. McGann remembers, 'I was in New York at the time meeting a prospective agent and she said to me, "I'm sure you're in a film around the corner." I've only done one film, I thought, it can't be that. And it was. It was playing in the basement at the Carnegie Hall. I went down there. I had to go and see. And I spoke to the girl on the tickets and she said, "Oh my God, it's you." I remember standing outside and people coming out laughing. It was lovely. I said to Bruce, "It's here!" '

It was also in America where the cult of *Withnail* really first started, long before it was embraced by the college kids of Britain. Brown says, 'It was almost immediate in Hollywood because there was always a little coterie of people in Hollywood that would walk around quoting lines from it. And that's how come we've all worked a lot since.'

Director David Fincher was a huge fan and wanted to reunite the *Withnail* cast in *Alien 3*. McGann and Brown appear, but Grant turned down an offer to play the doctor which, instead, went to Charles Dance. And Brown's role as a drug-crazed roadie in *Wayne's World 2* was specifically written with him in mind and very much based on Danny. Richard Griffiths also remembers being out in Hollywood making *Naked Gun 2* and cast members pointing him out as Uncle Monty. Indeed, so associated did Griffiths become with that role that the actor was assumed to be gay in real life. 'For the next five or six years, I was getting begging letters from every AIDS charity in the world to become its president or spokesman and I kept writing back saying, "I'm sorry, you're barking up the wrong tree." '

In Britain, the *Withnail* cult was slow to take off. It wasn't until the early 1990s that the film was 'discovered'. 'It was people who must have been too young when it was first released,' Brown says, 'so they've caught up with it on video and it was passed from hand to hand in student refectories and halls of residence. And I think that's been the heartbeat of the cult, really, it's been students and people who smoke marijuana.'

McGann, living as he does in a university town, is a witness to the cult first-hand. 'I know come September there'll be a new intake of students and I get stopped by different 18- or 19-year-olds in the street. And they act out the scenes in front of you.'

One can argue that, back in 1987, if *Withnail and I* had received a mainstream release it might well have been a hit, thus precluding the huge cult status it enjoys today. With video and DVD sales, plus a deserved 1996 cinema re-release in the UK, one might guess that everyone concerned has done very nicely out of it, thank you. Certainly Richard E Grant's quite exceptional performance turned him into an international film star. 'I don't think there is a single film that I have done that hasn't been as a result of *Withnail*,' he said in 1996. 'That is the thing that has stuck in the head of whoever has employed me.' Indeed, all the principal actors have pursued solid post-*Withnail* careers. But financially, aside from their basic fee, and they did the film for British Equity contracts – 'the worst film contracts in the world, with the possible exception of India,' according to Richard Griffiths – they've received no extra financial benefits. Largely due to the ownership of the film changing hands so many times, even Bruce Robinson hasn't received a penny of the not inconsiderable profits *Withnail* has incurred since. Something of a scandal, but not that unusual for HandMade. Cooper says, 'Bruce hasn't had a reporting sheet on *Withnail* I think since he made the film. I don't think Bruce has had a day's cheque from it, from the point of view of profit, and I find that extraordinary.'

Many who worked on the film feel aggrieved that people not associated with its making are now reaping the subsequent rewards. 'When HandMade was sold off,' Griffiths states, 'the new owners had the fucking cheek to come up to me and say, "We're gonna relaunch the movie and we'd like you to do some promoting." And I said, "What's in it for me?" And they said, "What do you mean?" I said, "I know what's in it for you, you're gonna clean up. So if I come along and be Mr Nice Guy and sign an interminable number of autographs to dreary dweebs who think that I am as obsessed with it as they are, fine, but I shall need some money for that because that for me is onerous work, above and beyond …" And they were, "Oh, we can't." And I said, "You're gonna make millions and you can't give me a few grand? Well, fuck you." And they sort of took four paces back with a horrified look in their eyes. It was pathetic.'

Then along came a documentary crew wanting to chronicle the whole *Withnail* phenomenon. Griffiths remembers: 'I said, "How much are you paying for it?" They said, "But … but … we're a documentary." I said, "All right, I'll do it for nothing. Is everybody else making it doing it for nothing? Are you gonna send free copies down the internet? In that case, I'm your man." They said, "No, it's a film." I said, "Yeah, that's right, you sell it to TV companies round the world and make a fucking fortune." So, yet again, I had this attitude of being the mercenary guy. And yet it's OK for everybody else to make money and exploit it, rip George off and take the piss out of Bruce, but we get fuck all out of it except the opportunity to help them make even more money. That's what I find offensive.'

Not surprisingly, there has been talk over the years of a possible sequel, though Robinson has made it plain there will never be one. What could you do? What's left to say? McGann recalls, 'But I do remember once at a party in LA around 1997 Bruce said to me, "A couple of people recently have sent me whole scripts for a *Withnail* sequel. Of course, they don't work and I'm quietly horrified that they even want to send me them." I said, "Tell me about one." He goes, "It starts at the theatre and Marwood goes on stage on the first night of *Journey's End* and Withnail's in the audience." And I go, "Well, there's a beginning ..." But Bruce was going, "We couldn't do it. We can't go back. Never go back." He'd had a few and was talking in slogans. He goes on, "Anyway, even if I decided that we could do a sequel, it's plainly ludicrous, you guys are now ten years older, so I'd have to set it a decade later on. So what are we talking about, 1979, and what the fuck was happening in '79 that's of any interest?" And then he went, "Thatcher! Winter of discontent ..." And I'm standing there with this producer and he goes to me, "Shhhh," as if to say, "Let's just leave him for a few minutes." And Bruce suddenly turned into Zero Mostel from *The Producers* – "I see it now!" '

CHAPTER 11

THE AMERICAN GAMBLE

*W*ithnail *and I* was really the last great film HandMade ever produced, certainly the last one that you could say had the look and feel of a HandMade production. The team that had made such distinctive films as *Time Bandits* and such quintessentially English comedies as *A Private Function* were about to fall into the trap sprung so many times before of a British film company overreaching itself by trying to crack the American market. Of course, they'd tried that already with *Shanghai Surprise* and failed dismally. Lessons obviously hadn't been learnt.

In a 1988 interview for *Film Comment*, George Harrison went public about his concerns over this radical shift in policy, making it firmly understood that it hailed from O'Brien and not from him. 'Denis is interested in broadening the base. I personally wouldn't like us to become some big swanky American company. At that point, I'd probably bail out. Even if we made hundreds of millions of dollars, once we moved out of our tiny, overcrowded office in London and got into the Big Time, I'm sure the bottom would all fall out. The answer is to be humble. For me, as an ex-Beatle, I'm not into that trip of being a big-shot. I peaked early. I got all that out of my system in the Sixties.'

Unfortunately, O'Brien hadn't, he was peaking now and eager to expand the company's horizons. Stephen Woolley believes, 'HandMade were starting to go into the big casino. In casinos, you get the $100 table, you get the $200 table and you get the big table. So Denis was trying to get on to that big table, which is what we all try to do, to play on the higher stakes because you realise the limitations of making small films that do quite well, you wanna make slightly bigger films that do very well.'

O'Brien's desire to get a foothold in the American film market can be traced back to the mid-Eighties. Gilliam says, 'Denis would spend a lot of time in Hollywood, because that's what he loved.' John Kelleher was another who voiced disquiet over the direction in which O'Brien was steering the company. 'I'm so glad I left, really, because Denis was totally out of control. He'd become completely bound up in the whole American film world. I think a lot of people who worked at HandMade, like me, would've been keener to keep things small, maybe to build on the relationship with Palace that was struck up with *Mona Lisa* and do more films in that vein. But Denis wasn't interested in that, he wanted to Americanise things and impress his American friends and his blonde girlfriend. Somehow he went right off the rails. I don't know how anyone could go so badly wrong. Those small Indie pictures he was to make in America, he only had to look at them to see they had none of the elements that the earlier small British films had.'

Increasingly, O'Brien was spending the bulk of his time away from Cadogan Square, planting roots for the company in America. Palmer recalls 'Denis started to be around a lot less. He'd always had big holidays in the summer and now he was taking most of the summer off and it was increasingly difficult to get hold of him. He was spending more and more time in the States.'

So it came as no real surprise when, in December 1987, O'Brien established a HandMade office in New York to handle all of its US production development. There would also later be an office in Los Angeles. David Patterson, an old family friend of O'Brien's – in the words of Wendy Palmer, 'a really up-market, East Coast, Ivy Leaguer' – who'd been at Cadogan Square since 1982 serving in a business affairs capacity, was given the task of heading the New York operation.

It was a radical step and a clear statement of intent, one that was met with mixed feelings back in London. Cooper recalls, 'During HandMade's last four years, the Cadogan Square office was virtually a token situation. We were doing little out of London creatively. It was being driven by American projects which ended up being fairly disastrous.' But there was also a feeling of some inevitability that if HandMade were to begin producing American-orientated features, they'd need some form of base out there. Brian Shingles says, 'There was the idea of expansion; you had to look further afield than the UK and those, I suppose, slightly parochial films that weren't always easy to sell on a worldwide basis. That was a logical step. It was only the choice of films that ultimately let us down.'

One of the most important people O'Brien met during his trips to America was Tony Bill, a maverick director, producer and sometime actor. They were introduced through a mutual friend, John Calley, then head of Warner Brothers, around 1984. Bill had no idea of O'Brien's desire to make US-based movies until the subject happened to crop up over dinner one evening. 'Denis said, "Gee, we'd like to do an American movie." And I said, "Hey, Denis, I've just optioned a script, maybe you'll be interested in reading it." And he said, "I'll read it right away." And he did indeed read it right away and called me the next day and said, "We'd like this to be our first American film." And I said, "OK." And it was pretty much as simple as that.'

The script was called *Five Corners* by John Patrick Shanley, a young writer new to cinema, which had been part of the fascination for Tony Bill. 'I'm particularly attracted to first-time writers. Most of the movies I've made are with first-timers. I like the freshness of point of view of a first-time writer. They haven't written for a market, they've written for themselves.'

Steeped in genuine feeling for the era and environment in which Shanley had grown up, a Bronx neighbourhood circa 1964, *Five Corners* takes place during a time of great social change, with Martin Luther King's civil rights crusade serving as background to an often dark tale about a potential rapist let loose from prison. Essentially, though, it's a coming-of-age story about a group of disparate young people and Bill was so taken by it he bought the rights using his own money with the intention of directing the piece himself.

With HandMade on board, Bill sent the script to Jodie Foster, who was impressed by its originality and the fact it was an ensemble piece, not a star vehicle. But no sooner had she accepted than Bill came under pressure not to hire her from a television company partly investing in the project. 'They were absolutely dead set against Jodie Foster. They didn't think she was a good enough actress or name. She'd been away at Yale College and hadn't been acting in a lot of movies. So I had enormous resistance to casting her.'

Bill won the argument and Foster was cast. A year later, she'd win an Oscar for her performance in *The Accused* and be elevated to superstardom.

Joining Foster were two then unknown actors called Tim Robbins and John Turturro. 'One of the interesting things about the cast,' Bill says, 'is that virtually everyone has gone on to be a director. Jodie, Tim and John have all directed movies. Our author, John Patrick Shanley, later went on to win an Oscar for his screenplay for *Moonstruck* and the guy who composed the score, who was actually suggested to me by Ray Cooper, James Newton Howard, is now one of the biggest composers in the movie business today. It was only his first or second movie. I dare say that no movie, except maybe *American Graffiti*, has ever launched so many careers.'

To make a period film in New York on a tight schedule and a low budget, a little over $5 million, was, in Bill's words, 'a dare'. Most of the film was shot on location during the late summer of 1986 in Queen's, which more closely resembled the Bronx of the mid-Sixties, even down to the ethnic mix of mostly Irish and Italian working-class people. Bill remembers being pretty much left to his own devices during production, meeting George Harrison just once. 'I went over to visit him and he was totally the gentleman and supportive and charming. The only thing we had to talk about that had any bearing on the movie was that he was resistant to the notion of my using The Beatles' song "In My Life" as the film's title song because he didn't want it to seem self-serving. Using that song was totally my idea. I thought the lyrics were perfect, it's all about remembering a neighbourhood, in effect. I just pleaded my case for using it and George finally relented."

It was a little different with O'Brien, although Bill insists there was no major wrangle over the editing of the movie. 'There were some odd suggestions that came out of England from people who were nameless and faceless to me, but eventually I think the movie was edited without any real compromises. There was a bit of Denis wanting to edit it his way but in the long run we wore him down and ultimately we made the movie we wanted to make.' Brian Shingles, however, admits that some O'Brien tinkering did go on. 'Denis certainly did have input on the final cut. It was trimmed down because it was felt to be too long and too slow. It didn't quite work, and yet now I'm sure if people saw it they would be impressed.'

Few did catch it back then, mostly because O'Brien had entered into the film without an American distribution deal. It wasn't until February 1988 that a company called Cineplex Odeon picked it up for release, a situation Bill found far from satisfactory. 'It never got a decent release so it never had a chance to catch fire. It ended up in the hands of an upstart company that wasn't in the distribution business and did a terrible job. I think if *Five Corners* had been a studio movie, it would have been a success.'

In Britain, too, HandMade struggled to find a distributor and *Five Corners* remained unseen until March 1989 when it received a limited release and a smattering of decent notices. 'An odd, volatile and mostly intriguing mix of violence and nostalgia,' said the *Independent*.

As for Tony Bill, he and Denis O'Brien never crossed paths professionally again. Although, funnily enough, Bill's assistant, Kate Smith, did end up working for O'Brien as his secretary at Cadogan Square.

Late in 1986, HandMade were once again cast in the role of saviours of an interesting project facing TV oblivion. Shades of *The Long Good Friday*, but there the resemblance sadly ended. *Bellman and True*, directed by *The Missionary*'s Richard Loncraine, started life as a television film for Euston about an alcoholic ex-con whose stepson is kidnapped to force his participation in a robbery. A month before filming was due to begin, Euston suddenly pulled out claiming the budget was too high. Loncraine says he 'went to Denis and within days he'd given me a million pounds to put into the pot. Not many people will do that. Talk about an easy deal. At the time, Denis had a deal with Cannon, the dreaded Golan and Globus, where they would buy any movie he made for a million. I didn't get anything out of it financially, but at least I was able to make the movie.'

That left one big problem. Loncraine's lead actor was Bernard Hill, who'd suffered so miserably on *Shanghai Surprise*. Hill remembers, 'Just before we started rehearsing, Richard said, "Denis O'Brien is involved now and I'm giving you the option of pulling out. I'll understand and Denis will understand if you pulled out given what happened between you both." And I said, "I don't know what to do. Maybe I need a bit more time." So he said, "Go off and have a coffee and think about it. But one thing you have to remember is, I think this is a vote of confidence from Denis. If he thought that you weren't capable of doing this, he wouldn't have put a million pounds in. So treat it as a vote of confidence." So I decided to go along with it. And I never actually met Denis on the film.'

Filming went smoothly on locations around London. Hill says, 'It was great fun. And working with Richard was a wonderful experience. He's hyperactive. He's a child, really, playing with toys. He used to have a thing on his desk saying "He who dies with the most toys wins". Which is very typical of him. He's a very technical director and a bit like Jim Cameron (with whom Hill worked on *Titanic*) in that he'll look at the acting in as passionate a way as he will the technical side. He does actually leave a lot of it to the trust of the actors.'

Perhaps the biggest hurdle was the film's action set-piece, the bank robbery itself, the complexities of which were so vast Loncraine spent some time with a few contacts of dubious repute from the East End in an attempt to get it looking just right. Indeed, the robbery was so realistically presented that Loncraine was approached by the police afterwards and asked how he knew what he knew.

As usual, there was never enough money and the film began to creep over budget, anathema to O'Brien. Loncraine recalls, 'They tried to fire our producer Michael Wearing and they brought in another producer called Christopher Neame. He came in as a kind of hatchet man, but we got on quite well, he recognised it was a good film and was quite well behaved. But having a producer come in who was there to cut things down when you're trying to direct a movie is not easy. It's tiring; directing is exhausting enough.'

Relations worsened considerably over the editing of the film. 'Denis did behave like an arsehole at the end,' Loncraine states. 'He came to a screening and at the end of it said, "Well, I'd like to get the material and I'm going to do some work on it and I'll talk to you in a week." And I said, "Denis, don't you dare do that to me, you tell me whether you think it's a piece of shit or it's good … don't you dare just dismiss me like that." And we had a big screaming match in the theatre, because it was out of order what he did. In the end, I don't think we changed the film that much.'

Bellman and True opened in London in April 1988 to mixed reviews. 'Action thriller brinkmanship combines with smartly cynical dialogue to produce a thumping British crime yarn,' said the *Financial Times*. The *Observer* noted, 'I have come across colanders less leaky than the plot of this unconvincing movie.'

Loncraine's film also did no business at all. Neither did it find an audience in America when it opened a month later, finding instead the scorn of this critic from the *Village Voice*: 'This is a dull, contrived affair. Purposefully underlit, the movie looks as though it was shot through Hill's bottle of scotch.'

Loncraine is adamant that *Bellman and True* was sold short in the States and never given a chance. 'It definitely wasn't backed well. Denis sold it to Island Pictures and they were going bust at the time and whenever I was in LA on other business they rang me up asking if I had any money I could put into the advertising campaign. And "No" was the answer. So I kind of knew it was dead from then on. One of the things that is exhausting about movies, it's not enough to make a great movie, you have to be lucky as well, you have to find the distribution, and it has to be the right time.'

HandMade's next production was another American venture, shot on location in north Carolina, though fuelled by a trio of British artistic eccentrics – writer Dennis Potter, director Nicolas Roeg and star Gary Oldman. *Track 29* was a post-modernist American update of the Oedipus myth. Roeg's actress wife Theresa Russell, whom *Time* magazine once called 'the criminally beautiful slut-goddess of art-house movies', plays Linda, the wife of a sexually promiscuous doctor (Christopher Lloyd), who escapes the boredom of her marriage by imagining the son she had after being raped as a teenager has returned in the shape of a mysterious stranger (Oldman).

After playing contemporary (if dead) figures like Sid Vicious in *Sid and Nancy* and Joe Orton in *Prick Up Your Ears*, both films elevating him to the top of the current crop of British actors, Gary Oldman found it a welcome change and a wonderful release to play a fictitious character and Nicolas Roeg gave the actor plenty of freedom to make of the part whatever he wanted. It should be added, though, that when he signed on, Oldman reportedly told Roeg he didn't know what the hell the story was all about;

which was fine, as it placed him in the same predicament as most of the audience when they went to see it.

Like many HandMade films before it, *Track 29* was to chart a perilous course through choppy post-production waters, attributed in print by Oldman to O'Brien having 'a bit of a problem. I don't think he understands or likes it.' O'Brien wasn't alone. Roeg's seriously weird movie was evidence of how far his fortunes had sunk after the early brilliance he displayed with masterpieces like *Don't Look Now* and *The Man Who Fell to Earth*. There was a curious disparity, too, in how critics welcomed the film on both sides of the Atlantic when it opened late in the Summer of 1988. '*Track 29* is clever, painstakingly perverse, seeks to disturb and may well strike you as an expensive waste of time,' reported the *Daily Mail*. The *Daily Telegraph* decided, 'Stylish it may be, but *Track 29* is notable for the artistic progress of Gary Oldman, not of Nicolas Roeg.'

The Americans liked it much better. 'Flawed but fascinating. Roeg's talent as a stylist and purveyor of the bizarre and kinky keeps this alive and humming. Definitely worth a visit,' said the *Chicago Reader*, and the *Washington Post* declared, 'Though preposterous, the movie is watchable, if only for the glee Roeg invests in its excesses.'

Thus far, one could say that O'Brien's American gamble had backfired somewhat. Still, the majority of new projects under consideration lent heavily towards the American market. In all, HandMade hoped to put something like $50m into some eight prospective features. These included *The Storyring*, a live action/animation children's story to be filmed in Mexico; *AnotherWorld* from Bruce Gilbert, the producer of *On Golden Pond*; and an adaptation of Kurt Vonnegut's novel *Breakfast of Champions*. Like so many projects mooted around this time, none ever saw daylight, at least not under the HandMade banner. *Breakfast of Champions* was finally made in 1999 with a stellar cast that included Bruce Willis, Albert Finney and Nick Nolte. Having left HandMade, Wendy Palmer recalls the script landing on her desk once again like some demented boomerang. 'I couldn't believe it was back on my desk. I said, "I'm not reading this script again. I read it 50 times 10 years ago and I'm not reading it again. It was shit then. Who wants to go and see it?" and no one did. Fancy that.'

By far the most intriguing project was something called *TVP*. The brainchild of Dave Stewart of the pop group Eurythmics, *TVP* was a fantasy musical about a planet that serves as a kind of Club Med for aliens. HandMade ploughed a considerable amount of money into its development but, early on, the signs were clear that this was never going to work and, if it did, it was going to be very expensive. Palmer says, 'That was just bonkers. Dave Stewart, he's a lovely man, great with music, but the first treatment I read of *TVP* was just virtually illiterate. But George wanted to make that. George was obsessed about that. That was a George project.'

With the exception of the Dave Stewart project, most of the films under consideration around this time left Harrison cold and he began expressing concern that, like those cabaret acts where plates are kept spinning on sticks all at once, O'Brien was taking too much on. 'If you don't watch out,' Harrison was quoted as saying, expanding on the spinning plates motif, 'they all go crashing on the floor. I want to be careful not to get too carried away. I don't like to have too much going at the same time.'

But it was already too late. HandMade had become almost unrecognisable from George Harrison's original grandiose concept of a philanthropic production outfit. 'The tone of the office started to change,' Cooper observes. 'We started to do instead of one or two projects a year, we were dealing with four or five, because we had to, the overhead was increasing and therefore the creativity tends to be a little bit less selective because you need films to feed this thing that you're propelling along.'

HandMade's next duet of films saw them return, albeit briefly, to its British roots and an actor who, besides the Pythons, was very much the cinematic face of HandMade – Bob Hoskins. After the success of *Mona Lisa*, Hoskins had signed a three-picture deal with HandMade and chose as his first project *The Lonely Passion of Judith Hearne* for veteran director Jack Clayton, who'd been trying to make the film for almost three decades, ever since he read Brian Moore's acclaimed novel about a woman fallen on hard times who moves into a Dublin lodging-house where she encounters a ne'er-do-well just returned from America and romance inevitably leads to tragedy. In the past, both Katharine Hepburn and Deborah Kerr had been linked to the part but it was Maggie Smith, making her third and final HandMade appearance, who was cast opposite Hoskins and the two of them give beautifully judged performances.

But despite the star presence of Bob Hoskins and Maggie Smith, backers for the film were decidedly thin on the ground and it was Ray Cooper's music connections which saved the day. 'I pulled in Elton John as part of the financial package of *Judith Hearne*. It was the first film he'd ever been involved in, and now he's got Rocket Films. I think he enjoyed being a part of an interesting movie, albeit very bleak, and being involved with Bob and Maggie.'

Another larger-than-life character was Jack Clayton himself, who hadn't made a film for five years ever since Disney's macabre live-action drama *Something Wicked This Way Comes* was wrenched out of his hands by the Disney management and drastically altered in post-production. In the press, Clayton ranted about 'non-professionals interfering in something they don't understand'. So a collision course with Denis O'Brien seemed almost inevitable and it duly arrived one day on the set when Clayton threatened to kill the businessman. 'We're the best of friends now,' O'Brien joked later. 'But he swears to this day he was serious.'

Clayton certainly had a reputation. On the last day of shooting on *The Great Gatsby*, he single-handedly tore down most of the sets. Shingles says, 'I felt there was always a lot of pent-up anger there. But he was a real craftsman. Jack had been ill and we lost a couple of weeks shooting at the very outset in Dublin, so you were already behind schedule. Denis was aware of Jack's personality. I don't think Denis would knowingly rub someone up the wrong way. There was a threatened incident, but I think that was just Jack's character.'

The Lonely Passion of Judith Hearne opened in America towards the end of 1987 to mixed notices. 'It's the feel-bad movie of 1987, just in time for the suicide season,' opined *Village Voice*, while *Variety* stated, 'An ensemble of sterling performances, an intelligent, carefully crafted adaptation.'

The film is rather dour and drab and that probably, more than anything else, frightened off the public. 'I remember going to a screening,' says Shingles, 'and they say, "Be honest," and all the rest of it, but honesty isn't always appreciated. It's the last thing you should be to a director. And Jack said, "What do you think?" And I said that it was unremittingly grim and he looked at me and just said, "Really." And I knew I'd just committed the most heinous of crimes. But Jack, he let that pass.'

In England HandMade ran into even bigger problems when a suitable distributor for *Judith Hearne* couldn't be found resulting in the film languishing on the shelf for almost a year before Cannon planned to release it in November 1988. Then the shit hit the fan in October when HandMade took legal action against the already financially beleaguered Cannon for £1.6 million in back payments which O'Brien claimed had been owing for six months. Cannon held the video rights to several HandMade films from a deal previously made between HandMade and Thorn EMI, which Cannon had bought in 1986.

Wendy Palmer remembers, 'Cannon were really proud of the fact that they had HandMade, because that was class for those guys. Menahem Golan and Yoram Globus used to call me "the handmaiden", which used to really irritate me. Then Menahem and Yoram, who are not bad deal-makers themselves, just realised that the EMI deal was too generous and they just stopped paying. It was a bad deal for them and they didn't want to do it. It all got very messy.'

Ten days before *Judith Hearne* was due to open, Cannon, then the UK's largest cinema chain, barred all HandMade films from being shown in any of their screens until the case was resolved. 'My patience has now gone through the roof,' O'Brien said in a press statement. Money that had been spent on producing trailers, posters and advertising material was wasted. Worse, HandMade were left with a release date but no cinemas to put their film in.

Finally, in January 1989, *Judith Hearne* opened but in small, limited venues scattered across the country. Shingles recalls, 'The problem was it was booked in for one or two weeks and we couldn't extend it and the film opened to such good business and, had it been able to move on properly, we might have done something with it, but we never got that opportunity. Once a film loses momentum, it's very difficult to pick that up again. Jack Clayton was very depressed by what happened with Cannon. And I remember him saying, "I don't know if I will ever make another feature film." ' After *The Lonely Passion of Judith Hearne*, Clayton made a film for the BBC before passing away in 1995. He never did make another film for the cinema.

Despite its lack of visibility, *Judith Hearne* was generally well received by British critics. 'An excellent piece of work ... one of HandMade's best,' raved the *Scotsman*. And *Films and Filming* declared, 'Despite faults, the film still gets three stars for courage in tackling some difficult and potentially unprofitable themes and for some quite stunning acting. Maggie Smith deserves the recognition best brought by packed houses.'

The Cannon fiasco rumbled on for a few more years and was finally settled in 1991 when the British High Court ordered Pathe Communications, the company who'd bought out the bankrupt Cannon Group, to pay all outstanding money owed to HandMade. The Cannon lawsuit was the first of several lodged by HandMade in the late Eighties, almost all of which sought to recoup monies allegedly owed them under a variety of distribution and exhibition agreements. In the end, entities as diverse as Virgin, Island, Embassy and Warner Brothers all found themselves entangled to varying degrees in HandMade's increasingly complex web of litigation.

Bob Hoskins followed up *The Lonely Passion of Judith Hearne* with an even more remote and uncommercial project, one he himself had developed, basing much of it on stories told him by his gypsy grandmother. *The Raggedy Rawney* tells of an army deserter (Dexter Fletcher) who dons a dress and tribal make-up to blend in with a band of gypsies, duping them into thinking he's a 'Rawney' woman possessing magical powers. Hoskins deliberately set his film in an unspecified time and place, believing as he did that it wasn't nations but the very concept of war itself that was the real enemy.

Sadly, the film didn't amount to very much, being notable today only as Hoskins' début as a film director. Directing movies never was a burning ambition but as he felt so close to the material it was probably the natural thing to do. It was O'Brien who made it a condition of his financing the picture that Hoskins also take one of the leading roles. Hoskins the director wasn't as marketable as Hoskins the actor. Cleverly, Hoskins cast the movie, both in front and behind the camera, almost exclusively with people he'd worked with in the past. This was a huge learning curve for him and there was no time for egos or clashing personalities. Shot on location in Czechoslovakia in the late summer of 1987, *The Raggedy Rawney* was completed on schedule and under budget. Hoskins reportedly returned some £170,000 to HandMade's bank account. That must have pleased O'Brien.

The Raggedy Rawney was Hoskins' second film to be delayed a release by HandMade's ongoing dispute with Cannon. When it finally opened in

Britain in July 1989, the critics gave it a decidedly dodgy reception. 'The whole affair resembles a version of Brecht's *Mother Courage* commissioned by UNICEF from the authors of *EastEnders*,' slammed the *Observer*. The *Financial Times* stated, 'This fey, portentous movie undoubtedly represents Hoskins' urgent summons to return to full-time acting.' And the *Sunday Telegraph* believed 'Hoskins' visually assured directorial début is a pacifist statement rendered incoherent by Hoskins' own screenplay which is rather more feeble than fable.'

As for America, the film's release was delayed a year. HandMade were now having to cope with the kind of fraught difficulties other small independent companies faced, that of getting proper distribution for their movies in America. Their next project suffered a similar fate to *The Raggedy Rawney*, although that was to be the least of its problems. Denis O'Brien had agreed to finance, to the tune of $3.2 million, an off-beat film called *Powwow Highway* about a pair of native Americans travelling across the West in a battered Buick from first-time director Jonathan Wacks, the celebrated producer of Indie cult hit *Repo Man*. Shot during November 1987 on location in Wyoming, Santa Fe and Montana, at the site of a Cheyenne reservation, everything seemed to be progressing well. 'Through pre-production and production Denis O'Brien was a prince,' Wacks recalls. 'He never interfered; he was never there! He basically let us make the movie that we wanted to make.'

It was after Wacks had completed his first cut of the movie that a request by O'Brien for a copy of it on tape to be sent over to London unnerved him. Wacks assumed he just wanted to see it, but a fortnight later the director received a series of instructions of changes and cuts O'Brien wanted made to the film. 'I went though them out of respect to him as the executive producer and sent back a fax saying, "Some of your points sound like good ideas, others can't be made in terms of the footage that we have and some make no sense to me at all." And literally minutes later, my producer, Jan Wieringa, got a call from Denis and his opening gambit was, "Jan, do you want to stay on the picture?" She said, "Of course, Denis. What are you talking about?" He said, "Well, if you want to stay on the picture just make sure he makes these cuts." And Jan came in all ashen and said to me, "Listen, Denis insists that we make all these cuts." And I said, "There's no way I can make some of those cuts." She called him back and then my phone rang and Denis gave me the same "do you want to stay on the picture" speech. And I said, "Denis, listen, I'm willing to make whatever works for the picture. I'm not that egotistical or stubborn, but some of these things are just plain ridiculous and they won't work. So the answer is no." So he said, "Well, you'd better make up your mind because either you make the changes or you're off the picture." And then he hung up.'

Wacks proceeded to cut his film the way he thought it should be cut and heard nothing more until he was in the middle of the final mix when Jan Wieringa got another call from O'Brien to say he was coming in personally to make sure that all the changes had been made. 'Impossible,' retorted Wacks. The film was all broken down into separate reels and in no fit state to be shown. 'He doesn't care,' said Jan. 'He just wants to see it in whatever form you can possibly show it.'

The next day, O'Brien showed up at the preview theatre, but the real surprise was that behind him was George Harrison and his wife Olivia. Wacks says, 'That was just devastating to me because I thought, when I get to show it to George, I want it to be in the best possible condition. And apart from anything else, it was the first time I'd met George Harrison and that was a little unnerving, albeit exciting. So we started running the movie and, as we went past the first section that was supposed to have a cut in it, I looked at Jan and she looked at me and we waited for something to be said and nothing happened and we moved on until the last reel was shown and George turned to me and said, "I love it. Don't change a thing." And Denis O'Brien walked out and I've never spoken to him since. That was the last time I ever saw him.'

So bad did relations become that, during the last few weeks of post-production, Wacks, who was renting an editing suite at a studio run by Tony Bill, went to the incredible lengths of locking up the film in his own home every night, so concerned was he that an associate of HandMade who worked in the studio offices might have a key and seek to remove the film in order to make the changes O'Brien wanted. 'It got pretty nasty,' Wacks remembers. 'But my feeling about it was that there were certain non-negotiable changes and, even though I didn't formally have final cut, it was done in such an obscene way that I just wasn't willing to co-operate. With Denis, there was no discussion on anything. I remember chatting to Tony Bill about this and there really was a feeling that, actually, Denis didn't give a shit one way or the other about what the cut was, what he really enjoyed was just messing with creative people's heads. He just wanted to go in there and stir it up and have that control. But at the end, George came in and saved the day.'

Wacks can only guess at why Harrison felt he needed to be on hand at that preview and not allow O'Brien to attend it alone. 'My instinct is that George wanted to make this film, Denis didn't. Denis had these fantasies of moving into the American market and George couldn't be less interested, so he and Ray Cooper really were the cheerleaders for this film. I'd been in touch with Ray and told him how appalled I was by this whole procedure, so I imagine he communicated that to George and, because George was in LA, he personally attended that screening.'

O'Brien's dispassionate approach to the film also affected how *Powwow Highway* was treated upon release. It was shipped around to various distributors before Lorrimar picked it up. Lorrimar was then almost immediately bought by Warner Brothers, who ended up releasing *Powwow* Stateside in March 1989. It wasn't an ideal situation for Wacks who'd have preferred a smaller independent distributor, someone who understood the 'art-house' market, a company like Miramax. Warners simply shoved *Powwow* out there with no publicity whatsoever, not caring if it lived or died, and Wacks' film never found an audience, this despite the fact it had won the top award of The Filmmaker's Trophy at that year's Sundance Festival.

1989 was really the year that Robert Redford's Sundance Festival took off in a big way, thanks partly to the success there of *Sex, Lies and Videotape* which walked away with the Audience Award. Wacks observes, 'What was interesting about *Sex, Lies*, which really won the consolation prize, because the Audience Award is just like a popularity contest for people who show up, is that Miramax did an incredible job of distributing the picture, whereas Denis did absolutely nothing coming out of Sundance. We got great reviews and all this press attention and he went nowhere with it.'

In Britain, the film fared even worse, scarcely being shown at all, again despite a clutch of excellent reviews, such as the *Daily Mail*'s: 'Ironic that Britain's HandMade should launch one of the best American films in ages.'

Wacks even had to stage his own opening night for the film, getting as he did no support from O'Brien. Held at the Director's Guild in Los Angeles, it was a charity event in support of a local native American museum. 'George showed up and brought some of his friends — Joni Mitchell, Bonnie Rait and Kris Kristofersson were there. It was a great evening. George greeted everybody and congratulated the actors. Looking back, I feel very honoured that George got involved in my film and I feel very grateful that he stood by it. As for Denis O'Brien, it was absolutely clear to me that this was the work of one rather twisted individual rather than how things have to be. I've made other films since then and I've never had that experience. There are always battles and differences, but that kind of cold, calculated insistence that you work in a certain way I've just never encountered before or since. Denis was basically a businessman who was trying to work with creative people and didn't really have the first clue how to do that.'

CHAPTER 12

THE PARTY'S OVER

After their less than successful foray into American drama with *Powwow Highway* and *Five Corners*, HandMade made a decision to go back to what it knew best – comedy, but with haphazard results. On paper, *How to Get Ahead in Advertising* looked extremely promising, reuniting as it did *Withnail and I* collaborators Bruce Robinson and Richard E Grant. Robinson first drafted the story in the form of a novella in 1979 and reignited the idea around the time of *Withnail*, believing as he did that Grant was perfect for his central character of Dennis Bagley, an ad man who has a nervous breakdown and develops a boil on his neck that grows into a head that starts talking to him.

Grant recalls, 'Bruce asked me to do another film with him during the second week of shooting *Withnail*. As I was so thrilled to be doing my first film at all, the prospect of another one seemed unlikely and, indeed, took a couple of years hence to get up and running. Although the part of Bagley was already written, Bruce claimed I was the actor who spoke with his "voice".'

Casting Grant, however, came with a price. Was Bagley going to be seen as the natural progression of the Withnail character – the wasted, booze-soaked Sixties drop-out becomes the late-Eighties greedy manipulator? Certainly, Grant's performance in *How to Get Ahead* is just as memorable as his Withnail. Few, if any, other actors of his generation could have reached and sustained such frenzied heights. 'Playing that part was eight weeks of high-pitched mania that was physically exhausting to maintain,' adds Grant.

How to Get Ahead in Advertising is typical Robinson, sometimes deliriously, sometimes disastrously over the top. But deliberately so. Robinson told one critic that he likened the film to a 'pantomime' and was looking to 'kick the British in their bollocks'. Certainly, no prisoners are taken in this savage assault on the advertising business and the consumer capitalism of the late Eighties in Thatcher's Britain. It was a rant, pure and simple, and although informing this author that, apart from George Harrison and one or two others, he found HandMade to be a 'disreputable organisation', Robinson was nevertheless beholden to it for coming up with £2 million for him to have a good rant. Robinson was also a much more confident director two years on from *Withnail and I*, though still nervous, playfully telling one reporter that he'd drawn a big 'D' on the back of his hand so if he ever got into trouble, he could look at it and think, Fuck, I'm the director!

Opening in the early summer of 1989, *How to Get Ahead in Advertising* met with some admirers. 'A vigorous, cheerfully outrageous British satire,' declared *Rolling Stone*, and the *Financial Times* said, 'The film is a showpiece for Grant, who more than ever resembles a regency dandy converted to hellfire preacher.' But on the whole, the film divided critical attention, particularly in Britain, with many feeling it to be a tirade too far against a pretty obvious target. Today, *How to Get Ahead* is all but forgotten in the wake of the cult phenomenon over *Withnail*. Grant says, 'I'm still fond of the experience and the people I worked with on *How to Get Ahead* and the friendship it afforded. It perhaps lacks a counter-viewpoint to balance its crusading ferocity.'

David Leland, who'd written *Mona Lisa* and had a smash hit on his hands with *Wish You Were Here*, had been sent a script by Joe Eszterhas (later the writer of *Basic Instinct* and the infamous *Showgirls*) called *Checking Out*, a black farce about an airline company executive (played by Jeff Daniels) who is so gripped by his own mortality that he comes down with a chronic case of hypochondria. Leland liked it but thought the script needed major revision. Ultimately disappointed with the end result, Leland left the project, only to be told by HandMade that they wanted to go ahead with the film and he could rewrite it himself to his own satisfaction.

Shot on location in Southern California, it was only when the film was test-screened that doubts began to be expressed. HandMade and Warner Brothers, who were distributing the film in America, were worried Leland had created something too dangerous to be successful, a hybrid of a film that couldn't be conveniently categorised. They also believed Jeff Daniels' character was too unappealing for mainstream audiences. The result was that Leland's film was taken off him by O'Brien and re-edited in a way he found totally unacceptable, reduced to a run-of-the-mill wacky comedy instead of what he'd originally intended, a story that trod a fine line between comedy and tragedy.

Leland knew he didn't have final cut and that HandMade were well within their rights to do what they did, but it seemed to him a sour irony that, after they'd specifically stated he could write and direct it the way he wanted, they'd, in his view, 'totally destroyed' the picture. In a letter to this author, Leland expressed his feelings about how he was treated: 'My experiences of working with Denis O'Brien were utterly unpleasant. He re-cut *Checking Out*. I hated what he did to it and the way he did it. My version of the film will never be seen. Nothing worse can happen to a film-maker. As Jeff Daniels said to me after the event (you must imagine this in Jeff's drawl), "I think we made a good film, you think we made a good film, but somewhere between us makin' it and them showin' it, it got fucked." Precisely.'

It was later particularly galling for Leland that some of the criticism the film received, particularly in America when it opened there in May 1989, was the direct result of vital scenes left on the cutting-room floor. 'I heard *Checking Out* just became a nightmare,' Gilliam says. 'The film is not, by any means, a perfect film, but it's really interesting. In particular, there are two scenes that are I think brilliant, and those are the two scenes Denis wanted out. I began to feel after a while Denis had this incredible unerring ability to go to the very core of the thing and rip its heart out. He was like some Aztec priest.' But others felt that no amount of tinkering could have saved what was almost from inception a poorly conceived project.

Shingles believes, 'I don't think *Checking Out* would have amounted to anything anyway, no matter who directed it, if it had been re-cut, re-shot or whatever. It lacked any direction or any point. With all the best will in the world, it was poor.'

Checking Out did indeed receive some devastatingly bad reviews. 'In a closely fought contest between this dire, rambling tale and *Erik the Viking* for worst comedy of the year, I think Mr Leland gets the gong on a photo finish,' said *Today*. The *NME* stated, 'Disappointing for someone like Leland. This is HandMade's plumpest turkey since *Shanghai Surprise*,' and *Variety* called it 'a dreadfully unfunny one-joke black comedy. Warner Brothers is advised to bury this stiff as quickly as decency allows.'

As usual, when O'Brien started intimidating and interfering, it was Ray Cooper, in his role as creative middle-man, who bore the brunt of it. *Checking Out* was particularly messy. 'Ray got himself in a terrible state with David Leland,' Terry Gilliam says, 'because he tried so hard to mediate and it was an unmediatable position because Denis was so extreme. David then started blaming Ray for conspiring against the film. That was really painful because Ray cares incredibly about the art of film and to be damned by David didn't please him.' By this time, Ray Cooper had sadly become little more than a mouthpiece for O'Brien, a gofer, and his friends were getting increasingly concerned. Richard Loncraine tried his best. 'I said, "This is just demoralising, you're too bright and nice a man to be walking around doing Denis's dirty work." You could tell what he was saying to you was not what he believed, but the boss had told him to go and say it. He was kind of the hatchet man for Denis and Ray's too nice to be a hatchet man. I always felt that Denis did not treat Ray with the respect he deserved.'

Cooper himself was also beginning to feel the strain. 'I'd get phone calls from people like David Leland saying, "Ray, what are you doing?" And at the end of the day it was, "Well, that's my job." And then I had to look at myself in the mirror and say, "That's no justification." So, occasionally, I would have to make a stand against Denis. But it was working away at my soul at the same time. It was all becoming quite painful. I was having anxiety attacks and all sorts of things.'

HandMade's two comeback comedies lacked considerably either the charm or popularity of their golden age comedies and, in the case of

Checking Out, left huge battle scars on the company that were never to heal. 'That caused such a furore,' Shingles remembers. 'I think George got dragged into it. A lot of people have said afterwards you can point to David Leland and say that the demise of HandMade starts around him and that movie.'

It was during the making of *Checking Out* in Los Angeles that David Leland got to know Harrison who was out there recording the first Travelling Wilburys album at the same time. 'George and I planned to make a film of the first Wilburys album,' Leland says. 'This did not happen but I did direct three Travelling Wilburys music videos. Working with George was always a pleasure and I greatly value the time I spent with him.' Almost certainly Leland confided to Harrison the problems he was experiencing with O'Brien, something along the lines of: 'Do you realise that this man is taking over creative control from the artists?' As Harrison always had more affinity with the artists than with the business end of things, he acted upon his friend's concerns causing a huge rift to open up between himself and O'Brien, forcing him, perhaps for the first time, to look at what was happening to the company and to re-evaluate his position within it. The strain was beginning to tell and, although the whole tragedy was more or less played out behind closed doors, the atmosphere of ill feeling was tangible. Shingles remembers, 'I did some work remastering George's concert for Bangladesh for video release, and there were costs, and I was always told that you had to bill for whatever work you did. At that point, Denis wasn't around and I asked, "Who should pay for this?" in a letter to George, and the note came right back – "Brian, you still don't understand. I'm paying for everything!" It was then I thought, Patently, things aren't going well.'

*   *   *

It was one of the biggest parties the British film industry had ever known, a celebration of HandMade's first 10 years. Held inside a giant marquee at Shepperton Studios in September 1988 with over 120 people in attendance, the event was an enormous success. Those that were there still remember it with excitement and fondness. Few, though, could have realised that the company was 30 days away from catastrophe.

The job of organising the party fell to Wendy Palmer, an immense task which consumed most of her time for the next three months. As the invites went out, one name was conspicuous by its absence – Stephen Woolley. O'Brien, it seemed, had still not forgiven the producer for their clash on *Mona Lisa*. 'It was just weird,' Woolley states. 'HandMade sent an invitation to my partner Nick Powell, 'cos Nick was fine, he didn't have to get into any of these bruising matches that I had to get into. But I didn't get an invite and Nick said to HandMade, "There must be something wrong with the post because Stephen didn't get his invite." And they rang back and said, "There's nothing wrong with the post." And Nick said, "I'm going to bring him as my guest, is that OK?" And they said, "If you want to bring him as your guest, then we're going to rescind your invite as well." So I was written off the history books.'

The decision to exclude Woolley was one that infuriated Wendy Palmer. 'Denis would not have Steve Woolley at that party. I begged him to reconsider. I begged him. I said, "Then don't invite Nick," because to invite Nick and not Steve was worse. But he would not change his mind.'

The party didn't come cheap. £50,000 was the first estimate until, at the last minute, George Harrison decided he wanted to invite his hero Carl Perkins over to jam with him live on stage, a request that bumped up the overall price of the function to nearer £85,000. 'But it was a humdinger of a party,' says Shingles. 'Whatever else HandMade achieved, they achieved a wonderful party. The New York office flew over for it and coaches were laid on from Cadogan Square to take us all out to Shepperton. And you thought, not that we'd made it, but ten years on and we're still here.'

The only real downer was the food. Palmer says, 'Denis chose the caterers. This is how involved Denis was in things if he wanted to be. He went for someone who catered for the Queen, because that was very Denis.' The food however, was hardly touched. The studio's location caterers came to the rescue by rustling up a traditional English fried breakfast in the early hours of the morning. When the assembled masses suddenly smelt the reassuring odour of bacon and egg, they made an instant beeline for it. Palmer insists, 'It was the best food we had all night.'

Besides the HandMade staff, producers, directors and actors from all of HandMade's films were well represented, amongst them Paul McGann. 'It was the first proper swanky do I'd ever been to and we all got plastered. I remember Denis standing up and giving this speech with mathematical equations in it, as accountants are want to do, giving the "we'd like to thank" sort of speeches. And he reeled off this list of names, of all the marvellous people he'd worked with in the last 10 years. Now you'll have to picture me there … I'm sitting with my wife and George Harrison shouted, "And what about Paul McGann?" And my wife said, "Your hand gripped my wrist so tight it left an indentation in my arm, and you said something to me so stupid like, 'A Beatle just said my name,' and you just gushed like a baby." I said to her, "What else did I say?" She said, "I'm in his thoughts." Jesus. It was a funny old evening.'

By far the best speech of the night was courtesy of Michael Palin. It was delivered so beautifully that no one there that night has probably ever forgotten it. A condensed version of the speech is presented below by kind permission of Michael Palin.

Ladies and gentlemen, we are here to celebrate 10 years of HandMade Films. Denis rang and asked me if I could deliver a fawning tribute — no stick, no undue criticism — or else he would re-release The Missionary *on a double bill with* Water. *Though many of you may not be aware of it, the real founder of HandMade Films is sadly not with us tonight. I refer, of course, to the late Sir Bernard Delfont. He it was who, one spring morning in 1978, decided on an impulse to read one of the scripts his company was filming. And what he read he didn't like at all. It was called* Monty Python's Life of Brian *and he thought it blasphemous. Nowadays, as any good film producer knows, blasphemy is almost as good as Tom Cruise at the box office. If, for instance,* The Adventures of Pippi Longstocking *had managed to incorporate a scene where Pippi fantasises over the Messiah changing a car wheel in a pair of boxer shorts it might well have found the box-office success that so eluded it this summer.*

Anyway, Sir Bernard pulled EMI out of the deal, leaving us with 20 crosses and 60 nails of minimal second-hand value. The film's chances of being made were about to expire when a good Samaritan in the guise of George Harrison happened upon us. And HandMade Films was born. The name was coined by George who wanted to call it

British HandMade Films but wasn't allowed to. At roughly the same time, Terry Gilliam tried to call his company the British Film Industry Ltd but was refused on the grounds that there already was one. How times have changed.

It is exceptional to have someone like George involved, even if it does take him so long to read scripts. I once asked George how he liked the script of A Private Function. 'I'm up to page seven,' he said apologetically. I asked him again three months later and he said he was up to page 11 and really enjoying it. But to know that one of the driving forces behind the company is someone who knows all about the trials and tribulations of showbiz from the artist's point of view is one of the great attractions of working for HandMade.

It's exceptional also to have someone like Denis, who manages time after time by some extraordinary balancing act to be able to persuade someone somewhere that people, who in many cases have only the tiniest of track records, are worth a few million. And to do this with the minimum of physical force. I once asked Denis how he did finance the operation. He was a little vague but mentioned a great many islands whose names I hadn't heard since stamp-collecting days, and various 'partners' whose names sounded awfully redolent of the Vercotti Brothers' sketches.

And, of course, it's not just Denis and George we're saying thank you to tonight, we're also acknowledging the countless thousands who have toiled away over the years at Cadogan Towers or in remote parts of the world trying to sell the Costa Rican rights of Bullshot. They have all contributed to HandMade's extraordinary record. It's a record of generous encouragement for first-time talent. It's a record of investing not in press conferences and glittering lunches but in a steady succession of interesting, unusual, individual and memorable movies. It's a record of taking appalling risks. It's a record of persisting with innovation rather than resting on laurels. It's a record of valuing independence at a time when so many companies are looking to eat up or be eaten up by someone else. And it's a record of trusting rather than fearing the film-maker. Never was a name for a company better chosen. As a beneficiary, more than once, of their policies and their judgement, and being fully aware that without

them very few of the films that have brought us here tonight would
ever have been made, I ask you to raise your glasses, or contact lenses
if you prefer, to HandMade films.

Regardless of the party atmosphere, George Harrison was unusually
grouchy and low for much of the evening. Even jamming with Carl Perkins
failed to lift the gloom for long. Many of his friends and acquaintances
were in attendance, but also a disagreeably large quotient of bankers,
lawyers and accountants, to whom Harrison purportedly blew his stack,
abusing them with profane language. The word 'freeloaders' was certainly
used. 'I hate fucking films anyway,' he declared, and later announced, 'He's
the only one who knows where all the fucking money's gone,' while
pointing in the direction of an accountant. Palmer remembers, 'George
got up and just gave an absolutely scathing speech, something like, "What
are you fuckers doing here? Here I am spending more money on you." So
things were pretty rocky at that point. He was angry. He didn't like anyone
in the film business at that point. Great party, though.'

What Harrison did next took everyone by surprise – he sacked the staff
at Cadogan Square. The bombshell arrived in the form of a fax, impersonal
in the extreme, and dated 21 October 1988. Palmer recalls, 'The list of
who was fired is fascinating – it was only those who he could remember.
The people that weren't fired were the people that he didn't know. That
really indicated what he knew about the company. He just fired the people
he knew, which kind of made it worse, really. But it's a major claim to
fame, being fired by George Harrison.'

Something like this had been expected. The directors at HandMade
were all aware that trouble was brewing, as were key employees like Ray
Cooper and Wendy Palmer. Some staff members were even secretly
looking for other jobs. Wendy Palmer was already in conversation with
Working Title to set up a sales operation for them. But for the majority of
workers, Harrison's fax was a bolt out of the blue and it sent everyone
reeling. 'I think that fax was a very instinctive move on George's part,'
Palmer believes. 'It was temper. Something had gone on between George
and Denis and George's attitude was, "This film company's giving me
headaches, I'm sick of it, I don't want it any more, I'm just going to close
it down." He woke up one day – he was in the States when he fired us –

and he phoned up his PA and dictated this thing. She faxed it to him, he faxed it back, and then she put them on each of our desks.'

Denis O'Brien was in America, too, when he heard the news and was as shocked as anyone. He had to be sent the fax personally before he could believe it. Immediately, he returned to England, but Harrison at first refused to meet with him. Meanwhile, it was mild panic over at Cadogan Square. 'We were just told to come into work as normal,' Shingles says, 'business as usual, and we weren't to breathe a word of this to anybody outside. It was a very sad and traumatic time for everybody. I don't know if the writing was on the wall, because you always hoped against hope that things will improve and it appeared that the bridge had been healed between George and Denis, but obviously not. The seeds had been sown and, whatever happened after that, obviously HandMade was never going to survive in its original form ... how could it? Things were never quite the same. I used to say to Kate Smith, Denis's secretary, "You know, life will never be as good as it is here, if we all leave." And it's true, because everyone refers to it as the good old days. We were a small company making movies ... what more could you ask for? And you were involved, you might not be a producer, but you were involved.'

After a while, a series of negotiations took place between Harrison and O'Brien with the result that a compromise was reached. Instead of sacking everyone, there would be a substantial reduction in staff numbers. Everyone was called together for a meeting in the conference room where O'Brien told them straight out that there were going to be radical changes but that the company would continue to operate and no one should be unduly alarmed. But behind the scenes, things were happening. A list was drawn up of those who were to get the chop. 'And I was on it,' Palmer says. 'Someone had told me. There was 10 of us that had to go. Denis phoned me up, it was six o'clock. "Oh, Wendy, could you remind me tomorrow morning that I have to see you." And I knew what he wanted to see me about and I'm like, "Well, do you need me to prepare any papers for this meeting?" He said, "No, I just want to see you." And I said, "You can see me now if you want." And he's like, "Well, I'm going to the opera, but I've got 10 minutes." I went up to his office and he said, "All I really wanted to say was, Wendy, if you get offered another job, you should take it." I said, "Denis, it sounds to me like you're making me redundant." He said, "No,

I wouldn't go as far as to say that." I said, "Let's just try to make this more clear cut. If you're going to make me redundant, then just make me redundant." And we had a bit of a barney for a few days and then I got my redundancy. That was just a very Denis thing. I remember going up there and he's all dressed up, black tie, to go out to the opera and "Bye!" But you know, it adds to the story, doesn't it?'

Wendy's dismissal was a surprise to many. 'Wendy was Head of Sales and excellent at her job,' says Cooper. 'Everyone liked her. And when Wendy left, she was very, very hurt. She was bitterly hurt by Denis's action. And Denis made the wrong decision getting rid of Wendy, and has admitted as much since, because there were other people who should have gone instead. And I thought, Why did they choose Wendy and not so and so? I don't know how they made those choices.'

Wendy Palmer had the last laugh, though, going on to carve out a highly successful career in movies, becoming one of the most influential female figures in the UK film business, so there are no regrets. 'I certainly don't feel bitter and twisted about it. I know lots of people do. But it was also wonderful. I had this incredible education there. I'd learnt a tremendous amount – from nothing. They gave you all these opportunities and it was sink or swim.'

Besides the staff reductions, HandMade also radically scaled down its production output and, in perhaps an acknowledgement of the fact that their American odyssey had been more or less a failure, closed down its New York office. The one in Los Angeles remained active, however. O'Brien put a brave public face on matters when the press got hold of the company's misfortunes, claiming that the unstable situation in America for all independent companies necessitated such cutbacks. In an interview for *Variety*, he tried to be optimistic. 'The hallmark of our company is low budgets and low overheads so we're in the best situation to make it through any period. We're staying with our strength, which is comedy.' True to his word, HandMade's next two films were comedies. They were also to prove the last films HandMade were ever to make.

First up was probably the owner of the least edifying title in cinema history. It also sadly turned out to be one of the least edifying movies in cinema history, too – *Cold Dog Soup*. The project belonged to Alan Metter and was a black comedy about two guys racing around Los Angeles trying to get rid of the corpse of a dead dog. O'Brien was a fan of Metter's 1986 comedy *Back to School* and, when the script of *Cold Dog Soup* landed on his desk, he hailed it as 'a quintessential HandMade film'. Others weren't too sure. Dick Clement recalls, 'Myself and Ian La Frenais were around at this time and read a lot of scripts and I remember looking at *Cold Dog Soup*, which was dreadful. HandMade did make some very, very odd choices towards the end, having started off so well. I think there was talk of us doing a rewrite but we just didn't get it at all. And then, lo and behold, it got made!'

For Metter, the very involvement of HandMade gave his project a certain cachet, even though he recognised the company was no longer the force it had once been. 'I always thought that HandMade was what Apple Records was when it first started up, when they signed James Taylor. It was an artist-oriented endeavour, so it deserved the utmost respect. Denis may have turned it into something slightly different. I don't feel like I made a film the way *Life of Brian* was made. I was aware that this was a Denis project more than a George project. I was never aware that George even read the script. At the beginning, they were making films for the reason they started the company, but by the time we arrived it was filling a pipeline a little bit, I got the feeling.'

Metter, in fact, had met George Harrison back in the mid-Seventies when the musician was in Los Angeles and needed someone to shoot a music video for him to take on *Saturday Night Live*. 'I was brought up to his house in LA on Hallowe'en. We knocked on the door and George answered. I said, "Trick or treat," and he laughed. I told him my idea for the video, he liked it and we sat down and wrote this video at his kitchen table in about two or three hours.'

During the shooting of *Cold Dog Soup*, however, Metter scarcely had any dealings with him. 'George dropped by one day. He happened to be in LA. It was great to see him again. He looked at 15 minutes of rushes and left and that was the only contact I had with him on the entire project.'

Metter's relationship with O'Brien was equally non-existent, though mutually pleasant. 'I didn't see Denis a lot, he was building a house and he was on a sail boat. But I can't say a bad thing about him. He honoured everything he said he would. I'm sure there are a lot of guys that can knock Denis; I'm not one of them. He was very enthusiastic about making this film and anybody that comes to me with that kind of attitude I automatically like. He was a very positive guy.'

The biggest creative disagreement Metter had with O'Brien was over casting. 'I thought Little Richard might be good for it. Originally, the lead role, eventually played by Randy Quaid, was written for a black man from the Caribbean. We met with Little Richard but Denis didn't approve of casting him. Randy's wonderful in the part, but I always wonder what it would have been like off the wall with Little Richard.'

The lowest point of the production came when Metter was in the editing room and heard that Warner Brothers, who were handling US distribution for HandMade, didn't want to touch his film with the proverbial barge pole. The result was that *Cold Dog Soup* went virtually unseen in America and, for that matter, Britain. Just as well for the public if the critical reaction was anything to go by. 'Quite possibly the worst film ever made,' slammed *Sight and Sound*. 'Even the hungriest film hound is likely to conclude that this is a dog's breakfast,' barked the *Daily Telegraph*.

But Metter is philosophical about the rough ride his film received. 'We made the picture on a shoestring. Did it come out as good as we hoped? Maybe not, but we gave it a go. I've seen worse. From a film-maker's perspective, it was a totally positive experience.'

For many, *Cold Dog Soup* represented how much O'Brien had lost his way. 'Denis just had the most appalling taste,' says Palmer. 'While I was still at HandMade, I tried selling *Cold Dog Soup* but I couldn't find a distributor. You'd start telling people what it was about and they'd just go, "Why are you making this movie?" And I'd be going, "Mmm, that's a good point." It was just terrible.'

Cold Dog Soup seemed to sum up perfectly the point financially and creatively the company had reached – rock bottom. 'It was a disastrous movie,' confirms Shingles, 'an awful movie that had no redeeming points. I haven't seen it for years and I've no desire ever to see it again. And that bloody stuffed dog they used in the movie turned up at the London office and we always felt that was an omen. It looked so realistic and we moved it from office to office because nobody wanted to keep it, they felt it was jinxed, but no one had the nerve to throw it out. It was like what happened with *The Missionary*. All these witch doctor things had come back from Kenya and they said, "You can't throw it out." And that went from office to office for years and years because no one had the nerve to throw them out. But *Cold Dog Soup* was really the end of the road.'

Not quite. HandMade's last film under the auspices of Harrison and O'Brien was partly to redeem the company, proving to be their biggest hit in America and the UK for years. Too late, of course. The film was *Nuns on the Run* and had ridden a curious path to Cadogan Square. Jonathan Lynn, writer of TV's *Yes, Minister*, was in an LA hotel room fearing the box office failure of his Hollywood directorial début *Clue*, and guessing that he'd better come up with an idea for another film pretty quickly. Suddenly, this notion of two soft-hearted crooks who disguise themselves as nuns to escape marauding gangsters danced into his head. Lynn pitched the idea to Peter Guber at Warner Brothers and settled down to write the script, setting it in Boston. 'But Warners had a problem with the script. I wrote another draft and they had problems with that. Then I went to a meeting at which, as is the way of the movie business, a 27-year-old executive gave me a lecture on comedy. This executive never having produced, directed, written or acted in a comedy. Basically, the tone of the meeting was I had to cut out all of the religious jokes which he said were going to cause offence. I said, "You can't have a film in which two guys hide out in a convent without touching on religion." And I was told I was wrong and they knew better, because they were Warner Brothers. And I just walked out of the meeting.'

For the next five years, Lynn pitched *Nuns on the Run* around the other Hollywood studios but no one wanted to know. Then he had a brainwave – why not rewrite it as a British movie? For the two leads Lynn sought out his old Cambridge Footlights cohort Eric Idle, together with Michael Palin. Idle loved the script, but Palin declined due to other work commitments. Idle then suggested Robbie Coltrane, which Lynn thought was inspired, and was also instrumental in passing the script over to HandMade. 'I was at the Cannes Film Festival and walking down the Croisette,' recalls Idle, 'when I bumped into Denis and he said, "You want to do this film?" And I said, "Yeah." And he said, "Great. We'll do it." '

Shot on location in London in April 1989, the film was made on a tight schedule and budget. Lynn had actually re-set his story to take place in Glasgow, but O'Brien ruled out shooting in Scotland because of the cost involved – air fares, hotel bills and so on. Lynn adds, 'Also, the week before we started shooting, Denis said, "The script's too long," and I said, "No it isn't." He said, "Yes it is." I said, "What don't you like about it." He said, "I like it all, it's just too long. Too many pages." So I said, "What are you saying?" He said, "You can't shoot this number of pages in 43 days." And I said, "Yes I can." He said, "Directors always say they can, but they don't. Now, I will make it really clear … there is no more money. This is not an American studio. There is no contingency. There is not a penny extra. So anything you've not shot at the end of 43 days does not get shot. That's it." I said, "OK." I understood the rules. In fact, we did mange to shoot it all in 43 days but there was a tremendous amount of pressure.'

Much of that pressure was relieved by the congenial and fun atmosphere that was infectious on the set. Lynn remembers, 'It was tremendous fun. Eric and Robbie were hilarious. They were a wonderful double act. They were as funny off camera as on camera. Between takes, the crew was laughing continuously because of the non-stop cabaret that was going on with Eric and Robbie.'

Both comics, though hailing from different points in the comedy universe, hit it off from the word go. Coltrane confirms, 'Nuns is the only film I have done that was as much fun to do as it looks! Eric and I had an ongoing competitive gag about alternative lefty comedy (Thatch is a bitch) and smarty-pants Oxbridge comedy (Kierkegaard is hilarious), which we enjoyed enormously, as did the crew.'

The two actors also found much to enjoy in playing, what was essentially, two characters at once, choosing close relatives to be their female alter egos. 'It was a great shoot,' Idle says. 'Johnny Lynn is fantastic and working with Robbie was just hilarious. We'd sit around dressed as nuns having a good laugh. I remember once we were sitting outside the church and we were both dressed as nuns and Robbie had his gear hoisted up and was smoking a cigarette and this little old lady came up and said, "Good morning, sister." It was like, "How could you think that was possibly a nun?" '

It soon became a source of amazement just how anonymous the actors were in costume. 'It was such a drag getting out of the gear,' Coltrane observes, 'that Eric and I sometimes nipped to the shops in costume and people would go, "Good morning, sisters." We gave up explaining after a few times and would just "Good morning" back to save the hassle. It was interesting, though, because you realised that nuns have an anonymity which made a lot of the plot easier to play; we knew that in real life the boys could have got away with it.'

Not since *Powwow Highway* did George Harrison take as much of an active interest in a HandMade film as he did with *Nuns on the Run*, no doubt due to the involvement of Eric Idle. 'George was on the set a lot, I'm glad to say,' Coltrane adds. 'Rock 'n' roll and comedy are close compadres. He sent me a letter after the film came out saying I was fab. I showed it to my sister and she nearly fainted. It's a generational thing. It must be said, George knew what he was doing, there was nothing dilettante about his involvement. As for Denis, he was always very cool and liked to play the producer in the camel coat.'

O'Brien was also keen for Harrison to provide a song for the film. Lynn remembers, 'George came in one day with a song and played it and I loved it, and the next day I tried it up against the sequence in the film and it killed the scene, it turned it into a kind of music video. The music was just too powerful. So I had the unenviable task of calling both a Beatle and the executive producer of the film saying, "I can't use your song." So I was a little apprehensive about this. But when I phoned him, he said, "Oh that's all right. It's not compulsory," and went back to his dinner. Later, I got messages that he liked the film via Eric.'

Early test screenings, however, revealed a different story. Audience reaction was good up until the last five minutes when it nose-dived. 'And Joe Roth,' Idle continues, 'head of Twentieth Century Fox who were releasing the film in America and who used to be a film director so knew about movies, he said, "You need a new ending and here's some money, go and shoot a new ending." I've never heard such intelligence from a film-maker.'

No doubt on the back of the recent success of *A Fish Called Wanda*, *Nuns on the Run* opened in America in March 1990 to good business and some rave notices. The *Village Voice* said, 'Idle and Coltrane are physically in the tradition of Laurel and Hardy.' 'This movie is hysterical. It's a divine comedy,' gushed *Good Morning America*.

The exception was Siskel and Ebert, a sort of excruciatingly annoying double act of TV reviewers – just think of Barry Norman cloned and you've got the idea. Ebert particularly loathed the film. 'Apparently,' says

Idle, 'Ebert was brought up by nuns in some kind of orphanage and, for some reason, he got very upset about the movie on behalf of all the nuns who were actually not upset by the movie. And he couldn't leave it alone. He kept attacking it everywhere.'

It was when Siskel and Ebert began holding the film up to derision outside of their regular show that Fox took swift action. 'Joe Roth went nuts and withdrew all screening privileges from them,' Idle says, 'which was great because it just showed them who they're dependent on. Without films to view and review, they don't have a job. I always thought they reacted completely ridiculously, but Ebert is a nun really, isn't he.'

Despite the film's Stateside success, O'Brien had a problem when it came time to release *Nuns on the Run* in Britain. He'd no confidence in Twentieth Century Fox's London office to get behind the film wholeheartedly, and so reluctantly came round to the view that, whatever his feelings and personal animosity towards Stephen Woolley, Palace were in the best position to make a hit out of it. That's if they wanted it. Woolley recalls, 'I saw it and thought it's got three funny moments in it and I likened it to a kind of *Carry On* film. It was basically a one-joke movie, which was Idle and Coltrane dressed as nuns; if you think that's funny, you'll like the movie; if you don't, you won't. As usual, Nick Powell went in to do the deal and they made Nick take *Cold Dog Soup*, and Nick comes back saying, "Oh, I've signed that film *Nuns on the Run* and I've done this other deal with *Cold Dog Soup*." I said, "What the fuck's that? No one's seen it." He said, "Oh, Denis wanted to get rid of it." I bet he did.'

So Palace Pictures released *Nuns on the Run* in the UK where it did extremely well, in spite of mixed notices. 'There are few screen farces which can sustain themselves without flagging for 95 minutes, and even fewer British ones. *Nuns* is an outstanding achievement within its genre,' said the *Sunday Telegraph*. The *Observer*, however, believed it to be 'a pre-cooked microwave version of *Some Like it Hot*'.

Former HandMade director Richard Loncraine made no bones about what he thought of it. '*Nuns on the Run* was one of the most unspeakable films, I thought, and that it did so well made it even more depressing.'

Indeed, it did do very well and therein lay the problem. Jonathan Lynn was unaware that HandMade was close to collapsing about itself, as O'Brien kept calling him all the time trying to set up other movies. But he was aware of financial goings-on that never made any sense to him. 'For instance, we made the film for about $5 million. It was sold outright to Fox for American distribution for $4 million. So it virtually recouped before it opened anywhere. However, you will not be surprised to hear that none of the profit participants have ever received a penny. The film is unquestionably a profitable movie, although the books seemed to show something different – "creative accountancy".'

Part of the problem was that Palace refused to give HandMade any of the profits from the film's UK release, citing the fact that O'Brien still owed them money from *Mona Lisa*'s cinema run. That cuts no ice with Lynn. 'Stephen Woolley seems to think that's an ethical argument. He had no legal basis for holding that position. I'm not happy about it and neither is anybody else who worked on *Nuns*, it was a great deal of money that was withheld. And then Palace went bankrupt. Palace's dispute with HandMade was nothing to do with any of the people that made *Nuns* and they had no right to withhold that money. They were separate disputes.'

Lynn's still waiting for the money and so, too, are Idle and Coltrane. According to Woolley, 'Denis was telling Eric Idle that he wasn't going to give Eric any money because we weren't paying him, not telling Eric that we were actually owed money from *Mona Lisa*. And Denis very much personalised it towards me, he said, "Stephen Woolley owes us the money." I was taking Eric Idle's money now. And it's a bone of contention with Eric, I swear, to this day, and even though I've had late nights with him at Cannes explaining it and he goes, "Yeah, I understand now," I know that like three weeks later he'll say, "That bastard Woolley owes me money." So Denis was very cruel to do that because it was an internal business thing, it was nothing to do with any individuals.'

But the bitterness hasn't gone, particularly as Idle, Coltrane and Lynn deferred their fees in order to get the movie made, so to be financially shafted at the end of it made the pill even harder to swallow, especially when Palace, having gone bust, started up again a little time later as a different company. 'I don't take kindly to working very hard,' Idle says, 'deferring my money, making a success – God knows, which is rare enough in movies – and then having someone take the money and just keep it. So whatever he feels, I felt they shouldn't be allowed to come back into the business and I really find it very hard to forgive that. It's our money they took. They had an argument with Denis – they're not the first people to do that – but the effect of that was to just take all our money and keep it. So the minute he pays it back, I'll be happy with him.'

The last word on all this is probably best left to Robbie Coltrane. 'I am still very fond of *Nuns on the Run*, but every time I see it on Channel 4, getting huge ratings, I get severely pissed off thinking about the money I am owed. And it's a shame because a lot of goodwill went into that film, the crew and everyone else alike. It was all legal, but in the scheme of things, legal isn't everything.'

Just before cameras rolled on *Nuns on the Run*, Eric Idle told a reporter that he'd done the first film with HandMade and that this would probably be the last film with HandMade. 'And that got printed and Denis was furious. But, of course, it turned out to be true.' Ironically, O'Brien's downfall was to be at the hands of a man especially brought in by him to raise funds in order to keep his ailing company afloat. His name was John Reiss, a film accountant, and what he was to discover at Cadogan Square sounded HandMade's death-knell.

CHAPTER 13

THE WHISTLE-BLOWER

In November 1988, Ray Cooper and film accountant John Reiss visited George Harrison at home at Friar Park to tell him they'd discovered that Denis O'Brien was robbing him blind. During the meeting, Reiss warned Harrison, 'One of these days, you'll open a newspaper and you'll find a headline BANKRUPT BEATLE.' He also urged Harrison to call in an independent accountant and lawyer to investigate. But Harrison either didn't believe what was being said to him or simply didn't want to hear it. Whatever, Reiss and Cooper were all but thrown out. Palmer remembers, 'George was the kind of person who'd shoot the messenger because he didn't want to know. He wanted to believe that everything was hunky dory and fine.' It wasn't.

John Reiss had previously been Finance Director at Thorn EMI Screen Entertainment where he'd been involved in various negotiations with O'Brien over video rights for HandMade films. 'I remember Denis being a very tough and shrewd negotiator. His reputation as a tricky bastard preceded him.'

In early 1988, O'Brien began to court Reiss to join him at EuroAtlantic. 'Clearly, what Denis wanted was to raise a lot of film production finance for HandMade,' says Reiss. 'I'd been quite successful in doing that at EMI. We'd raised a bank facility of $175 million for film finance there and an equity fund from the City of about £36 million, which did various films including *Passage to India*. And I think Denis thought that perhaps I would be a link to the respectable side of the City, to use my bank contacts to raise substantial credit for the company.'

Reiss became a part-time consultant at EuroAtlantic in May 1988 and almost immediately sensed an atmosphere within Cadogan Square, one of fear; and particularly the fear of one man – Denis O'Brien. 'Denis could be very personable. He was superficially extremely charming. But he ran the organisation with a rod of iron, everyone was in total fear of him. And there was no wastage, except in his own lifestyle. Denis actually was not there very much and the place used to relax when he wasn't around. When he was there or when he was coming back, everybody used to get tense. Key people were highly paid, most people were badly paid and he traded on their loyalty to George. It was the atmosphere of fear – you co-operated. But, obviously, he had something to hide so he had to be very careful.'

Just what O'Brien was hiding gradually grew apparent as Reiss discovered that EuroAtlantic was merely the tip of the iceberg of a complex network of companies, which O'Brien told him were for tax-saving purposes. Reiss even drew up a chart listing each and every one of O'Brien's 'funny companies' which ended up being so complicated that today it makes no sense to him at all. Companies existed all over the place, some with bizarre sounding names like Harikrishna SA and Clog Holdings. Most of them appeared to operate out of Panama, a popular country for people like Denis O'Brien to do their business because of the lack of any disclosure laws there. One didn't have to bother about such legal niceties as filing your accounts and so forth, so once something went to Panama it was as if it was lost for ever. Very convenient.

O'Brien was also reluctant to explain the group structure when confronted about it and would look at Reiss with a charming expression whenever fundamental questions were raised like, "Why does George Harrison need to borrow so much money?"

Though he'd been with EuroAtlantic some months by this time, Reiss had yet to even lay eyes upon the elusive Harrison. 'I'd kept saying to Denis, it would be nice to meet George some time. I suppose nothing to do with work, but because he was a Beatle, me being a child of the Sixties. And when I finally met him it was in very controlled circumstances. Denis never left the room when I was there. I remember thinking beforehand, What do I say to a Beatle? I ended up saying to him, "The last time I saw you was at the Blackpool Odeon in 1964." And he said, and I'll never forget this, he said, "Yes, you were on the seventh row, weren't you?" '

Previously, many of HandMade's films were financed by partnerships, which were a tax device to get tax relief for high network individuals like Harrison. A small amount of money, in essence equity money, was put into these partnerships, and the rest was financed by bank loans, something like 90 per cent of the cost of the production, secured partly against any pre-sales there had been, and very often these were quite small as the films in question were not necessarily mass-market films. The rest was financed by just the security of a guarantee which the bank got from Harrison. A lot of banks at the time were more than happy to take the personal guarantee of a Beatle, enjoying as they did the benefits such an affiliation engendered, going to premières and the like. Reiss recalls, 'Denis was very good at enticing people with all that. Everyone wanted to be associated with a Beatle, particularly senior bankers who were probably children of the Sixties like myself. They just assumed the balance sheet of a Beatle, without ever seeing it, was enough.'

All that changed one day when the Soho Square branch of Barclays, which handled a lot of film banking, suddenly and quite sensibly asked to see the personal balance sheet of George Harrison to make sure that it did, in fact, support the guarantee. 'I had to mention this to Denis,' says Reiss, 'and we started to compile this balance sheet and it became quite obvious as you got more and more of the information together, sensible values for the physical properties, the flow of income coming from the music royalties and so on, that perhaps we were heading towards a pretty substantial deficit. I calculated at the time, and it is a figure I shall never, ever forget, that the deficit was $32 million.'

Reiss began to dig a little deeper and made a startling discovery. 'I found documents to suggest that Denis had been telling George that he and George were equal partners in backing these films and that the bank guarantees would be signed by them both. But, in fact, Denis never signed them himself. So it was a single guarantee.'

Harrison was almost like a walking credit card for O'Brien that the American used whenever HandMade's coffers went bare. Wendy Palmer states, 'That was the thing that most of us felt most culpable about, that George really did not know what Denis was doing with his money, and what he thought he was doing with it was not an accurate picture. Every time Denis needed more money for films, he would basically use George's personal guarantee to guarantee the loan and George had no idea and, of course, the bank assumed he was mega-rich and they never checked and he had personal guarantees that were far greater than his net worth. I remember clearly Denis going off to see George, clutching the document, and coming back with a signature and we'd have more money again.'

It suddenly dawned on Reiss what had been going on and the realisation made him go hot and cold. 'You think, my God, you don't discover these things very often in life, and I began to see the whole thing was a pack of cards. I'd assumed all this network of companies was because George and Denis were obsessed about tax but then I began to realise it was far more than that, it was a massive moral breach of trust.'

How exactly was O'Brien doing this and how had he been getting away with it for so long? First, he had an easy victim in George Harrison, a trusting man and a simple man in terms of business, although there's no reason why Harrison should have been an expert in business matters; that's what business advisers are for, after all. 'George was mesmerised by Denis,' Reiss believes. 'What would happen, occasionally they'd meet and he would actually lie down on the chaise longue in his office and Denis would talk to him for three or four hours, a bit like a shrink with a patient. And what Denis used to do was terrify George above all about the tax man. And, to me, that is the critical thing. George was terrified about tax, and probably didn't have any reason to be, so Denis used to frighten him about tax and say, "This is for tax reasons." He just took advantage of George.'

Harrison relied on O'Brien totally and gave him unchecked control of his affairs. In effect, he placed his entire financial life in O'Brien's hands. What's even more ironic is that O'Brien often received lavish gifts from Harrison. One Christmas, for example, O'Brien was presented with a black Mercedes from his unsuspecting client. 'It's the worst sort of abuse,' Reiss adds. 'George gave him total trust and it's a total breach of that trust. I got the impression that Harrison's wife Olivia was probably more wise to it but then probably wasn't able to change things. It was so sophisticated the nature of the fraud.'

Much of the problem was that Reiss couldn't actually analyse where all the money was going because it was all being mixed up and recycled over and over again. To complicate matters further, a lot of funds from Denis's companies were intermingled with funds belonging to Harrison. 'There was also no reporting of stewardship which was what a manager should do to his client. Denis also took a very large salary from EuroAtlantic. But it went beyond the professional breach of trust and went into actual, I believe, probably criminal fraud, and certainly moral fraud. He borrowed the credit of a Beatle and used that to his own advantage. I know, for example, that George's income flow from various sources was at that time financing a house Denis was building in New York. I don't believe Denis ever spent a penny of his own money. Everything was borrowed from somewhere.'

Even Harrison's participation in the all-star group the Travelling Wilburys, which he must have taken huge creative solace in at times of stress over HandMade, was open to exploitation. 'Everyone was very excited about the Travelling Wilburys,' says Reiss, 'but Denis was so deprecating about it. He thought it was a load of nonsense and was very negative, until, of course, it started to be successful and he was delighted that it was going to be a vehicle to raise money. And when the sad news came that Roy Orbison died, and George was clearly devastated at the loss of a personal friend, Denis was devastated because it would stop the royalty flow on the Travelling Wilburys. I'll never forget that.'

Reiss took his findings to Ray Cooper, whom he knew to be the closest associate to Harrison. Cooper needed no persuading that what he was being told was true; indeed, he'd all but guessed as much. For a while now, a lot of the senior people within the company had an inkling that O'Brien was taking advantage, but none guessed the scale. Now, what to do about it?

Sensitive to Harrison's feelings and determined not to cause him any embarrassment, Reiss and Cooper decided instead to visit the musician quietly at Friar Park. 'We were there for quite a few hours,' Reiss reveals, 'we had supper with him and his family, Olivia and Dhani. And I remember thinking how bizarre this is, here I am in a Beatle's kitchen and George is tossing a salad.

'I told him that most of his assets were in the films and properties, he hadn't got any liquid capital. His portfolio was totally out of skew in the sense that he hadn't got resources to meet his day-to-day needs, it was all in celluloid and properties. He also had no pension provision for old age. And then there was the contingent liabilities, the bank guarantees *not shared* with Denis. And also he'd personally given completion guarantees on films. But he really didn't want to know and he virtually threw us out … even his old mate Ray. And that saddened me. I think he half-knew, he just didn't want to hear the terrible news. Let's face it, he had been the victim, as had all The Beatles, of bad practice by managers in the past. But he'd been warned by the Pythons, because they knew Denis and they'd left, they'd all got out. He was warned.'

Harrison was to confront O'Brien about the issues raised that evening, but obviously any worries he had were laid to rest because O'Brien next hauled Reiss into his office where he accused the accountant of totally unwarranted allegations. 'You've been speaking to George without my permission,' he said. 'How dare you!' Then the following January Reiss was sacked.

He'd been enjoying a day off and returned to the office only to be unnerved by the number of work colleagues looking at him with puzzled expressions. 'I said, "What's the matter?" And Kate Smith said, "Didn't you receive the letter?" Apparently, a letter had been sent to me saying that my contract was terminated. Denis hadn't got the balls to tell me to my face. So I realised what had happened. He wanted me out of the way. And I actually took him to court because I had a three-month notice period. The court case lasted about four minutes, the judge just threw it out because Denis had no case. He tried to raise all sorts of spurious arguments but he couldn't say, "Well, m'lud, I fired this person for no good reason." So judgement went in my favour.'

There are many theories as to why the relationship between Harrison and O'Brien finally fell apart – David Leland opening Harrison's eyes to the abuse his partner was regularly dishing out to the film-makers, the financial situation … and so on. Another theory is much more simple, and surprising given how much Harrison took a back seat in creative affairs, almost from HandMade's inception. 'George suddenly wanted to have more of a creative role in the film making,' Palmer says, 'and, of course, Denis didn't want anybody's creative input, even George's. Denis just didn't want him involved. He wanted George to be a sleeping partner who took the kudos and stumped up the dosh. George was happy to be a sleeping partner for a long time, but his wanting to be more involved started with *Shanghai Surprise*. And that really did put a rift in the relationship and that was really the rocky road, when it began to unravel. That was the beginning of the end.'

The initial chemistry between Denis O'Brien and George Harrison was magical, there was an alchemist thing happening. Unfortunately, the chemistry changed. 'And for me,' Cooper says, 'it was an overwhelming feeling of sadness, not of anger or bitterness, but just sadness that such a wonderful situation had changed; but then all things change. Those last few years were difficult, you had to be a comedian every day, you had to keep the morale of that company up, in London especially because there was so much being done in America. This feeling of impotence was creeping in and I couldn't allow that to be seen through me. It was like a divorce, except one party's not telling the other party they want it and you're left with that terrible taste in your mouth of "What have I done wrong?" Well, I did nothing wrong, none of us did anything wrong. Denis should have come down and said, "Listen, I love you all, thank you very much but the wind of change is on." None of that was really stated. So I formed the film police, an underground movement of naughtiness which was hopefully very funny and played out in the office, in moments unseen to Denis. Anything to keep the morale in that office buoyant. But at the end of the day, it was impossible, the office became an extremely sad, desolate place.'

Things were to go from bad to worse, especially for Ray Cooper, as people began to sense that, like Wendy Palmer and numerous others before her, he was working on borrowed time. 'Clearly Denis didn't like Ray being there,' Reiss believes. 'He'd obviously been quite involved creatively at the beginning. Denis just didn't want him around because he was associated with the old regime.'

After ten years as a director of HandMade, the end for Ray Cooper came in the form of a telephone call from O'Brien in America. There was no handshake. There was no goodbye. No thanks for everything you did. Nothing. 'I ended up on the psychiatrist's couch,' adds Cooper. 'It took me a long time to come to terms with it, in the sense of my own personal life. My psyche had been chipped away by O'Brien. I wasn't aware of it at first

... well, maybe I was, but I thought I could deal with it, but there was an undermining all the time. What I am sure of, is that Denis would have thrown me out years before if it wasn't for the support of George.'

So traumatised was Ray Cooper by how foully he was treated by O'Brien, that it wasn't until the late 1990s that he involved himself in the movie business again.

Though not the end, Ray Cooper's departure was another substantial nail in the HandMade coffin. Shingles confides, 'Ray going was very sad for HandMade. I think he was very unfairly treated. But we had great times. I remember one incident. We used to have production meetings on Wednesday. Denis, Ray, Kate, Wendy and myself, and others, too, we'd be talking and Ray wouldn't be there and Denis would say, "Where's Ray?" And someone would come up with a reason, but if you looked in *Screen International* and saw Terry Gilliam's *The Adventures of Baron Munchausen* shooting in Spain, in the cast list was Ray Cooper. And we'd think, let's hope Denis hasn't looked.'

It was when the banks stopped lending and instead started to pile on the pressure that the whole sorry house of cards built by O'Brien really began to tumble. 'Once the shit hit the fan, we saw very little of Denis,' says Shingles. 'We used to have birthday parties for all the staff up in his boardroom. During the last one we had, there was a power cut, there was thunder and lightning, everyone was there that was left; very atmospheric. And that was it ... you knew then this was the end somehow.'

Looking back on the whole venture, there's no way, even taking into account the two big early hits, *Life of Brian* and *Time Bandits*, that HandMade was a commercial success. 'It must have been a massive financial disaster,' Reiss believes. 'It was a private business and the ownership of it and the films were spread about all over the place. People talk about HandMade, but HandMade didn't really exist as such, it was a network of partnerships, distribution companies and so on. If it had been HandMade Plc and everything had gone into one company, it would have collapsed financially massively long before. It was only because it was spread about no one really knew.'

Everything only came to a head when the banks finally sussed out that these films weren't going to generate the income that Denis O'Brien had projected for them. One such bank seemingly blinded by all the showbiz razzmatazz was American Express in London. It was only after a change in management that they began to realise that perhaps this was a loan that should be called in. 'American Express kept trying to chase Denis all the time,' Reiss confirms, 'and the Chemical Bank in America, a very experienced film banking operation, they began to get suspicious. And what Denis would do was to borrow from another bank, on another film, and use the money to pay off something else. He kept borrowing from one bank account to support another.' Always to postpone the inevitable.

And when the inevitable finally came and Harrison uncovered the truth, he was utterly devastated and $25 million in the red. 'I know that George never forgave Denis,' Eric Idle says. 'He hated him with an intensity that was quite rare for George. He felt bitter, betrayed, angry and let down. In fact, he wrote a song called "Lying O'Brien" which he played me. It took him a long time to get over all that. I don't think George was ever ready to relive a lot of that stuff. Then he lost half a lung to cancer, and then half a lung to some fucking loony stabbing him. One of the last times I saw him, he said gleefully that Denis had been forced to sell his last house. But it was never the money with George, it's about, "How could you deceive me ... how could you use my good name?" I'm sorry that it worked out the way it did for George. One always hoped that Denis was on the level; you hope that they're right. It turned out that he wasn't.'

CHAPTER 14

'I JUST HOPE DENIS DOESN'T TURN OUT TO BE A MADMAN'

This quote made by George Harrison in a 1988 interview was prophetic indeed. But it wasn't as if nobody warned him about it. As early as 1982, his Python mates were questioning O'Brien's *modus operandi* and telling Harrison of their concerns. Eric Idle states, 'George always said to me afterwards when he found out about it, he said, "Yeah, I know, you warned me, you warned me." '

Gilliam also warned him. 'HandMade had really been rolling along based on George's fortune that was tucked away somewhere and Denis was very clever at using that as equity to get more money to keep things going. So he played pretty free and easy with George's money. It was an incredible power base for Denis. But George didn't want to know until it was too late. In a way, you can't blame him after having the hassles he'd had.'

It is remarkable indeed that George Harrison did not learn from the lessons of his past, from the years of financial litigation with Allen Klein, who from 1968 to 1973 managed The Beatles' affairs and was in charge of Apple Corps, The Beatles' business vehicle. Klein and Apple were finally disentangled in 1977, but only after the company was placed into receivership. The man who replaced Klein as Harrison's manager was Denis O'Brien. 'One of the things that George always liked,' says Idle, 'was for someone to take care of things. He needed that, in a way, because he was an artist and if someone could take care of the business that was great. He worked on absolute trust, George, he always told the truth, he never lied, even when it was painful. So the idea that somebody would not be telling the truth to him didn't actually enter his head. He was susceptible.'

Since the release of *Nuns on the Run*, HandMade was still functioning but no longer making movies. It was in a strange sort of limbo, like a zombie walking aimlessly around the graveyard of the British film industry knocking into the tombstones of other departed film companies like Goldcrest and Palace. O'Brien and Harrison's business association was finally dissolved in 1993. Then, in August 1994, HandMade was sold for $8.5 million, in cash, to Paragon Entertainment Corp, a Canadian media giant. The largely token sum indicated to many just how little the dormant company had come to mean to Harrison and O'Brien amid their increasingly acrimonious partnership.

When he came to sell HandMade Harrison said he would only sign his name once. He hated what had happened and didn't want to think about it. He would turn up to one meeting, and sign his signature, once. But the lawyers still produced twenty different contracts. Harrison refused to sign them. So the lawyers had to put them all together in one agreement. Harrison signed, and walked away.

For many of the old staff, this was the end of an era. 'There was Hilary Davis,' Shingles recalls, 'myself, Gareth Jones, a few others that were left, we were all up at HandMade physically moving out of Cadogan Square. George was there with Olivia helping to clear out, there were computers and bucket-loads of stationery to move. And we didn't know what the future was. We arrived at the Paragon office and found out that we'd all been made redundant except Hilary and Gareth. They said, "Sorry, you've been made redundant, here's your cheque, goodbye." We were absolutely stunned and went back to what we called the HandMade pub, the Australian in Milner Street, which is where we used to go at lunchtime. We couldn't go back to Cadogan Square because it had been sold, so we all sat in this pub and discussed what had happened. That was the real end of HandMade. It was sad because HandMade felt like a second home to me. My 14 years there were the happiest of my working life and this was a very sour end to what had been a wonderful time.'

Although in selling the company Harrison had broken all ties with HandMade, his feud with Denis O'Brien was far from over. In January 1995, he filed a $25 million lawsuit against his former partner for allegedly mishandling his investments and deceiving him for 20 years. The entertainment world gasped.

Harrison's complaint was long (18 pages in length) and dramatic: 'This case involves the tortious misconduct of a faithless manager. Pretending to serve the interests of his musician client, he misused his position and his client's assets and credit to finance secret profit and a lavish international lifestyle for himself, while subjecting his trusting client to massive economic risks and losses.' It also alleged that O'Brien 'drastically reorganised Harrison's financial and business holdings into a complicated, Byzantine structure, involving multiple offshore corporations and other inter-related entities all under O'Brien's direct or indirect control.'

The claim, which was lodged with the Los Angeles County Superior Court, also alleged that O'Brien encouraged Harrison to rack up massive debts to finance more films and that 'he made secret decisions, concealed and misrepresented the facts and took actions contrary to Harrison's wishes and directions, and through his improper and inept management caused the film organisation to lose huge sums of money'. The papers went on to claim that O'Brien told Harrison, 'That in order to keep the film organisation as a going business it was necessary and advisable for Harrison personally to borrow massive amounts of money. Harrison did so, acting in reliance on O'Brien's advice and thereby incurring personal liability in excess of $25 million.' In conclusion, the papers stated that 'Harrison suffered enormous losses and liabilities as a result of O'Brien's improper and inept management and deceitful conduct'.

Harrison also contested that O'Brien had backed out of a 1978 agreement to cover half of the losses incurred by HandMade. It was claimed that O'Brien 'carefully avoided telling this to the lenders or signing any notes or loan documents'. It appeared that O'Brien bore none of the risks of film-making, yet half of the potential profits.

In essence, the whole case hinged on the large sums of money Harrison had to borrow on behalf of HandMade and the personal guarantees with which he buttressed HandMade's borrowings. According to court papers, it was these loans and guarantees that led to Harrison's $25 million liability.

John Reiss only heard about Harrison's court action when he saw an article about it in the *News of the World*. 'I wrote to George and explained why I was glad he was making progress against The Evil One and sorry he hadn't listened to me in the first place and offered to help. And, in fact, I later gave a deposition to his solicitors.' Harrison, it seemed, had taken Reiss's earlier advice and had got independent people involved. He brought in Ken Roberts, an accountant at a medium-sized practice called Shipley's, who specialised in the music industry and film, and one of the partners at Ernst and Young, Garth Tweedale, again a music specialist. 'I think they both got the confidence of George,' Reiss says, 'and probably helped towards the end in assembling the information for the legal cases. But if only George had been persuaded to do all that earlier on.'

Denis O'Brien, now a director and Vice-Chairman of Union Illinois Co Bank in St Louis, naturally contested the action and lodged a vigorous defence denying each and every allegation. Despite the belief of some professional analysts that an out-of-court settlement seemed the most likely outcome, it looked more and more certain that Harrison was going to get his day in court.

One of the most interesting facts brought up by the case was that George Harrison still owed some of that $25 million figure to various creditors, putting him in the position that, if he were to lose and be forced to meet costs, his rock 'n' roll lifestyle would be in serious jeopardy. The press speculated that if that were to be the case the former Beatle would be down to his last £10 million. Still bloody rich by normal standards, so not a huge outpouring of sympathy, but when you think at the time that fellow Beatle Paul McCartney, after years of careful management, had an accumulated wealth in the region of £500 million, it was a sorry situation. And one considerably more serious than people might have imagined. According to Reiss, 'O'Brien milked George directly or indirectly in every conceivable way possible that I believe George would have become bankrupt. It was only the launch of The Beatles' albums on CD in the early Nineties that came to his rescue. A big flood of money came in and also later with subsequent Beatle re-releases. So I imagine he died a wealthy man, but he wouldn't have done had his fortune been wiped out at that stage, which wouldn't have been very nice and he didn't deserve it because he was an honest, decent man. I think he was taken advantage of horribly.'

Despite Harrison's London solicitors succeeding early on in the case in obtaining important documents from O'Brien's EuroAtlantic office in Guernsey, it wasn't until January 1996 that judgement was passed in Harrison's favour and he was awarded $11 million in compensatory damages in the Los Angeles Superior Court, roughly half of what had been originally claimed. The judge's ruling hinged on Harrison's allegation that O'Brien had contractually assumed personal responsibility for half of any debt incurred by HandMade, but concealed that information from lenders, did not sign any loan documents and, in fact, assumed none of the losses himself. Afterwards, a spokesman for Harrison said that, although his client was pleased with the decision, 'Winning's one thing, collecting's another.'

During the case, O'Brien went to extreme lengths to stave off the inevitable financially. 'When I later met Noel,' Reiss remembers, 'Denis's former wife, I heard that Denis had even used her personal house in New York as some sort of security, probably to hold up a crumbling empire, and she was trying to get that back so she could actually either live in it or sell it. But I think it had been charged as part of the settlement by the court order in favour of George.'

Not surprisingly, Denis O'Brien appealed against the court's decision on the grounds that the case should have been tried in England, and that it had been erroneously decided. As the case dragged on further, the toil started to show on Harrison physically; he was greying and at times appeared haggard. Terry Gilliam recalls, 'I actually saw George well into the case and it looked like he'd aged 10 years.'

Eventually, in February 1998, the California Court of Appeal affirmed the original trial court's judgement to award Harrison $11m. Reiss says, 'I later heard that George's lawyers were trying to collect the money from Denis who kept hiding behind legal processes and eventually hid behind bankruptcy. So Denis became bankrupt and now he's protected. So he had the last laugh financially.'

While HandMade's past was being decided and laid open to scrutiny in the law courts of America, Paragon chief Jon Slan was attempting to steer the new HandMade towards a brighter future by announcing a slate of projects for the born-again production company. Principal among them was a sequel to, arguably, HandMade's most successful ever film —*Time Bandits*.

Paragon had approached Terry Gilliam to write a sequel and persuaded Universal to put up development money, though, in the end, the studio was to turn the project down. 'I said we could do it for $30 million,' Gilliam says, 'but they didn't think so. Or maybe they just didn't like the script. The plot's about saving the world from God's wrath on the millennium. God had bottled out on the first 1,000 years, because he was going to destroy the place, it was a disaster, and now come 2000 he's finally going to do it. Actually, God is a total schizophrenic at this point, he's got a devil hand-puppet that he talks to all the time; this was before *South Park* and the schoolteacher character with his puppet. And there were going to be new Time Bandits, the daughters of the old guys who have worked their way up through the creation departments and are finally getting equal pay as women. It's a really good tale.'

Time Bandits 2, sadly, never saw daylight. What did emerge during Paragon's reign was mostly a bedraggled collection of Indie pictures and comedies, the sort of fare that O'Brien was churning out dismally in the death throes of his tenure. But at least Paragon did try and maintain the Harrison/O'Brien tradition of low-to-medium-budget, off-the-wall, intriguing pictures from mostly first-time writers and directors. Operating from new premises in Golden Square, the whole operation was considerably smaller in size to the Cadogan Square office and mostly run by the two last remaining links between the old HandMade and the new – Hilary Davis and Gareth Jones. 'Paragon set us up again to go back into film production,' Davis says. 'It was quite a smooth transition. When Paragon took over, it was myself and Gareth, we set up the new HandMade, as it were, and we were the feature film division of Paragon.'

First up was the black comedy *Intimate Relations* (1996) from first-time director Philip Goodhew, a true tale of sexual obsession, hypocrisy and murder in Fifties Britain that starred Julie Walters and Rupert Graves. *Sweet Angel Mine* (1996) was a psychological thriller from first-time film-maker Curtis Radclyffe. *The James Gang* (1997) was a comedy about a young family forced to become fugitives and starred John Hannah and

Helen McCrory. *The Wrong Guy* (1997) was a spoof of TV show *The Fugitive* and the feature début of David Steinberg, who'd previously directed episodes of *Seinfield* and *Friends*. *The Man with Rain in His Shoes* (1998) was a romantic comedy and a Spanish co-production, notable for giving Penelope Cruz one of her earliest roles. *The Secret Laughter of Women* (1998), directed by Peter Schwabach, starred Colin Firth as a man beginning a love affair with a Nigerian exile living with her young son in the south of France. And *Dinner at Fred's* (1999) was a comedy from director Shawn Thompson about a young businessman forced to spend Christmas with an eccentric family and starred Christopher Lloyd.

The failure of these films, both from an artistic standpoint and most crucially at the box office, quickly impacted upon Paragon. In March 1998, the company was struggling so badly it was forced to lay off 50 per cent of its staff. In April, Jon Slan stepped down as Chairman. And in June, Paragon began stripping off its assets. A buyer for HandMade was being actively sought.

Ironically, the one film that could have saved the company's bacon was allowed to pass through its fingers. In November 1997, HandMade announced shooting had begun on a low-budget British gangster picture by first-time director Guy Ritchie. It was called *Lock, Stock and Two Smoking Barrels*. HandMade had agreed to buy the worldwide rights for $1.2 million, but when the film wrapped, Paragon were in such financial straits it couldn't afford to pay. Polygram gratefully stepped in and made a killing. Amazingly, *Lock, Stock and Two Smoking Barrels* made more money at the British box office than the price Paragon paid to buy HandMade back in 1994.

As Paragon headed for bankruptcy, the last thing it needed was what actually happened next. The company was involved in a bizarre court case involving the Monty Python team who had taken great exception to how cheaply Paragon were selling off the TV rights to *Life of Brian*. Although it formed part of HandMade's library of films, something like 50 per cent of *Life of Brian* was owned by the Pythons themselves. 'In fact,' Idle adds, 'when George was trying to sell the catalogue, he kept saying to me, "I'd love to sell you *Life of Brian* but unfortunately I can't separate it from the catalogue."'

Steve Abbott was brought in to handle the case and discovered that

Paragon's acquisition of HandMade back in 1994 had created a cash squeeze at the company, putting them almost immediately in the position of scrambling around for money, and so the films were sold off fast and cheap. 'I'd gone to see Jon Slan at his office in LA to let him know, just in case his lawyers hadn't told him, of the powers we were entitled to over *Brian* and that they couldn't just make any old deal. Even after Python split from HandMade, the deals Denis made for *Brian* were pretty fair and they reported to us, by and large, on time and I could go in and audit. So Slan didn't have to be a genius to work out I was really letting him know that we'd be keeping an eye on him. It was all very polite.'

Paragon were also late in reporting and some of the deals they were making were mysteriously absent from their statements. The writing was on the wall. One deal in particular that Paragon had made with Channel 4 for a paltry sum incensed the Pythons and was clearly breach of contract. Abbott remembers, 'I think Paragon and Channel 4 thought we were little pip-squeaks that would go away ... I think they thought we wouldn't go through with it. But very few things have united the Pythons over the years I've known them more than this, it was a sense of, "This is outrageous, we can't let them get away with it." So we took out legal proceedings. It was kind of scary, even though we knew we were on good ground. Terry Jones came in one day and nothing in films means more to Terry than the director's rights. The words "final cut" are like the holy of holies for Terry and he was there to hear this Channel 4 representative saying in court that, no matter what was said in the contracts, the channel must always have the right to cut films. This was Channel 4, the film-maker's friend. It was just wonderful for him to hear that, even though it was illusion shattering.'

Another Python witness was Michael Palin. 'I took the stand. It was a very Pythonesque location, the Law Courts, like something out of Gormenghast, all very gothic, beautifully carved panels and seats and then taped to the side of the desk was this cable for the recording device. The architect would turn in his grave if he could see this thing stuck on with gaffer tape. And I remember it didn't work to start with so the court had to rise while they mended it.'

Paragon and Channel 4 argued that, because *Life of Brian* was a notoriously controversial film, this made it harder to sell and therefore reduced its value. Palin observes, 'It was a very silly point to make because

Brian had been out for nearly 20 years, was enormously popular, had proved itself as a film that despite reaction would still do very well. I was being cross-examined by Paragon and Channel 4. The Channel 4 lawyer was by far the toughest. Channel 4 should've known better because they'd done a quite shameful deal over the whole thing. I'm a great Channel 4 fan, but I thought this was really their low point to try and actually defend a deal which gave them the right to show *Brian* for 25 years for $100,000. I mean, "Up yours," really, absolutely indefensible.'

After a month, the judge ruled that the deals made for *Life of Brian* were null and void and all the rights reverted back to the Monty Python team. Abbott says, 'Basically, they picked the wrong people to have a fight with. It was the fact that the Pythons' film had been mistreated and that's what they were fighting for. Paragon and Channel 4 relied on the fact that, once the costs started mounting up, they thought, These guys have got to cave in. Every time they suggested a settlement, we went and tried to work it out and always they were taking the piss. I think they thought we could never afford to go the whole hog.'

Perhaps the biggest tragedy to come out of the whole Paragon débâcle was that the negative and unused footage from *Life of Brian*, and other films like *Time Bandits*, that HandMade had been looking after and preserving, were simply junked by Paragon, without consulting anyone, because they weren't prepared to continue to pay for storage of such material.

So it was goodbye and, frankly, good riddance, to Paragon. Out, too, went Hilary Davis and Gareth Jones, the last vestige of the old HandMade gone for ever. Davis and Jones were later to form their own London-based production outfit. Shingles comments, 'It's funny, together with Wendy Palmer, Gareth and Hilary went to a recent Cannes Film Festival, saw Denis O'Brien coming into Nice and they all hid.'

In 1998, HandMade was once again up for sale. There were numerous takers, including the US/UK private investment company Rubicon and British production company Parallel Pictures, based at Ealing Studios. Another interested party was Ray Cooper who tried to form a consortium to buy back HandMade but, in the end, couldn't raise substantial funds and was forced to pull out.

The victor was entrepreneur Patrick Meehan who purchased HandMade in 1999. Meehan began in the music business back in 1969.

One of the first bands he managed was Black Sabbath and later prog rock giants Yes. Meehan also bought Nems, an old Beatle company and in 1973 took over the likes of Elton John, Pink Floyd and Deep Purple, who were all looked after by Nems. In the eighties, conglomerate management companies had a rough time. Bands didn't want a company managing them, they wanted their own individual managers. So Meehan gave up management and went into semi-retirement in the Caribbean. In 1997 he returned to the entertainment business. 'As I hated the music business, I decided I wanted to do something in films. I saw that HandMade was for sale and I called up to try and buy it. And basically I did the deal and came up with the money and bought it personally. HandMade attracted me because it's a classic period and they're classic films, and the name, it's one of the most special names in the world, everybody knows the name HandMade. Next to the studios I think it's one of the best-known names there is.'

Meehan immediately announced plans to back several sequels and remakes of classic HandMade films, including Gilliam's *Time Bandits 2* and a long-awaited follow-up to *The Long Good Friday*. Ever since the gangster film hit screens back in 1981, there had been plans for a sequel. 'But I wasn't interested,' John Mackenzie states. 'I said, "That's the end." They said, "Oh no, the IRA car goes round the corner, hits a lamp-post and Harold jumps out." "Fuck off," I said, "I've killed him in my head."'

In the mid-Eighties, Bob Hoskins and producer Barry Hanson managed to talk Mackenzie into a script idea where Harold Shand escapes to America and sets himself up as a local mobster, all the time pining for the washed-up England he left behind. But nothing came of it. Then, following in the wake of numerous Brit gangster flicks that spread like a cancer across cinema screens after the success of *Lock, Stock and Two Smoking Barrels*, *The Long Good Friday* received a deserved cinema re-release in May 2000 and was again hailed by critics as an all-time classic. Chief among its fans was premier film magazine *Empire* who voted it the best British film ever made, narrowly beating another HandMade film, *Withnail and I*, to the title.

In the face of its successful re-release, talk of a possible sequel resurfaced with a script idea from Hoskins himself which he called *The Business* and had Shand returning from self-imposed exile. Mackenzie says,

'It was a very good script. Shand had gone to the Caribbean, taken all his money and got out of the business. He only comes back because he loses it, his brother-in-law embezzles the money, so he has to come out of retirement to get it back. Then it's all about can he be the man he once was against the new crowd, whether they're blacks in Brixton who shoot you as soon as you open your mouth, or whatever. It's all about him being completely lost, trying to get back the power. But Bob just lost interest; he keeps expressing interest but it doesn't last. We had a huge argument. I was working with the writer, it was about the third draft, and Bob came in on the day we were going to talk about casting and he said, "Maybe it needs another two or three rewrites." We said, "No, it doesn't." So Bob lost interest. He inaugurated it and then walked ... typical fucking actor. Anyway, we've talked since.'

Meehan moved to Los Angeles and set up offices there and in London; HandMade was a production outfit again. After the troubles getting the sequels going for *Time Bandits* and *The Long Good Friday*, Meehan bought the rights to Eloise, the classic and popular children's character and turned it into a TV feature film starring Julie Andrews. And there are more films in the pipeline. 'New HandMade films will be mostly Hollywood-type films. But I'll do a few of the English-type movies because I do want to keep the company as an English company, that's important. I don't want us to become an American company. We'll always have our base here in England. We're looking to make three to five films a year. I want HandMade to be, again, the top English production company that it was and generating a lot of films.'

Whatever path Meehan steers HandMade in the future, past glories can never be recaptured. It's doubtful that we will ever see more films of the energy and quirkiness of *Life of Brian*, *Time Bandits*, *A Private Function* and *Withnail and I*, which are up there as some of the best British comedies ever made. It's down to George Harrison and Denis O'Brien that they exist at all. HandMade took enormous risks in that respect and had the courage to give fresh talent the money and space to express themselves, launching, into the bargain, the careers of now huge names like Bob Hoskins, Terry Gilliam and Bruce Robinson. Wendy Palmer suggests, 'I guess if there is a legacy, it is that they did support a lot of people and created a lot of careers. There was a bravery to take on things that most other people wouldn't necessarily touch. And that was Denis.'

Unfortunately, the dark side of Denis O'Brien always tended to negate the positive. His habit of fiddling in post-production drew the most wrath from his artist employees, though admittedly it's a practice not uncommon in the film industry. Richard Loncraine believes, 'They all get God-like complexes. Very few producers will come on the set when you're making a movie. You've got to have quite a lot of bottle to come up and say, "Richard, excuse me. Are you sure you really want to track here … maybe you should be over here?" Not many will do that because they're too exposed, because people say, "Excuse me, you don't know what you're fucking talking about." But it's very easy once you've shot a movie to go into the editor, it's one guy who you can intimidate … you can fire him and get another one. You can't ruin the movie … well, you can ruin the movie … but it will still come out and it's always someone else's work so you're hidden, you're not exposed as a producer then, so it's much easier for them. That's why Denis, like many producers, would come along and screw around in post.'

But there are those who'll defend his method of post-production supervision. Shingles' point of view is that 'Denis enjoyed that side of being a producer and I think he found it difficult to let go of his babies. That's what they were, all these projects, he nurtured them like everybody else. We all were very protective of them, even the ones you weren't so keen on, you had to rally. It's like having a premature baby, you nurture it and hope it will succeed. Denis was very charming and very plausible, a smooth-talker, and after you'd spoken to him you always felt really reassured, and that was a knack. His judgement, I suppose, in movies was suspect, but he was a banker, not a film person. Whatever claims are laid against him, he got the films made. And people seem to forget that when they complained, he was getting their films made.'

Others too will, to an extent, also excuse the man himself. Cleese admits, 'I have feelings of goodwill towards Denis, although I didn't want to get suffocated by his embrace. He was so clever about tax and moving money around that he was able to survive even on films that didn't work very well. But when everything started to go wrong, I was very sorry because he was a jolly fellow to be around. He laughed a lot. So I had nothing but goodwill towards Denis for making all those films. But he did make an awful lot with rather bad scripts, like *Bullshot*. I mean, they were really pretty terrible, weren't they? And when I heard it had all broken up with George, I was very disappointed. I suppose that tendency of Denis to do things behind closed doors without explaining what he was actually doing, that side of his personality must have taken over too much. I have a sense of disappointment at what eventually happened.'

Perhaps the biggest tragedy in the whole HandMade story is that, given the right circumstances, a little bit of luck and a whole lot more honesty, HandMade could have gone on and survived a lot longer. Don Boyd says, 'It didn't surprise me at all when I began to read things about the degree to which the company had had problems. What I think is tragic about HandMade is that George's money and what O'Brien had as an idea carried through properly could have led to a very vibrant, powerful movie company, but it seems as if ego and the rather peculiar nature of the financing arrangements were such that that was never going to happen.'

John Kelleher agrees. 'A lot of us who worked there just thought that there was this fantastic opportunity and amazing people around and amazing material and Denis always seemed to take the wrong option. Having lucked out with his first two movies, he almost got nothing right after that. The more Denis got involved in the making of the films, the more they went downhill. He understood the deals, but I don't think he understood the movies. But you have to give Denis some credit. If it weren't for him, I suppose some of those terrific films wouldn't exist. You can't knock him completely.'

Or perhaps you can, especially when your name is Stephen Woolley. 'I think Denis was in a position he shouldn't have been in. He was like so many people who find themselves in a position of responsibility and power without the experience of what they're doing. Denis could have been making cheese or been bottling champagne. Denis likes making money. If you're making money out of sweat shops in Korea or making jeans, after a while you think you're a fashion designer. Denis had this fantasy that he was a film producer, that he actually knew something about films, and because of his power, because of his access to money, people would allow that fantasy to flourish. I would describe HandMade as a dysfunctional company. The great thing about them was George and Ray, they were fantastically smart, funny and tasteful people who understood other artists. The downside was that you had an accountant running the business and, as anyone will tell you in Hollywood, once it's in the hands of the lawyers and accountants, the creativity stops flowing.'

Perhaps it wasn't just ego but O'Brien's paranoia that stifled the company out of existence. 'I just thought, what a pity,' Steve Abbott says, 'he could have had everything, he could have had something really good but he alienated a lot of people, he wanted to control absolutely everything, so he ended up disillusioning his clients and, over the years, disillusioning very good staff. I suppose Denis was probably paranoid. He wanted control where perversely he could've got more by just easing off a bit, certainly in terms of the people in his kingdom. It would have been a great organisation but it foundered and it was always Denis refusing to yield any of the power. It's such a bloody shame. He had the intelligence, he had the ambition and the foresight and blew it all. He wouldn't ultimately trust people. I suspect if he had his time again, he'd probably be more paranoid. He'd be worried that too much information was available to enquiring minds in the office like John Reiss.'

But despite the horror stories, the cock-ups, the rows, the betrayals, everything, in fact, that would make for a damn good TV mini-series, HandMade is looked back on almost uniformly with massive fondness and nostalgia. Robbie Coltrane suggests, 'HandMade produced a lot of good films and with Channel 4 was responsible for a renaissance of low(ish)-budget British film-making. There was a sense that they were a spearhead for a lot of talent whose Time Had Come.'

Richard Griffiths is another who looks back on his time with HandMade with great affection. 'I thought they were wonderful. They were just so brave and daring. They didn't have big resources or deep pockets, but they would try. And George Harrison, I felt so sorry for him because it was his free-spiritedness that allowed all that work to happen. I felt mostly for him and I just think he was stabbed in the back. Denis particularly fucked him up. And then the Cannon people should have been just put against the wall and shot.

'It seemed to me, George got nothing out of it except the opportunity to give all these wonderful people the chance to work. I think HandMade was the most important company in the second half of the twentieth century of British cinema.'

Ray Cooper has the last word. 'Not that George would have wanted it, but I would love to, at long last, have HandMade placed in its rightful position in film history. For me, it played a significant part in redefining what a British film could be ... it's something that happens maybe once every other decade, where great writing, great performances and great film-making all come together to suddenly represent a film that, although is British in its essence, is acceptable in Europe and America. George was very happy with what went on in the early days at HandMade. He was very proud of his films, very proud of *Withnail and I*, of all the formative films. We didn't often talk about HandMade afterwards, but if we ever did, it was only in reference to those good years. And he always asked very lovingly after Bruce Robinson and Terry Gilliam ... he always asked after his mates.'

After all, that's how it all began. George Harrison didn't have to get involved, but HandMade was his vision, his dream, his passion ... to help his mates.

HANDMADE FILMOGRAPHY

Monty Python's Life of Brian (1979)

Director: Terry Jones.

Producer: John Goldstone.

Screenplay: Graham Chapman, John Cleese, Terry Gilliam, Eric Idle, Terry Jones and Michael Palin.

Cast: Graham Chapman, John Cleese, Terry Gilliam, Eric Idle, Terry Jones, Michael Palin, Carol Cleveland, Ken Colley, Gwen Taylor, Charles McKeowan, Neil Innes, Chris Langham, Spike Milligan, George Harrison.

Running Time: 93 minutes.

The Long Good Friday (1980)

Director: John Mackenzie.

Producer: Barry Hanson.

Screenplay: Barrie Keefe.

Cast: Bob Hoskins, Helen Mirren, Dave King, Bryan Marshall, Derek Thompson, Eddie Constantine, Pierce Brosnan, Paul Freeman.

Running Time: 105 minutes.

Time Bandits (1981)

Director: Terry Gilliam.

Producer: Terry Gilliam.

Screenplay: Terry Gilliam and Michael Palin.

Cast: John Cleese, Sean Connery, Shelley Duvall, Katherine Helmond, Ian Holm, Michael Palin, Ralph Richardson, David Warner, Peter Vaughn, Craig Warnock, David Rappaport, Jim Broadbent.

Running Time: 113 minutes.

Monty Python Live at the Hollywood Bowl (1982)

Director: Terry Hughes.

Producer: Terry Hughes.

Screenplay: Graham Chapman, John Cleese, Terry Gilliam, Eric Idle, Terry Jones, Michael Palin.

Cast: Graham Chapman, John Cleese, Terry Gilliam, Eric Idle, Terry Jones, Michael Palin, Carol Cleveland, Neil Innes.

Running Time: 77 minutes.

Scrubbers (1982)

Director: Mai Zetterling.

Producer: Don Boyd.

Screenplay: Roy Minton and Mai Zetterling.

Cast: Amanda York, Chrissie Cotterill, Elizabeth Edmonds, Honey Bane, Kathy Burke, Robbie Coltrane, Dana Gillespie, Pam St. Clement.

Running Time: 93 minutes.

The Missionary (1982)

Director: Richard Loncraine.

Producer: Neville C. Thompson and Michael Palin.

Screenplay: Michael Palin.

Cast: Michael Palin, Maggie Smith, Trevor Howard, Denholm Elliott, Graham Crowden, David Suchet, Michael Hordern, Phoebe Nicholls, Timothy Spall, Neil Innes, Frances Barber, David Leland.

Running Time: 86 minutes.

Privates on Parade (1982)

Director: Michael Blakemore.

Producer: Simon Relph.

Screenplay: Peter Nichols, based upon his own play.

Cast: John Cleese, Denis Quilley, Michael Elphick, Joe Melia,
Nicola Pagett, John Standing, Simon Jones, Neil Pearson,
Julian Sands.

Running Time: 113 minutes.

Bullshot (1983)

Director: Dick Clement.

Producer: Ian La Frenais.

Screenplay: Ron House, Alan Shearman and Diz White.

Cast: Alan Shearman, Diz White, Ron House, Frances Tomelty,
Michael Aldridge, Mel Smith, Billy Connolly, Geoffrey Bayldon,
Ray Cooper, Nicolas Lyndhurst.

Running Time: 88 minutes.

A Private Function (1984)

Director: Malcolm Mowbray.

Producer: Mark Shivas.

Screenplay: Alan Bennett.

Cast: Michael Palin, Maggie Smith, Denholm Elliott, Richard Griffiths,
Tony Haygrath, Bill Paterson, Liz Smith, Alison Steadman,
Jim Carter, Pete Postlethwaite, Don Estelle.

Running Time: 94 minutes.

Water (1984)

Director: Dick Clement.

Producer: Ian La Frenais.

Screenplay: Dick Clement, Ian La Frenais and Bill Bersky.

Cast: Michael Caine, Valerie Perrine, Brenda Vaccaro, Leonard Rossiter,
Billy Connolly, Fred Gwynne, Maureen Lipman.

Running Time: 95 minutes.

Mona Lisa (1986)

Director: Neil Jordan.
Producer: Stephen Woolley and Patrick Cassavetti.
Screenplay: Neil Jordan and David Leland.
Cast: Bob Hoskins, Cathy Tyson, Michael Caine, Robbie Coltrane, Clarke Peters, Sammi Davis.
Running Time: 104 minutes.

Shanghai Surprise (1986)

Director: Jim Goddard.
Producer: John Kohn.
Screenplay: John Kohn and Robert Bentley.
Cast: Madonna, Sean Penn, Paul Freeman, Richard Griffiths.
Running Time: 97 minutes.

Withnail and I (1987)

Director: Bruce Robinson.
Producer: Paul Heller.
Screenplay: Bruce Robinson.
Cast: Richard E. Grant, Paul McGann, Richard Griffiths, Ralph Brown, Michael Elphick.
Running Time: 108 minutes.

Bellman and True (1987)

Director: Richard Loncraine.
Producer: Michael Wearing and Christopher Neame.
Screenplay: Desmond Lowder (based on his novel), Richard Loncraine and Michael Wearing.
Cast: Bernard Hill, Derek Newark, Kieran O'Brien, Richard Hope, Frances Tomelty.
Running Time: 122 minutes.

The Lonely Passion of Judith Hearne (1987)

Director: Jack Clayton.

Producer: George Harrison and Denis O'Brien.

Screenplay: Peter Nelson.

Cast: Maggie Smith, Bob Hoskins, Wendy Hiller, Marie Keane, Prunella Scales.

Running Time: 116 minutes.

Track 29 (1988)

Director: Nicolas Roeg.

Producer: Rick McCullum.

Screenplay: Dennis Potter.

Cast: Gary Oldman, Theresa Russell, Christopher Lloyd, Sarah Bernhard, Colleen Camp.

Running Time: 91 minutes.

Five Corners (1988)

Director: Tony Bill.

Producer: Tony Bill and Forest Murray.

Screenplay: John Patrick Shanley.

Cast: Jodie Foster, Tim Robbins, Todd Graff, John Turturro, Elizabeth Berridge.

Running Time: 93 minutes.

The Raggedy Rawney (1988)

Director: Bob Hoskins.

Producer: Bob Weis.

Screenplay: Bob Hoskins and Nicole de Wilde.

Cast: Bob Hoskins, Dexter Fletcher, Zoe Nathenson, Zoe Wanamaker, David Hill, Ian Dury, Jim Carter.

Running Time: 103 minutes.

Powwow Highway (1988)

Director: Jonathan Wacks.

Producer: Jan Wieringa.

Screenplay: Janet Heaney and Jean Stawarz.

Cast: A. Martinez, Gary Farmer, Joanelle Nadine Romero.

Running Time: 91 minutes.

Checking Out (1988)

Director: David Leland.

Producer: Ben Myron.

Screenplay: Joe Eszterhas.

Cast: Jeff Daniels, Melanie Mayron, Michael Tucker, Kathleen York.

Running Time: 95 minutes.

How to Get Ahead in Advertising (1989)

Director: Bruce Robinson.

Producer: David Wimbury.

Screenplay: Bruce Robinson.

Cast: Richard E. Grant, Rachel Ward, Richard Wilson, Jacqueline Tong, John Shrapnel, Jacqueline Pearce.

Running Time: 94 minutes.

Cold Dog Soup (1989)

Director: Alan Metter.

Producer: Richard G. Abramson and William E. McEuen.

Screenplay: Thomas Pope.

Cast: Randy Quaid, Frank Whaley, Christine Harnos, Sheree North, Nancy Kwan.

Running Time: 88 minutes.

Nuns on the Run (1990)

Director: Jonathan Lynn.

Producer: Michael White.

Screenplay: Jonathan Lynn.

Cast: Eric Idle, Robbie Coltrane, Camille Coduri, Janet Suzman, Doris Hare, Winston Dennis.

Running Time: 92 minutes.

APPENDIX

These documents were created by John Reiss in an attempt to understand the complex relationships between the companies associated with HandMade. However, they cannot be seen as a definitive or complete description of HandMade's structure, past or present.

CHART A

1. Subafilm SA. (Panama)
2. Lansdowne Investments SA (Panama)
3. EuroAtlantic S.A. (Luxembourg) - Chart C
4. Glenbrook Securities Corporation S.A. (Panama) - Chart D
5. Loka Productuctions S.A. (Panama)
6. Dark Horse Publishing S.A. (Panama)
7. Multicetera Investments S.A. (Panama)
8. Borough Services S.A. (Panama/Guernsey?)
9. Tritan Marine & Trade S.A. (Panama)
10. Immobilie Sorrento S.A (Panama)

CHART B

11. Latchmere Charitable Trust
12. Harikrishna S.A. (Panama)
13. Haribol Publishing Ltd (UK)
14. Idees et Services S.A. (Panama)

CHART C

Euroatlantic S.A. (Luxembourg) from Chart A

15. EuroAtlantic International S.A. (Luxembourg)
16. EuroAtlantic (Channel Islands) Ltd (Guernsey)
17. Bow Bells Securities Corporation (Panama)
18. EuroNovege S.A. (Panama) (50% with Glenbrook)
19. Euroatlantic Ltd (UK)
20. HandMade Films (Productions) Ltd (UK) (50% Harrisongs Ltd)
21. HandMade Films (Distributors) Ltd (UK) (50% Harrisongs Ltd)
22. Partnership Interests

50% of HandMade Films (1981) Partnership withHarrisongs Ltd

1% of HandMade Films (EJ) P'ship with GH 50% & E John 49%

1% of HandMade Films (1987) P'ship with GH 50% & G Ronson 49%

CHART D

4. Glenbrook Securities Corporation S.A.

23. Clog Holdings NV (Netherlands Antilles)

18 Euro Norvege S.A.)Panama) 50% with EuroAtlantic Int. S.A.

CHART E

24. Dark Horse Publishing S.A. (Panama)

25. Dalstiching NV (Neths Antilles)

26. Angada NV (Neths Antilles?)

27. Ganga Distributors NV (Netherlands)

28. Ganga Productions NV (Netherlands)

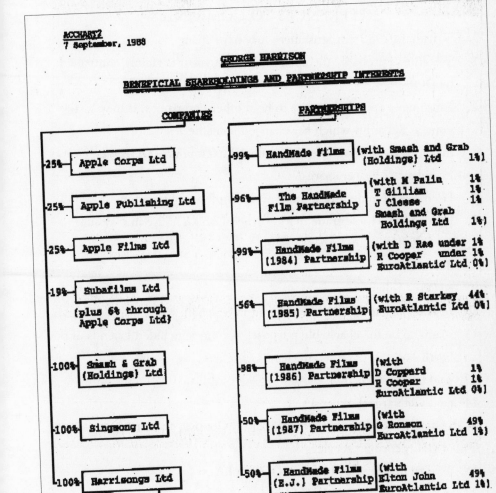

ACCHART2
7 September, 1988

GEORGE HARRISON

BENEFICIAL SHAREHOLDINGS AND PARTNERSHIP INTERESTS

COMPANIES

- 25% — Apple Corps Ltd
- 25% — Apple Publishing Ltd
- 25% — Apple Films Ltd
- 19% — Subafilms Ltd
  (plus 6% through Apple Corps Ltd)
- 100% — Smash & Grab (Holdings) Ltd
- 100% — Singsong Ltd
- 100% — Harrisongs Ltd

PARTNERSHIPS

- 99% — HandMade Films (with Smash and Grab (Holdings) Ltd 1%)
- 96% — The HandMade Film Partnership (with M Palin 1%, T Gilliam 1%, J Cleese 1%, Smash and Grab Holdings Ltd 1%)
- 99% — HandMade Films (1984) Partnership (with D Rae under 1%, R Cooper under 1%, EuroAtlantic Ltd 0%)
- 56% — HandMade Films (1985) Partnership (with R Starkey 44%, EuroAtlantic Ltd 0%)
- 98% — HandMade Films (1986) Partnership (with D Coppard 1%, R Cooper 1%, EuroAtlantic Ltd 0%)
- 50% — HandMade Films (1987) Partnership (with G Ronson 49%, EuroAtlantic Ltd 1%)
- 50% — HandMade Films (E.J.) Partnership (with Elton John 49%, EuroAtlantic Ltd 1%)
- 50% — HandMade Films (1981) Partnership (with EuroAtlantic Ltd 50%)
- 50% — HandMade Films (Distributors) Ltd (with EuroAtlantic Ltd 50%)
- 50% — HandMade Films (Productions) Ltd (with EuroAtlantic Ltd 50%)

NOTES TO CHARTS –
REFERENCES TO COMPANIES

Notes made in 1989-circumstances may have changed.

1. Subafilm is probably the apex of the tree, most certainly controlled by DOB.

2. Lansdowne appears to exist to hold other companies. It may be the same as Subafilm which has changed its name.

3. managed by Banque Internationale A Luxembourg. DOB was President. 7 bearer shares.

4. Used as a nominee sometimes as a completion guarantor.

5. Holds Dark Horse trade mark; owned Nahiku house in Hawaii

7. Peter Sellars management.

8. dormant.

9. re Peter Sellars

10. re Peter Sellars – hotel investment in Seychelles which was aborted.

11. seems to be for charitable purposes – donees included Friends of the Earth

12. paid fees to GH

14 paid GH's travel expenses

17. vestige of Sellars management; paid R Cooper; involved in provision of GH recording services

18. used to purchase a house for DOB in LA

23. used for Olivia H's salary

27. owns album masters

28. royalty conduit.

INDEX